D1031809

WHAT'S WRONG WITH WALL STREET

WHAT'S WITH WALL STREET

Short-term Gain and the Absentee Shareholder

LOUIS LOWENSTEIN

ADDISON-WESLEY PUBLISHING COMPANY, INC.

Reading, Massachusetts   Menlo Park, California
New York   Don Mills, Ontario   Wokingham, England
Amsterdam   Bonn   Sydney   Singapore
Tokyo   Madrid   San Juan

Material excerpted in Chapter 5 is from *Knights, Raiders and Targets: The Impact of the Hostile Takeover*, edited by John C. Coffee Jr., Louis Lowenstein, and Susan Rose-Ackerman, and is reprinted by permission of Oxford University Press.

Material excerpted in Chapter 2 and Chart 2–1 and Table 2–1 are from *The Intelligent Investor* by Benjamin Graham, copyright © 1973 by Harper & Row, Publishers, Inc. Reprinted by permission of the publisher.

Quotations cited in Chapters 1, 2, and 7 are from *Security Analysis* (1/e, 2/e, 3/e and 4/e), by Benjamin Graham and David L. Dodd, copyright © 1962. Reprinted by permission of McGraw Hill Book Company.

Many of the designations used by manufacturers and sellers to distinguish their products are claimed as trademarks. Where those designations appear in this book and Addison-Wesley was aware of a trademark claim, the designations have been printed in initial capital letters (i.e., Apple Computers).

Library of Congress Cataloging-in-Publication Data

Lowenstein, Louis.
    What's wrong with Wall Street : short-term gain and the absentee shareholder / by Louis Lowenstein.
        p.   cm.
    Includes index.
    ISBN 0–201–17169–4
    1. Stocks.   2. Institutional investments.   3. Stockholders.
    4. Tender offers (Securities)   I. Title.
    HG4521.L853   1988
    332.63′ 22—dc19   87–33000
                              CIP

Copyright © 1988 by Louis Lowenstein

All rights reserved. No part of this publication may be reproduced, stored in a retrieval system, or transmitted, in any form or by any means, electronic, mechanical, photocopying, recording, or otherwise, without the prior written permission of the publisher. Printed in the United States of America. Published simultaneously in Canada.

Cover design by Marge Anderson
Text design by Robert G. Lowe
Set in 12 point Bembo by Pine Tree Composition, Lewiston, Maine

ABCDEFGHIJ-DO-898
First printing, March 1988

HG
4521
.L853
1988
c.1

To
Helen
for the joy of it all

Contents

⤚ Preface ⤜

A Footnote to Black Monday

This book was essentially complete before the market break on October 19, 1987. Even in the immediate aftermath, however, some useful insights may have emerged. The concerns expressed in chapter 3 about the potential impact of portfolio insurance programs turned out to be rather prophetic, except that the "snowball" effects described there were not intended to suggest the possibility of a 500-point avalanche. While the presidential commission has yet to issue a report, portfolio insurance probably distorted the market in both directions, up as well as down. The selling on October 19 "required" the insured funds to sell stock-index futures, which in turn pushed the market still lower, requiring them to sell again, and so on. But what had not been appreciated, at least not by this author, is that these insurance or hedging programs induced many investors to hold large portfolios of securities long after they knew them to be overpriced. In short, portfolio insurance may have helped drive the market first up too high and then precipitously down.

It has been suggested that those who invented these hedging strategies should go back to the drawing boards to invent new products, ones better designed to "insure" against the next market break. We insure against auto accidents, we hedge against commodity fluctuations. Why not create products to hedge against market fluctuations? Overlooked, of course, is the fact that stocks are not commodities and market collapses are not random accidents. No tire or glass manufacturer in his right mind would ask his insurance broker for a policy to protect against a loss in market share. (He might ask the federal government for protection, but that is a different matter.) Why then would a shareholder of that company believe that he can insure against a loss in the value of the business? The answer is that shareholders have increasingly come to think of their stocks as a financial commodity, something divorced from the underlying business, assets to be traded rather than investments to be owned.

What was missing in 1987 was a better class of investors, not a better insurance product. Until we understand that, the primary lesson of Black Monday will continue to elude us.

What happened in the real world that could explain a 22-percent loss in a single day? One obvious answer is that the stock market is simply not as efficient as the cheerleaders would have us believe, meaning that it does not do a very consistent job of pricing stocks in accordance with fundamental, long-term values. Those issues are examined in chapters 2 and 3, and on the added evidence of October 19, the skepticism expressed there seems fully justified.

It is possible, of course, that Black Monday was only a hiccough in an otherwise steady march of stock prices toward still higher levels, but that is unlikely. So much of the advance was fed by the same euphoric greed that has driven investors in times past to pay bad—i.e., too high— prices for good companies. The rationalizations are never quite the same. This time it was the voracious appetite for takeovers—discussed in chapter 5—which, seizing on one industry after another for suitable targets, helped drive up the market as a whole. Or it was the widespread assumption that foreigners, particularly the Japanese, would continue to invest, because there was no place else to go. (In almost every bull market there is said to be a shortage of stocks, as if holding money, or the equivalent of money, were an unacceptable alternative.) Once bubbles burst, it is very difficult to create immediately credible new myths to replace them.

L.L.

December 20, 1987

Acknowledgments

This book grew out of a law review article on hostile takeovers that I wrote five years ago. At the time, William J. Baumol suggested that I turn it into a short book for a more general audience. That was a useful piece of encouragement, but I was not yet ready to act on it. Takeovers were then, as they are now, often regarded as a cure for whatever ails corporate managers. I was as skeptical then as now, but I needed time to reflect on the next step in the inquiry: if tender offers are not the complete answer, what is there that shareholders could usefully do to oversee the executives who day to day have control of the enterprise?

One cannot sensibly think about American shareholders without also thinking about the stock market that spawns them. In particular we need to consider the implications of the extraordinary share turnover—160 million shares a day and more—and the proliferation of new financial products. Investors shaped these and other changes in the market, but they have also been affected by them. The process is not yet fully understood, but no one understands it better than Warren Buffett. That is reflected in a number of passages of the book, but more importantly in the influence he has had on my outlook and analysis. (As S. J. Perelman liked to say, the trick is to steal from the best places.)

Those who are willing to read and criticize drafts, bit by bit, are a writer's best friends. There are others, too, but I am especially grateful to Meredith M. Brown, Edward S. Herman, Roger Lowenstein, Dennis

C. Mueller, William J. Ruane and F. M. Scherer. Their collective skills in law, finance, journalism, economics and money management would make a talented firm.

Bruce Ackerman introduced me to Albert O. Hirschman and Mancur Olson, who in turn helped to shaped some still inchoate thoughts about solutions to some of the issues raised here. The Columbia Center for Law and Economic Studies funded the statistical research that Ed Herman and I did with respect to tender offers. Dean Barbara A. Black of the Law School juggled the academic schedule so that I could keep to my writing schedule. The Law School library staff was remarkably helpful and responsive in finding materials, many of which were elsewhere. Riaz Karamali, Robert Rodriguez and James Wang provided valuable research assistance.

The usual procedure is to pick a publisher and then find out who the editor is. I reversed the process, picking first an editor, Jane Isay. Assuming that good judgment is as difficult to find in the publishing trade as elsewhere, that was a marvelous decision.

WHAT'S WRONG WITH WALL STREET

~ Introduction ~

T HE SPRING AND SUMMER of 1987 may seem like an odd time to have been writing a book that argues that investors are not doing their job well. The stock market had roughly tripled in five years, and in the first few months of 1987 alone it was up by almost 40 percent. How greedy could one be?

In fact, the market had some visibly bubblelike characteristics. Black Monday, October 19, was probably the best advertised financial collapse in history. There had been little in the way of earnings increases to explain the sumptuous price increases. Stocks appeared to be more demand driven than value driven. But the proper level of the Dow Jones Industrial Index is not the concern of this book. Prices have been too high (and low) before, and if they are out of line with business reality, the correction will come along, sooner or later, more or less painfully.

Instead we are going to deal with some more deeply rooted, secular problems growing out of the fact that pension funds, insurance companies, and other institutional investors have largely abandoned any notion of making a painstaking analysis of the companies whose stocks they buy. For some time now, almost uniformly, they have adopted a variety of strategies that differ in some respects but have one horrendous defect in common. They all reject the need or feasibility of making company-by-company judgments about price and value, industry structure, managerial competence, or many of the other factors that would affect the selection of one stock over another as a long-term holding. These are the

performance game, index fund, portfolio insurance, and other so-called
modern strategies. Mostly they inflict on investors heavy costs, and invariably they distract managers from their fiduciary and social responsibilities.

Responsibilities? Perhaps that is the key. Most of us, if asked about
our responsibilities as investors, would laugh off the question, replying
that our only responsibility is to make money. In other words, our goals
and responsibilities are the same. But if you think about it for a moment,
that laugh might carry just a hint of embarrassment. We all know at
some recessed level that going to the racetrack and going to the stock
market are not the same, even though we are "just trying to make a
buck" at both places. The racetrack has entertainment value, and nothing more. (Now that horses are no longer used to pull cannons or milk
wagons, no one takes very seriously the old saw about trying to improve
the breed.) But while we don't talk about it much, we do like to think
that the stock market serves important social objectives and that as investors we are both advancing that process and in some sense protected by
it.

If you don't think that stocks are different, try telling your spouse
that you put all the mattress money in a diversified portfolio of horses.
No, stocks are different, and investors do have an important function.
Actually several functions:

(a) to invest intelligently, if not brilliantly, so as to earn a reasonably
    satisfactory return on their own or their clients' money;
(b) to enable the marketplace to perform its function—the primary
    function of any capital market—to price securities as accurately
    as possible and thereby to allocate new resources to their best
    long-term uses; and
(c) to act as a monitor of the managements of the companies in
    which they own shares so that they in turn act with diligence,
    honesty, and competence.

Sorry to say, we shall see that investors have not done a good job.
The fault is partly theirs and partly that of a financial and legal framework that has never adapted to some realities that have been visible for
a long time. It is common knowledge, for example, that the stock market is a peculiar sort of market, one in which rules that might work
quite well elsewhere don't work well at all. These peculiarities help to

explain why so many investors, including the professionals, play some versions of that old children's game, follow-the-leader, that are very expensive and wasteful. In a sense, there are just too many distractions; and as we shall also see, Wall Street keeps inventing new ones. The result has been almost mindless behavior by investors, hyperactive financial markets for the society, and inadequate oversight and faulty governance for the corporations that are the ultimate object of the exercise.

Nor is the prognosis all that good. There has been a growing acceptance of modern finance theory, a much-too-simplified thesis that one stock is as good as another and that therefore one might as well buy thousands of stocks as any one of them. Modern finance theory, although a product of academic work, strongly resembles the old Wall Street adage "Don't argue with the market." One effect is that 30 to 40 percent of the equity money being managed by mutual funds and other institutional investors has been "indexed," either avowedly or in effect. Indexing* is a passive version of a follow-the-leader game. It means that the mutual or pension fund manager has abandoned making choices and instead buys, or sells, a market basket of stocks that dollar for dollar matches some index—often the Standard & Poor's 500 Stock Index. (You wouldn't let Bloomingdale's sell you a bit of everything; why let Merrill Lynch?) When Reebok, for example, was added to the Standard & Poor's 500, its value increased in one day by more than $70 million, because so many fund managers were "obligated" to buy it.

That is not to say that investing is easy. It is difficult, because it requires that the investor/fund manager make judgments about the long-term economic prospects of this or that business and about the price he is willing to pay for those prospects. He must then have the strength to stand by those judgments even when, as must happen, they are not shared by the crowd. (If everyone agreed, then almost by definition the price would be "wrong.") This is difficult in execution, but uncomplicated in concept, if we remember that the essential, and essentially simple, purpose of finance is to provide the money to those who do the "real" work of designing, manufacturing, and marketing goods and services. Those who invest funds without making any judgment about which companies to select have abdicated their own responsibilities. In

---

*"Indexing" and other terms commonly used in finance and in takeover contests are defined in the glossary at the back of the book.

so doing, they have made it more difficult in turn for the financial markets to do their job of allocating capital properly to the businesses best able to use it.

Modern financial theory tries to lead us down a seemingly simpler path—one that is in reality a cul-de-sac—in which stocks acquire a life of their own, with an elegantly phrased algebra of their own. This path is one in which the risks and potential rewards of a stock can be precisely measured by studying its price fluctuations without so much as a look at the company itself. How can that be? Stock prices might better be thought of as a vote or a bet, usually sensible but not always, on the progress and prospects of the underlying business. It is terribly wasteful to have bright young scholars doing elaborate studies of whether stock prices tend to move higher on Mondays or preparing graphs that describe so-called efficient portfolios with arithmetically precise risk/reward ratios. These attempts to make of finance a hard science, like physics or chemistry, distract us from the behavioral aspects of financial markets and obliterate the distinction between investment and speculation. Investors need to understand that; and because so much turns on the outcome, legislators and the rest of us need to understand it, too.

The reality is that a stock is a part-interest in a business, and nothing more. That is a marvelously simple reality, yet we can easily lose sight of it. Businesses do change over time, but mostly the changes occur quite slowly. (Think about the local supermarket chain, television station, newspaper, or car dealer. Like as not only the car dealer's business looks very different from how it looked five years ago, and even there the prospective changes were already visible.) Listening to "Wall Street Week in Review" or the nightly business news, however, one would think that something important is happening every day and that the real values are in constant flux. The subliminal message is that you can't afford to relax, even for a moment, at least not without a smart fund manager who will do the worrying for you, or better yet a financial adviser who will pick three or four fund managers to help you cope with this rapidly changing investment climate. Nonsense. Studies show that stock market prices fluctuate far more than the underlying business results or interest rates would warrant. Too much of that volatility is a function of stock market activity, not business activity.

This gap between business substance and market perception is seldom as visible as during the period of euphoria, such as mid-1987, that follows a long market run-up. The market then seems to acquire a life and substance of its own. In early 1987 there was said to be a lot of money chasing a shrinking supply of stocks. The stock market was also said to have "momentum," as if one should now buy *because of*—not despite—the price rise. Looking at market averages that had leaped ahead since 1980, however, it was striking how little could be explained by growth in earnings. But in a period of euphoria the attention paid to earnings seems to diminish in proportion to the enthusiasm. The behavior of stock prices, not the behavior of companies, increasingly becomes the primary topic.

Investors who thought of themselves as part-owners of a business would never "tax" themselves, as they in fact do, by turning over their portfolios—taking in each other's washing, as Ben Graham put it—at 160 million shares and more a day. Very few new stocks are issued; the supply is essentially constant. The professionals, the institutional investors, are simply exchanging stocks with each other at a rate and a cost that is wholly inconsistent with the attitudes of a business proprietor. More shares sometimes trade on the New York Stock Exchange in an hour than did in a month at the beginning of the 1960s. This trading enables money managers to stay close to the financial fashions of the day—that old game of follow-the-leader—but they, their clients, and ultimately society as a whole are paying heavily for the privilege.

These are important issues affecting the role of investors not only in their day-to-day trading, but elsewhere, too. In the first instance it may involve just investors playing a high turnover, "performance game," as they say on Wall Street. But recalling the simple reality of stocks as a part-interest in a business, we are ultimately forced to think, as few of us have done, about how shareholders might influence the companies whose shares they trade. How much should shareholders contribute to the management process, not directly, of course, but by watching the company store and monitoring those who are running it? We have been engaged recently in a major debate as to whether large public corporations should be free, by one device or another, to issue nonvoting shares and thereby disenfranchise the public shareholder. Sometimes it helps the analysis of this sort of issue to think of the shareholders as being 20 in number—with no trading, of course—rather than 20,000, and ask how the 20 would behave. The 20 shareholders of a local, closely held business would almost certainly insist on full voting rights, and we would almost certainly agree with them. Why change the rules when there are more rather than fewer shareholders? Someone still needs to watch over management, and indeed the larger the number of shareholders and the more removed they become, the less likely is the manager to be on his best behavior. On the other hand, it is sadly true that when there are many shareholders, they seem almost totally uninterested in such matters. The balloting at annual meetings is a boring formality in over 99 percent of the cases. (Nothing of much interest gets discussed until the shareholders leave the hall and the directors sit down to lunch.) Perhaps we should be thinking about how to help shareholders perform that function better, rather than stripping them of the few rights they have. But in so doing, we cannot help but wonder to what extent they are ready or able to assume the responsibilities of corporate citizenship.

THREE MAJOR TRAPS

The three goals, good results for investors, good markets for raising and allocating capital, and good watchdogs for companies, can be stated easily enough, but there are several large traps along the way. The first is that the business of finding good investments is, for the reasons already suggested, very arduous. An investor in an oil company today inescapably makes a judgment, even if by default, about the price of oil ten to twenty years hence. The correct price for oil over such a period is astonishingly uncertain. Money managers who don't like making judgments of that sort, and there are many of them, invest in those index funds *regardless of price and value.* Many of them are easily victimized by the salesmen of expensive "portfolio insurance" and other nostrums.

The second complication is that financial markets are a special breed of market, like the gold market, but very unlike the markets in wheat, clothing, or other products or services that are bought in order to be used in some manner. The difference is that almost no new stocks are produced, and very few are taken off the market or otherwise "consumed." Like gold, stocks trade in an almost wholly secondary market, simply moving from hand to hand. The result is that the "correct" prices are much harder to determine, and the always delicate balance between investment and speculation is easily tipped the wrong way. The whole enterprise begins to resemble nothing so much as it does gambling, except that the stakes are much larger. While we care when people lose at the dice table, it does not affect the rest of us so much as when they take a flier at the stock table. The stock market, one having at best a fragile structure, one easily bent from its useful purpose, is being asked to carry a lot of social freight, and, as we shall see, it often falls down on the job.

The third complication lies at the other end of the process, the publicly owned corporation. Corporations need long-term capital in order to build factories and to finance research and inventories. The stock market does a wonderful thing when it enables these corporations to sell stocks to investors. The companies have the long-term capital they sought, and yet for the investors the shares serve as quite liquid, short-term holdings, because they can be resold easily, quickly, and at prices that change little from yesterday's close. It has rightly been called an act of magic. But it may be black magic. If investors think of their stocks as being short-term commitments in *all* respects, they may lose interest in thinking about what's going on down at the corporate store they were supposed to be minding.

The fault is not just investors'. For a variety of reasons, mostly the almost unchecked ability of corporate managers to influence the state legislatures, we still distribute power within the modern public corporation much as if it were a nineteenth-century closely held, family-owned business. Independent directors help, but their independence is seriously compromised by loyalties to the managers who selected them. Very little has been done to deal with the fact that public shareholders are widely dispersed and have no bargaining agent to represent them on the issues where they need to be represented. The institutional shareholders, in particular—the pension funds and mutual funds—are too much on the move, trading stocks like kids with baseball cards or, no better, buying and holding an "index" group of five hundred different companies at a time, scarcely knowing which are in and which are out of the package. In either case, they seem not to think much about how to keep any particular corporation on its toes.

The investor is a wonderful prism through which to examine these various problems. The investor is the common link, and what is seldom perceived is that the solution to any of the problems depends on a solution to all. As their caravans roll on, gypsies do not think much about how they might contribute to the quality of life in this village or that. There have been numerous studies of corporate governance, but they rarely consider the dramatic changes over the past twenty to thirty years in stock ownership and trading.

The rules of the Securities and Exchange Commission generate a great

deal of valuable information for interested shareholders, but how useful
is it to the managers of the over $400 billion of index funds who have
little or no discretion about where to invest? Given the frenetic pace of
trading, given the fact that the pension funds and other institutional
investors who now dominate the trading are even more peripatetic than
the rest of us, is it useful to think of them as owners of a business rather
than rootless nomads? At issue are basic aspects of the corporate structure, but many of the answers are to be found only in the how and the
why that stocks are bought and sold.

On the other hand, it is also inadequate to insist, as many modern
economists do, on thinking solely about markets, without recognizing
the importance of the arrangement of power *within* the corporation. Corporations are not all that different from other organizations. They run
best when the managers are monitored by internal checks and balances
and oversight mechanisms, so that the executives receive "messages"
directly and not just through the noisy, ambiguous chatter—up $\frac{1}{2}$, down
$\frac{1}{4}$—of the Dow Jones ticker.

We need to avoid the analytic compartmentalization that has often
bedeviled such studies. The stock market and the public corporation are
not separate phenomena; the one ought not be examined, and its vigor
cannot be maintained, without the other. At the universities we teach
corporate finance, security analysis, and corporation law in separate
schools, with separate teachers, which is sensible if we are sure that teachers should be spending this much time writing books. For policy-making
purposes, they are but one.

AN OUTLINE OF THIS BOOK
1. The evolution of the modern stock market
The first chapters of this book have been written partly in a historical
mode, analyzing problems by tracing their development. Those who are
new to these issues may find that helpful. Chapter 1, for example, looks
at the development of the stock market in the 1920s and the growing
enthusiasm for stocks as a proper place for personal savings. A lot of
lessons were learned from the crash of 1929. But the rise in prices—and
to a degree, the collapse, too—was so spectacular, so divorced from business reality, that in some respects it is best thought of as a unique event,
a one-time bubble about as likely to repeat itself as the South Sea Bubble
two centuries earlier. Apart from the obvious excesses of the 1920s, even
after the boom and bust were over, there remained some intractable ques-

tions about our ability to insulate the investment process from the hurtful aspects of speculation. Those questions were seldom more acute than at present. The stock market was then, and still is, a very problematic affair.

2. What kind of market is the stock market?

People should not invest in stocks without some sense of what makes the market tick. Chapter 2 tries to do just that, relying primarily on two brilliant books written in the mid–1930s, Graham and Dodd's *Security Analysis* and Keynes's *The General Theory of Employment, Interest and Money*. (The relevant portion of the latter is the brief but remarkable chapter 12). The central and similar contributions of both books were three concepts. The first is that investing is so difficult primarily because business prospects are so very unpredictable. Second, because proper investing requires such painstaking, difficult analysis, and because the errors in stock selection can be so extravagant, it is tempting for money managers and others to beg off and look for shortcuts. (Just as you and I look to professional managers to shoulder the responsibility, it turns out that they are in effect doing roughly the same thing.) They tend to focus on what the stock market is doing rather than on what companies are doing, or at best on those short-term company prospects that will have an immediate market impact. The shortcuts are counterproductive socially and seriously hurt their individual results, too. The third and perhaps most critical aspect of the analysis turns on the peculiar nature of the stock market. Being an almost wholly secondary market, an almost stagnant pool of unchanging content, it is one in which the investor's judgment as to "true value" can be vindicated only if his fellow investors come to agree. Thus the stock market tends to aggravate the already considerable temptation to watch one's fellows, while they watch their fellows, all or at least too many of whom in turn may also have taken their eye off the ball.

Chapter 2 also looks briefly at the contrary views of those financial economists for whom the efficiency of financial markets is unquestioned, but only briefly. The idea is not to hold a debate, and certainly not a full and fair one, but many of the views expressed in this book are at odds with prevailing theory, and the differences need to be noted.

3. The performance game

For thirty years, there has been a growing institutionalization of the market, as pension funds and other professionally managed accounts have come to own a larger and larger share of publicly traded stocks. That should have produced more thoughtful, considered patterns of investing and a more careful, professional monitoring of corporate managers. That at least is the hope that has been expressed ever since the 1920s, but it hasn't worked out that way. The problem—and this is the critical development discussed in chapter 3—is that the market has begun to trade with a manic pace and turnover that have not been seen for sixty years, and indeed depending on the measure, exceed even the heady days of 1929. "Shadow" markets have developed in various stock-index futures and options. The immediate costs are much higher than is generally suspected, although until the recent panic very few of us had thought about it much. The indirect costs, the implications for rational market pricing and for a useful participation by shareholders within the corporate structure, are more difficult to measure but are obviously heavy.

4. The role of the shareholder
in supervising management

Chapter 4 is about the role of the shareholder within the corporation, why that is an important and necessary role, and the reasons that it has not been fulfilled very well. Some of the blame belongs to the shareholders as such, but as in any systemic problem it is often necessary to reexamine the rules and not just to criticize the players. Under our federal system, with power divided between the national government and the states, we have tried to separate two inseparable issues, with the national government writing rules for the trading of stocks and the states writing them for "internal" corporate matters. It doesn't work. If companies begin to sell nonvoting stocks once again, as they are seeking to do, is that an abuse of the market process that the Securities and Exchange Commission has, or should have, the right to prohibit? Or would federal action intrude too much on the powers reserved to the states? Or does the competition between the states to attract corporate charters effectively negate the possibility of effective regulation anywhere but at the federal level? There was a grand opportunity in the 1930s to unify these conflicting, disjointed regulatory schemes, state and federal, but it slipped away and has never reemerged.

5–6. Takeover bids

Against such a bleak background it is not surprising that hostile tender offers, which emerged in the 1960s, were soon welcomed as an answer to the long-standing question of how shareholders might best monitor managers. It was seen as a device by which target company shareholders could hold a referendum on their management in the marketplace, voting for the Christians (incumbents) by holding their shares and voting for the lions (raiders) by selling. Merger activity, largely fed by takeovers, rose from $12 billion in 1975 to $180 billion in 1985, and hostile bidders began paying premiums over market that averaged 80 percent.

Some very different views of takeovers have emerged. Under what might be called the "enterprise" view, ultimately it is only from the profits of the enterprise that the community can hope to gain. The presently frenetic trading of whole companies in the takeover market is no more productive than is the manic trading of shares of companies in the stock market. There is a limit to the economic and social value of takeovers. They do have a place, but for the reasons discussed in chapter 5, it is not so large a one as the president's Council of Economic Advisers and many economists would have us believe.

Unfortunately, the hot debate about the overall value of takeovers has tended to overwhelm the more specific questions of tactics; and, as a result, an unnecessary number of abuses have crept into the process. Takeover proponents have long argued for unrestricted tender offers, and that is essentially what we have. Two-tier bids, greenmail, bids without committed financing . . . bidders soon realized that almost anything goes. All of these and more have been matched by the almost equally unrestricted tactics of targets, such as poison pills, crown jewel lockups, and dual class voting stocks, most of which would have been unthinkable just a few years earlier. As discussed in chapter 6, excess bred excess.

Congress could have acted, and indeed enough bills have been drafted to do the job twenty times over. It did not, because while Congress feels free to restrict bidders' tactics, it hesitates to do so without also deciding what targets can and cannot do, and the latter is an area that has traditionally been reserved to the states. No attempt has been made to balance or rationalize the two.

7. A legislative package

In the course of the book, we will have examined a number of quite different, seemingly unrelated matters, such as shareholder voting rights, stock-index futures, and hostile takeovers. But these are not unrelated issues, even though they are often—too often—dealt with separately. Underlying them all is a view of what American capitalism is, and is not, supposed to be about. It is a view that emphasizes the distinction between what Bill Cary, chairman of the SEC in the early 1960s and a teacher at Columbia Law School, liked to call finance capitalism and industrial capitalism, between the trading of financial instruments and the real business of the nation.

A useful point of departure is a recent proposal by Warren Buffett for a 100 percent tax on all gains, including those of tax-exempt investors, from the sale of stocks or derived securities held for less than one year. The purpose is not to raise revenue but rather to force investors to push out their investment horizons, get away from the quick-turn, and change their perception of the function of stock investing. (One can believe devoutly in free markets and yet see the need for a more rational framework or structure within which the market is allowed to operate.)

This ''nontax'' tax is a necessary, but not sufficient, condition for creating a more important role for shareholders within the companies whose shares they hold. It is not sufficient because of the long-standing practice, known as the Wall Street Rule, which says that if you don't like the management of a company, sell the stock, don't try to influence the management. That inertia, that tendency to sell out of a problem rather than solve it, is individually quite ''rational,'' as economists say, but it is counterproductive for shareholders as a group and for the nation.

One major obstacle has been that the shareholders have no access to the nominating procedures or the proxy machinery, except by confrontation and contest. With the surge in institutional holdings, the time is ripe to consider giving to the shareholders the right to nominate and elect, *separately from the election of the other directors,* a significant although still distinctly minority, position on the board, e.g., 20–25 percent. The particular proposal is designed to encourage the nomination and election of candidates put forward specifically by institutional investors. Encourage them to participate in corporate governance before the event rather than vote with their feet after.

The hostile tender offer has a place in the scheme of corporate monitoring, but it has been much overdone and perhaps for that reason has turned out to be a more clumsy tool than was first thought. But even without tilting the balance between bidders and targets, a great deal could be done to eliminate some obvious abuses. The list of proposals is lengthy, more so than one might prefer, but that reflects largely the long period of political stalemate and neglect.

[T]he market is not a *weighing machine*, on which the value of each issue is recorded by an exact and impersonal mechanism, in accordance with its specific qualities. Rather should we say that the market is a *voting machine*, whereon countless individuals register choices which are the product partly of reason and partly of emotion. (Graham and Dodd, *Security Analysis*, 1st ed. [New York: McGraw-Hill, 1934], 23)

IT WAS NOT UNTIL the 1920s that common stocks matured as an investment vehicle. There had been both investors and speculators before then, but not many members of the general public had bought securities of any kind, and even fewer had bought common stocks.

Until the end of World War I, the distinction between investment and speculation seemed to be much clearer. Only a handful of common stocks qualified as investment grade. They consisted of a few that were listed on the New York Stock Exchange—many of the railroads carried too much debt—plus a good many bank and insurance company stocks that were unlisted. Mostly they were bought from bankers with whom the investor had a personal, ongoing relationship. The stocks were paid for in cash and then stored in a strongbox.[1] What could be better evidence of the proper attitude than a strongbox? Investors bought for current income and for increased dividends over the years. Given the emphasis on current income, and on the stability of income, price appreciation was a very secondary consideration. The attitude was not very different when buying stocks or bonds, stocks being regarded much like a second-grade bond. In either case, these investors, mostly businessmen, adopted much the same attitude as if they were buying into a private business, and with the same intention to hold for an indefinite period.[2]

The arrangement worked, not because there was a Securities and Exchange Commission (SEC) to police the market, not because the banks or insurance companies issued full and fair financial statements, but because the investor dealt on a continuing basis with a recognized investment banker who accepted responsibility for his customers' interests. The banker was a critical link between the shareholder and the corporation. He was the financial intermediary, in the present-day jargon, who assembled the funds, monitored (even if he did not assume) the risks, and took care that both parties were served, and served well if not always equally well. Individual shareholders had no better ability then than now to utilize their voting rights, but their "proxy" was J. P. Morgan and Company, Kuhn, Loeb and Company, or one of the others in a closely knit group that virtually controlled access to the capital markets at a time when new, capital-intensive industries were developing.[3] Many of the companies were under banker control, but Morgan and others like him thought of themselves as "responsible" bankers. During the years 1897–1902, for example, when there was a rush to amalgamate the companies of a given industry into a single, industrywide "trust," Morgan created the United States Steel Company out of blatantly watered stock—shares issued for other companies at inflated prices—but even then he saw himself as a builder of companies, not a stock jobber. While the stock was watered, Morgan had created in U. S. Steel a company that controlled 60 percent of industry output,[4] and he took pains to see that the management of the new company was in good hands. No other proxy was possible or, within limits, needed.

At the turn of the century the New York Stock Exchange was not the prestige market that it is today. The Exchange was where the speculators worked, and there were enough of them to make the wheels really spin. Except for a few railroads, the listed securities consisted mostly of common stocks of highly leveraged ventures with erratic or no earnings at all. Brokerage firms arranged margin credit of as much as 90 percent and used elaborate, pressured selling techniques. In fact, speculation and manipulation were inseparable, each feeding on the other. The market was in the hands of manipulators for days at a time.[5] Still no one complained or sought to institute reforms. For one thing, it was typically the less stable, marginal companies that were toyed with in this fashion. But the real explanation was that everyone knew the rules. When Congress later "exposed" the bear raids, the stock pools and other manipulations of the 1920s, many of the players on Wall Street understandably complained that these were old and time-honored games. One should not go to a bawd's house expecting to find virgins.

This investment-speculation distinction has always been difficult to define, even though we understand it well enough in familiar terms. When Mrs. Smith says that she and Mr. Smith, a pensioner, cannot afford to speculate, we know that she is probably referring to securities where there is not, in the definition of Graham and Dodd, a sufficient margin of safety that can be identified by recognized standards. Mr. Smith should not buy the securities of companies whose earnings are not substantial and stable, and not even those of companies that meet that test if the price does not satisfy established standards of value. (One does not pay $10 for a $5 gold piece.) But there is an additional connotation that is also important. Even if Mr. Smith's stocks are of investment grade, he would turn them into a *speculative* undertaking if he is doing no more than trying to benefit from short-term market swings, what in today's jargon is called the "performance game." The pursuit of price appreciation within a few weeks or even months is not consistent with a proper concept of investment, because its success depends more on a prompt change of attitude in the market than on anything in the underlying business. Such speculation may serve a function by filling in the gaps in trading, providing a more continuous market, with smaller spreads between bid and asked prices and between successive transactions, and by assuming risks that others do not care to carry. But its social value is limited. Investment is always desirable, while speculation is useful only within limits, beyond which its direct and indirect costs are mere burdens on the process. (Once the wheels have been lubricated, added grease helps only the merchant of grease.)

The distinction might be difficult to pinpoint, but at the turn of the century people seemed much more confident about the difference between investment and speculation. To paraphrase Justice Potter Stewart, you knew a speculator when you saw one—by the securities he bought, his expectations in buying them, and the breed of Wall Street firm with which he dealt. Investment issues were distinguished by having sound balance sheets as well as reasonably stable earnings. Investors bought mostly bonds, not stocks, the emphasis being on "securities that assured safe principal, stable income and [only] an eventual rise in price. These were . . . 'governments,' railroad and public utility senior securities on state 'legal lists' of investments appropriate for fiduciaries and a few . . . common stocks of seasoned, responsible railroads and financial institutions."[6] The investment-grade stocks typically had, first, a market price that was close to or exceeded the par value—the stocks were backed by real capital—and second, an ability to maintain or even increase dividends during periods of panic or depression.

The approach was remarkably similar to that of Graham and Dodd thirty-five or so years later, when they wrote *Security Analysis*, or that of their celebrated disciple Warren Buffett, thirty-five or so years after that, in rejecting as appropriate for a true investment operation the securities of companies that do not lend themselves to rigorous analysis or whose income streams are too uncertain. (The major difference is that as the pace of change in industry accelerated, tangible asset and other balance sheet values have lost much of their earlier relevance.) While there weren't many investment-grade stocks at the turn of the century, there were plenty of speculative ones. American Can and U. S. Steel, to take two that ultimately succeeded, had book values that consisted *entirely* of intangibles—all air and water, as Andrew Carnegie said of U. S. Steel,[7] the company to which he sold out. U. S. Steel issued $1.4 billion of securities, including more than $500 million of stock, resting on a bed of intangible and even fictitious assets of more than $700 million.[8]

Investors and speculators took their business to different firms. Arthur S. Dewing, writing in 1920, at the end of this era in American finance, reflected the still prevailing sentiment that among the investment bankers, the elite firms, "much emphasis was laid upon the fact that the banker had an established business in which his good-will consisted of a clientele of satisfied customers. . . . He must therefore restrict his promotions to those companies where the earnings, and therefore the stability, can be predicted with a reasonable degree of accuracy."[9] Their bond circulars, and many of them were primarily bond firms, adopted a tone that was absolutely devoid of demonstratives and superlatives. They made an after-market in the securities they sold, at discounts of 2–3 percent, but more as an accommodation to those who might be forced to sell than as a source of revenue—all of which was, of course, in sharp contrast to the promotion of low-grade securities, the techniques of which seem to have changed little over the years. The one notable change is that the "sucker lists" of the day included well-to-do farmers, in addition to the physicians, dentists, and teachers of a later period.[10]

Nothing was more symptomatic of the distinction between investment and speculation than the manner in which securities were bought and held. As one turn-of-the-century commentator noted, when a "security is bought and paid for in full, put away in a place of safe keeping and held for the income it produces—that is called an *investment*." But when

it "is bought on margin and held for sale as soon as the price advances—
that is *speculation*." The author concluded that the "great bulk of the
dealings in stocks are speculative."[11]

At the New York Stock Exchange, not many stocks were "held for
income." In the peak year of 1901, the stocks traded on the Exchange,
including those of some companies that rarely traded at all, turned over
300 percent. The capital of some of the more active companies, where
the speculation centered, changed hands ten to twenty times. A represen-
tative list of nine of them, mostly railroads and street railways, such as
the Erie and Brooklyn Rapid Transit, traded almost fifteen times over.[12]
According to one contemporary analysis, one-third of the volume was
by traders; another one-third represented outright manipulation; and the
last third was divided between pool operators, who also indulged in
manipulative tactics, and finally the public.

The Twenties

After World War I, the patterns changed. By the 1920s, American industry was maturing and with it came the realization—crystallized by a
celebrated study published in 1924[13]—that common stocks as a group
had become a valid investment vehicle. Stocks were performing better
than bonds, the traditional core of a prudent portfolio. It was an exciting
insight. After all, there were large, new middle and professional classes
with money to invest, and the supply of investment-grade stocks was
increasing to meet the emerging demand. Here was a long, new list of
companies—Westinghouse Air Brake, Diamond Match, United States
Rubber, and many of the other watered stocks issued at the turn of the
century[14]—whose earnings had been growing steadily and whose stocks
could be purchased not just at a banker's counter but in an auction market open to all.

This new awareness of the suitability of common stocks became, alas,
the occasion if not the cause of a speculative frenzy. From the risky
commitments they had once seemed, stocks appeared to become a no-
lose proposition. As the price levels advanced, so did the optimism, and
by then the attitude of "common-stock 'investors'" had become indistinguishable from that of speculators."[15] An investment operation depends
on a price that provides a margin of safety. It is true that there was a
premium on buying quality "growth" stocks, but within the group no
price seemed too high. Those who might have intended only to be pru-

dent investors had lost the attitudes of the strongbox days and begun to
expect price appreciation that was not tied to anything so modest as a
share of earnings over a substantial period of time.

It is easy to forget that underlying this manic behavior there were
good companies, and that often it was only the price that was speculative. During the six-year period from 1923 to 1929, National Biscuit's
earnings increased from $35.42 per share to $57.20, but the average price
of its common stock rose from 319 to 1,316. Essentially the same pattern
was repeated at Sears, Roebuck, American Can, and many others.[16] A
strongbox investor who had bought almost any of the "blue chips" in
the relatively normal, stable market of 1923–1925 and then held them
until the also relatively normal period of 1936–1938 would have done
quite well in fact.[17] Of course, there weren't many who had the necessary
resources or discipline.

There had been bull markets and panics before, but not until the 1920s
did we succeed in mixing up investment and speculation so thoroughly.
This confusion ultimately became evident even at Morgan. Formerly the
august arbiter of what was reasonable and responsible, a firm of bankers
that refused to appear on the floor of the Exchange, the House of Morgan
joined the rush to "manufacture" securities to feed the frantic demand.
Just as the stocks of sound companies can sell at unsound prices, so too
can sound, growing companies be used as the base for an unsound pyra-
mided capital structure. In 1929 Morgan floated United Corporation,
the last of the three utility super-holding companies. United alone controlled 27 percent of the nation's electric power.[18]

United Corporation was the nightcap of a long evening of financial
debauchery, one that was well chronicled by William Z. Ripley, in *Main
Street and Wall Street*, and others even while it was happening. Electric
lights were going on and gas stoves were being installed all over America, and the earnings of the public utilities were growing with them. So
too were the sales of public utility securities. In 1925 alone over $1.5
billion of new capital issues were sold by such companies, over a third
of all new corporate financings in the country. Between 1924 and 1930
utility holding companies floated, in all, some $5 billion of securities.
Little of it, however, was used for plant and equipment. Samuel Insull,
who controlled another of the three great utility groups of that period,
said that the holding company task was to strengthen and guide the local
companies. But in reality, strength was being turned into weakness. Insull and the others used the $5 billion primarily to purchase good operat-

ing companies and then to tie them together in a complex, fragile pyramid, as many as seven layers deep, each with its own array of senior securities. The businesses were superb, but the capital structures were paper thin.

The holding companies at the apex of the pyramid—the place where the control group invested its money—had two objectives, neither related to operations. By trading on a thin equity, with large amounts of senior securities, the holding company could magnify its earning power. As Ripley wryly noted, it would "operate something like the nozzle on a hose pipe—in speeding up the flow."[19] Second, holding companies permitted a remarkable concentration of power. An operating utility issued bonds and stocks to the public, retaining enough of the common shares in the first tier parent company to assure control. The process was repeated at the second tier, third tier, on up to the ultimate parent that controlled the far-flung system. The trick was to make a little of the promoters' capital go a long way. At United Light and Power, controlled by Hulswit and Company, $4 million of parent company voting stock controlled in all over $430 million of investments in seventy-five companies. There was nothing intrinsically new about some of these devices, but they were used in new and labyrinthine combinations. In the Associated Gas and Electric Company system the parent company alone had eighty-five different classes and series of securities with overlapping claims and rights.[20] Even the management was confused.

The earnings of these utilities, which should have been extremely steady, became extremely volatile. Small fluctuations in the revenues at the operating level were magnified at each intervening layer of the subsidiaries, each with its own fixed charges and dividends. Ripley calculated in 1927, before the process had run its full course, that at American Water Works and Electric Company, one of the largest of these systems, a 12 percent drop in operating income would make dividends on the parent company shares impossible and a 17 percent drop would cut off even the interest on its bonds.

The published financial statements frequently were worthless. United Light and Power, for example, reported consolidated net income in the three years 1935–1937 of over $12 million, but its corporate net income—the dollars that it was then able to take out from the system— was less than $1 million. The problem, of course, was that the flow of "earnings" frequently was blocked or diverted before it reached the parent company. The flow was interrupted because of the need to retire subsidiary debt or to invest in plant and equipment, or simply because the state regulatory agencies—which, fortunately, cared more about the maintenance of service than of dividends—prohibited further payments.

United Corporation, the holding company created by Morgan and its partner, Bonbright and Company, was not different from the others of the day. By trading on the magic of the name Morgan and coming to market early in 1929, just as the stock market was reaching its most fevered pitch, the flotation was a spectacular, if short-lived, success. The stock price rose from 25 to 73 in a few months; and Morgan, which had kept over one million perpetual warrants, profited handsomely.

In an industry essential to the nation's day-to-day well-being, no room had been left for an economic downturn. By 1936, despite a decline of only 15 percent in utility operating revenues from their peak, 52 holding companies and 36 operating companies went into receivership or bankruptcy, and 39 others defaulted on their bonds and offered debt "readjustment" or extension plans.[21] There is an old story on Wall Street about the trader who, having watched the market bid up a can of sardines to $100, entered the bidding. Having won the auction and opened the can, only to find ordinary fish, he complained. "Fool," he was told, "those were trading sardines, not eating sardines." The stock and warrants of United Corporation, and others like it, were trading sardines. The strongbox investor of an earlier day would not have bought them, nor would Morgan have sold them.

After the debacle, at the congressional hearings, the Morgan partners had little to say; their behavior had been no worse than that of others. The world had changed. It was no longer a place where a J. P. Morgan, the "Doctor of Wall Street," could time and again rescue banks and railroads and even, as he had in 1895, the currency and credit of the United States government.[22] Although mere private firms, the leading bankers had assumed a responsibility for maintaining order and liquidity—functions performed in other countries by central bankers. It is almost impossible to overstate the imprint that Morgan left on his times. He cared deeply for the public interest, in ways that John D. Rockefeller never felt, but it was the public interest in financial and industrial stability. He cared not a whit about the twelve-hour day, and at times of social unrest his response was to sleep on his yacht. But within that framework, he was more myth than man. At one time, in 1907, he put the fortunes of family and firm, and perhaps more, at risk behind a bold move to halt a dangerous panic, a move that saved the New York Stock

Exchange, the City of New York, and much of the banking system. As he said to the bankers whom he badgered to join with him, "What is a reserve for if not to be used in times like these?"[23]

Yet Morgan was equally capable of floating in 1901 the speculative securities of U. S. Steel and then manipulating the market to keep the stock above the offering price. Ultimately, the lesson of his achievements was that the role was too big for any one man. The process of change began as early as 1913, with the passage of the Federal Reserve Act.

A price had been paid for private bankers to act as guardians of the system; there was a "money trust," just as there was an oil trust, a rubber trust, and a window-glass trust. The bankers had divided up the turf. According to Andrew Sinclair's excellent biography of Morgan, "some twenty men dominated American finance and industry."[24] But they had succeeded to a remarkable degree in balancing the interests of their clients—the corporations that floated securities and the investors who bought them—with their own interest in making money and wielding power. By 1933 it was over. Finance had become more impersonal and decentralized, and Morgan, the man who had inspired so much hatred as well as respect, had been dead for years. In part the bankers had lost some of their control, and in part they had simply abdicated their role as arbiter and proxy. Even the House of Morgan had become speculators, no better than anyone else, only better situated.

THE DUST SETTLED, BUT THE ISSUES REMAINED.
Obscured by the frantic pace of trading, the rising prices, and the ultimate collapse, the securities markets had undergone major changes. The great army of investors foreseen by Morgan and Charles E. Mitchell, president of National City Bank, had arrived in the 1920s. By 1931 American Telephone and Telegraph Company had 642,000 shareholders, Pennsylvania Railroad Company had 241,000, and United States Steel Corporation had 174,000. It was not anyone's purpose to shrink those numbers, even if the clock could have been turned back.

Business would in time revive, and the Securities and Exchange Commission would help restore confidence in the financial markets. Eventually even new stock issues would reappear. When the dust had settled, however, there was substantial unfinished business still on the table. In particular there were three major issues, the resolution of one of which was important to the working success of the modern public corporation; the second to the credibility of the financial markets that serve it; and the third to the ability of investors, or their money-manager proxies, to put their savings to work without getting caught up in a trading game that, whatever the label or the perception, was almost certain to lead to disappointment. The three major issues were as follows:

1. It is all well and good to speak of the shareholders as the owners of a business, but what if there appears to be neither effective means nor interest in exercising the rights of ownership?
2. Congress had acted to make the market an honest game, to take out the fraud and manipulation, but it was difficult to know whether, even if free of abuse, the market would be still so hostage to speculation as to impede its primary job of allocating the flow of new capital resources.
3. Investment and speculation can and do coexist. In the wake of the Great Crash, however, it remained to be seen whether the public generally would have the skill and discipline to distinguish the one from the other and to what extent, therefore, stocks were an appropriate place for personal savings.

The three issues relate to three quite different concerns: (1) the ability of the nominal owners of corporations to monitor managements; (2) the role of the stock market in a system of private capital; and (3) the suitability of common stocks as a place to invest private savings. There is a common thread in that while positive answers to these questions are not assured even if strongbox investors predominate, it is almost certain that none of them will be resolved satisfactorily if short-term trading and speculation—a willingness to pay bad prices for good companies—predominate.

1. Shareholders as owners of a business

In some respects, to be sure, the events of the 1920s were a passing, isolated phenomenon. One could not help but notice, however, that the public had bought the stocks of holding companies and others like them, with little or no regard for voting rights. In some cases, the fact that control was firmly lodged in the hands of a particular banker or promoter seemed to have been a virtue rather than a detriment, even if the control group had invested little of its own money. The public quite clearly had not bought stocks in order to monitor managements.

In 1927, for example, Cyrus Eaton began to buy shares of various of Samuel Insull's utility holding companies, hoping to seize control. Insull responded by creating two super-holding companies that insulated him from the threat. After that there was no chance that Eaton, or anyone else for that matter, could challenge Insull's control. The public responded by bidding up these new Insull stocks, exchanged share for share for the old, by over 500 percent in a few months' time, as if somehow an Insull more entrenched than ever had become more attractive than ever. There seemed to have been an assumption, there and elsewhere, that the control group would deliberately allow the public to hang on to its coattails in some distributively fair fashion. In actuality, of course, the public was not treated as a partner any more than one invites a chicken—in the jargon of the 1920s it was a lamb—to sit at the dinner table instead of on it. The profits of the utility operating companies frequently were drained off by privately owned service companies and by other tricks. Morgan and other bankers did, it is true, have long coattails, but not for the public. They maintained preferred lists of people who would from time to time be allowed to buy new stock issues at a 40 percent or more discount from the public offering price. The Morgan list consisted of presidents of large corporations (e.g., Sloan of General Motors and Gifford of American Telephone and Telegraph), influential politicians (e.g., Senator McAdoo and Democratic national chairman Raskob), bankers (e.g., Wiggin of Chase) and the like, whose corporate business or other favors might be of value. The *public* was never invited to buy at prices below the *public* offering price.

In truth the public investor has never shown much interest in voting rights. In the tidy, smaller financial world of the 1890s it did not matter much, at least with respect to the investment-grade stocks, because of the paternalistic oversight exercised by reputable bankers. But that world could not survive the growing need to finance new industries whose furnaces and assembly lines needed large amounts of capital as much as they needed iron and coal. The once recognizable distinction between investment and speculation had been swept away. There were not enough strongbox investors to do the job, nor could they have been accommodated in any event by personal transactions at bankers' counting houses.

Perhaps this yawning disinterest in voting rights would prove to be short-lived, a function of a boom period that had now passed. In the two-tier market of the 1920s, the public had focused all its attention on that group of corporations—the "blue chips"— that were by definition successful and not in need of much discipline. With prices of the "good" companies, the blue chips, rising dramatically, it seemed pointless to in-

vest in the companies that were less well run, where the votes might
have mattered but whose shares were not participating in the boom.
Furthermore, so much of the activity was centered on pool operations
and other manipulative practices. People gathered around the brokerage
firms in the morning to pick up tips about which stocks the operators
were going to make move—tips that were disseminated by design. The
point was to get in on the operation to buy early enough on the way up
and then sell early enough to leave someone else holding the bag on the
way down. It was a game, not much different from musical chairs and
of about the same duration, but there was no point in pretending that
one was supposed to behave like the owner of a real business.

The shares of companies listed on the New York Stock Exchange were
turning over in 1928–1929 at an annual rate of about 125 percent, ten
times what the rate would be just a few years later. With people getting
rich so quickly and easily—everyone could become rich, according to a
national political figure—there was an inevitable and dramatic shortening
of investment horizons. As Keynes wrote, the "welfare of [the] enterprise in the relatively distant future weighs less [when] thoughts are
excited of a quick fortune and clearing out."[25]

It would be more agreeable to report that this problem of shareholder
disinterest was a temporary one, a function of the Roaring Twenties,
but it was not. Long after the bubble had burst, stimulating shareholders' interest in exercising the franchise remained extremely difficult.
Turnover is a problem, of course. If you're caught in a revolving door
at the entrance to the hotel, there is not much point in checking on the
quality of service on the twenty-second floor. But even by the 1930s,
the public ownership of too many companies had plainly become too
large and too well dispersed. The Pennsylvania Railroad now had a quarter of a million shareholders, the largest reported holding was less than
.40 percent of the outstanding stock, and the twentieth largest holding
was .07 of 1 percent. Whatever their collective interest, the stock ownership was so fragmented that no shareholder of the Pennsylvania Railroad individually had a stake in the venture sufficiently large or lasting
to justify much time or effort on the voting of shares or other acts of
superintendence. As the corporations grew in size and in number of
shareholders, the right of any individual shareholder to vote or even to
express his views to management diminished in value. Why expend all
that effort only to have 99 + percent of the benefits accrue to others?

For the Pennsylvania Railroad shareholders as a group, of course, voting rights were as important as, probably more important than, in smaller companies where there is less distance between owners and managers. With rare exceptions, however, the corporate voting process is not a collective one in which the parties can influence each other's decisions. There is no union hall for investors. The votes are already in before the doors open.

The election of directors is not like a political election. Business corporations are engaged in a competitive enterprise, and it is a mistake to think of a board of directors as being similar to a deliberative, legislative body. But allowing for that difference, the apathy of the voters in corporate elections is still too complete. No effort is made to stimulate shareholder deliberation or discussion. In most years, in most companies that may be appropriate, but it ought not to be so 99 percent of the time. (According to SEC data, less than 1 percent of the elections of directors are subject to contests.) When reading a management proxy statement, one does not learn anything about the directors. Some directors are very useful, some sleep through the meetings. There are no newspaper articles or editorials to provoke debate—ever. *Forbes* magazine frequently runs excellent muckraking articles, but so far as one can tell it never overtly attempts to influence the outcome of a corporate meeting beforehand.

With nothing to prod them out of their indifference and ignorance, with management enjoying unlimited access to the corporate treasury if a proxy conflict does arise, shareholders act as little more than rubber stamps. For the shareholders individually, each with only a nominal portion of the total ownership interest, that seems rational enough. Reading proxy statements is not the way to get rich, and there are better outlets for social service. But what is rational for the shareholder individually is not rational for shareholders as a community—or for the larger community's interest in them.

None of this might have mattered so much if the investment bankers had not lost their informal fiduciary role of an earlier period. Left to its own devices, however, the public was not about to act on the proxy voting rights carved out for them by the Securities Exchange Act of 1934. Some institutional framework was required to create incentives to crystallize opinion and to supply the block captains and other proxy soliciting machinery. In this respect, at least, one election is no different from another. The proxy rules created by Congress were like a freight train that could carry the goods but sat in the yard for the lack of an engine. Something has to drive the system, or so we believe, if corporations are to be kept efficient and honest.

2. The stock market's uneasy balance
between investment and speculation

The stock market performs, it has been said, an act of magic by permitting long-term commitments in plant and equipment to be financed by investors who, even if investing long-term, at least want the assurance that the funds can be readily withdrawn. The liquidity of the stock market is valuable. Investments that might otherwise be frozen become marketable at will, with low brokers' fees and small spreads between bid and asked prices. Stocks acquire some of the characteristics of money, because they can be exchanged for money quickly, cheaply, and at quite continuous prices.

The stock market is such a firm fixture of everyday life that we tend to overlook the fact that the primary purpose of the stock market is quite limited. Trading already issued stocks among existing shareholders is only a secondary purpose. The principal goal is to encourage the purchase of *new* stocks, whether issued by the company or sold by those who had theretofore financed it privately. The New York Stock Exchange creates a mechanism for pricing these new issues and a place where they can be resold by those who buy them, and those who buy from them, and so on. It mobilizes savings for research and development, factories, and other working assets. To the extent the market prices stocks accurately, in accordance with their long-term prospects, it helps to allocate those savings to their most profitable uses.

A stock market that is not refreshed from time to time by a stream of new public issues would still have value, as a mirror or token of changes in real wealth—the earnings of the underlying companies. It would also act as a mechanism for allocating risks to those most willing to bear them at any given time and as a device for making liquid the capital investments of individuals. People can, and do, think of stocks as being much like money, even though the *community's* investment still is fixed. But as a purely stagnant pool, the market's value would be far less, of course, and the aggregate cost of the heavy trading would be more difficult to justify.

Do we need very much participation by speculators, those buying for the quick turn? We do not really know that investors alone could not do the job. It is generally assumed that, without speculators, there would not be enough trading to oil the wheels of investment; stocks could be sold only at intolerably infrequent intervals and at intolerably unpredictable prices—although again we don't really know what the level of tolerance might be. We do not enjoy nearly so much liquidity in the real estate market, much of which turns over at about a 4–5 percent annual rate—less than one-twentieth of today's stock market turnover—and yet that is enough to support all the new homes and offices that are needed. And no one complains that the pricing is not exact enough, or that people are left for long with houses they can't sell for fair value.

The proper mix of investment and speculation rests ultimately on a great leap of faith, that the prices of stocks in the market will be determined by the investors who are focusing on fundamental, long-term, or enterprise values—or any other term that describes the present value of a stream of very long-term payments—rather than by the speculators whose function is only to fill in the gaps. The market mix is risky, because once inside the house—like the "cat in the hat" of Dr. Seuss— there is no assurance that the speculators won't rearrange the furniture. The issue is the relative impact of speculators on prices, and since for a dollar of capital the speculators trade much more often than strongbox investors, one can easily see how the balance can be tipped. As we shall shortly see, too, there is a great temptation for investors to behave like speculators, which aggravates the problem no end.

The prevailing view is that speculation is, without qualification, a good thing. Thus the then chairman, John S. R. Shad, of the Securities and Exchange Commission could say, as he did in 1986, that "arbitrage, and for that matter, speculation are good for the market, not bad. They increase market efficiency and tend to smooth out price fluctuations."[26] An "efficient" market would ordinarily mean a market that priced stocks in accordance with their intrinsic value. But Chairman Shad was using a different definition of efficiency—operational or trading efficiency—one that focuses on the smoothness of the process and the size of brokerage commissions rather than on the correctness of prices and their correspondence to fundamental values. Frank Easterbrook, now a federal judge, and Gregg Jarrell, until recently the chief economist of the Commission, also equate very active markets with efficiency, but they seem to assume that high turnover assures proper pricing.[27] This is as if to say that we would be richer, rather than poorer as would be the case, if all of us somehow bought and sold our houses more often.

What this conventional view overlooks is, first, that a trading game is expensive, whether in houses or in stocks, and needs to be justified by some benefit. Trading adds to liquidity, but at some point the added benefits diminish rapidly. In 1960, when the turnover on the New York Stock Exchange was a mere 12 percent, no one complained that the market was inefficient or illiquid. Eventually the value of the added liquidity becomes less than its cost, which is substantial. Also overlooked is the fact that the source and effects of the trading need to be examined to see to what extent the pricing can still be explained by "rational expectations," as the economists would say, or whether short-term trading does not, by focusing on short-term opportunities and on sentiment within the market itself, have a distortional effect. A study by John G. Cragg and Burton G. Malkiel, for example, suggested that the stock market may listen too much to its own voices. They found that the ability to predict near-term stock prices would be much better if one knew what the security analysts' predictions would be one year hence than if one knew what the actual growth would be five years hence.[28]

But whether the traders and analysts focus on developments at companies or merely on the stock market, much of the time and effort spent gathering this information are an utter waste. That may seem surprising, given the usual assumption that information is what economists call a "collective good" that helps to improve an otherwise imperfect market process. The anomaly here, as Jack Hirshleifer has pointed out, is that most of this information will, in due time and *without any effort*, be available to all; and in any event the information will be used to redistribute wealth rather than to produce it. Socially the information is useless, and the huge apparatus on Wall Street working to publicize or sell it only adds to the waste.[29]

During the boom and bust of the 1927–1933 period, speculation did overrun the trading market. There was clearly too much speculative activity in the public utility stocks, and the behavior of the blue-chip growth stocks, was not very different. The prices for United Corporation, for example, were beyond explanation by classical economics. The price approximately tripled in a few months' time from the original issue price fixed by Morgan and its partner, Bonbright and Company, even though the two had created the company for their own accounts as principals, knew its value, and kept a huge block of perpetual warrants— which ought to have acted as a damper on the market's enthusiasm. The Insull holding companies appreciated during one fifty-day period in 1929 at the rate of $7,000 a minute, or a total of over $500 million.[30] For the public trying to ride the Morgan and Insull coattails, it was as if there were a giant money machine at work. For a time there was, but it did not have much to do with fundamental values.

Sixty years—and a few market breaks—later there is still reason to ask whether the stock market serves us well. It may not be wholly stagnant, but the pool of stocks that moves about so turbulently from hand to hand provides an after-market for a trickle of new issues that is no more than about 1 percent of those already outstanding. The stocks traded on the New York Stock Exchange and other domestic markets had a total market value in mid-1987 of about $3 trillion, but the total value of the new common stocks offered publicly for cash averages no more than about $25–30 billion annually. Turnover of the already listed shares has returned to the level of 1928–1929, and yet leaders in Washington assure us that this hyperactive trading is good for the country.

3. Is the stock market too speculative,
too volatile a place to invest personal savings?
The role of the shareholder depends on his acceptance of common stocks as a legitimate place to put his savings, and by the early 1930s there was a good deal of concern that Wall Street was little more than a gambling hall. Investors and speculators had coexisted in the past, largely by buying different securities. If speculators toyed with the stocks of highly leveraged, promotionally controlled railroads, then investors stayed mostly with high-grade bonds and the stocks of a few banks. The 1920s changed all that. As the Dow Jones Industrial Average rose from about 90 in mid-1924 to 381 in September 1929, with remarkably little advance in the underlying earnings, those who might have chosen to conduct a true investment operation had no place to go—except to sell out altogether. At almost thirty times earnings, even National Biscuit was a speculation on market sentiment. Three years later, in 1932, the Dow had fallen to 41 and National Biscuit from 95 to 20.

It is true that an investor might have purchased the equivalent of the Dow average in the relatively normal period of 1923–1925 and held them as a strongbox investor until "normality" returned again in 1936–1938. His stocks would have appreciated approximately 33 percent,[31] which although not spectacular would have made him one of the most successful investors of the day. But that would have required that he ignore market prices almost completely, neither sharing in the enthusiasm of the crowd nor trying to play against it. After a period that had ignored fundamental values so completely—the blue chip index quadrupled in value, and then even more rapidly fell by 90 percent—it was fair to ask whether there was still room for those who chose to invest on fundamentals.

Sixty years later, there is still reason for private investors to view our financial markets with suspicion. We have seen the good company / bad price syndrome reappear, as it did in the 1970s, when the so-called "nifty-fifty" stocks sold at price-earnings ratios that exceeded even those of 1929. We are seeing in the 1980s the reemergence of the old funny money game of the public utility holding companies—financial entrepreneurs using good businesses, such as television stations, as the base for capital structures so weak as to leave no margin of safety even for the bondholders. We are again seeing investors exchange stocks with each other at a rate as costly as it is pointless. As will be seen, professional investors, including the pension and mutual funds, having led the way in these and other developments, cast some of the longest shadows.

➤2 ➤   Rule No. 2: Never Forget Rule No. 1

"[The] man who grasps the morning paper to see how his speculative ventures upon the exchanges are likely to result, unfits himself for the calm consideration and proper solution of business problems. Andrew Carnegie. (Andrew Sinclair, *Corsair* [Boston: Little, Brown, 1981], 44.)

A S THE NEW DEAL UNFOLDED, the overriding issue in corporate finance was whether the genie of unbridled speculation could be put back into the bottle. The stock market had gorged itself on the notion that no price was too high for a company with good earnings, and then went into reverse and allowed stocks to trade at fire sale prices. Investors paid too much on the way up and then abandoned their positions, or were forced to sell, as prices collapsed.

The stock market had not behaved well for investors nor efficiently for the economy. During the peak period, 1927–1929, inflated stock prices sucked money into all sorts of wasteful, misguided ventures, such as the utility holding companies mentioned in chapter 1. So much money was drawn into margin accounts as to raise interest rates and restrict credit for the real work of the nation. On the way down, real business was hurt again, but now it was the exorbitant cost of new equity, rather than debt, that did the mischief. With stock prices at woefully depressed levels, even in the context of the times, access to the capital markets was almost completely cut off.

During those New Deal years, there appeared two remarkable books that explored the distinction between investment and speculation and the complex, confusing embrace of the public shareholder and the securities markets. They were *Security Analysis* by Graham and Dodd, published in 1934, and *The General Theory of Employment, Interest and Money*, by Keynes, published in 1936. By a happy coincidence, each book—and the Keynesian analysis is almost entirely contained in a single chapter of less than twenty pages—focused its primary attention on a separate aspect of the newly emerging dilemma, Graham and Dodd on the investor and Keynes on the market mechanism.

Graham and Dodd

Security Analysis would have been a remarkable achievement at any time, but it was particularly so in 1934. The unlimited optimism of a few years earlier had given way to despondency. There seemed to be no room left for a positive and yet analytic attitude to securities and, therefore, little if any room for a private capitalist system. Graham and Dodd is a book that would have appealed to President Roosevelt. The authors had faith in capital markets over time, coupled with realism about human fallibility in the short run, all seen through a richly documented history of finance. Their insights are so long-lived that the book, even in the 1934 edition, is still the single best source for an understanding of Wall Street and its participants.

Graham and Dodd's analysis of speculative bonds when purchased at or near par, for example, would have saved potential grief for many a junk bond buyer of recent days. Junk bonds, although they weren't called that, had been widely used in the 1920s, particularly by public utilities. Such bonds were then, and for several years now have again been issued on a basis that offers so little protection—with interest obligations that frequently exceed the company's earnings—that they are very little different from common stocks. If analyzed as such, many of these bonds would undoubtedly be rejected. There is substantial risk of a loss of principal, but unlike common stocks, there is no substantial opportunity for appreciation of principal. As Graham and Dodd said in 1934, quoting the French maxim, "The more it changes, the more it's the same thing."[1] (Chapter 5 contains a discussion of junk bonds, including a description of a 1987 issue by Allied Stores Corporation.)

The heart of the Graham and Dodd analysis was that the influence of analytic factors and fundamental values over the market price was both partial and indirect—partial in that it frequently competes with purely speculative factors, and indirect in that "the merits of an issue reflect themselves in the market price not by any automatic response or mathematical relationship but through the minds and decisions of buyers and sellers."[2] Subjective factors influence the market and are in turn influenced by it. And this is true not just of speculators. Even for those committed to a purely investment program, market prices cannot be ignored, because they have a strong psychological, if not financial, impact. Thus, Graham and Dodd concluded, as in the quotation at the beginning of chapter 1 of this book, that "the market is not a *weighing machine*, . . . [but rather] a *voting machine*, whereon countless individuals register choices which are the product partly of reason and partly of emotion."

Graham and Dodd rejected what we now call the fair-game or fundamental-value version of efficient market theory, saying that it was too glib to speak, as many did in 1934 and still do today, of the wisdom of the market. "Don't argue with the market" is the way it's usually phrased. But as various academic studies have subsequently shown, the market tends to extremes. Euphoria and despair are as much the faces of the market as objective analysis. The favorites often are marked up too much and others down too much. They rejected also that other (and opposite) conventional wisdom of the day that common stocks are inherently and necessarily a wholly speculative undertaking. Common stocks are an appropriate vehicle for an investment program, because for a patient investor the stock market is efficient over the longer term. "There is an inherent tendency for these [shorter term] disparities to correct themselves." In the meantime the investor could be entirely satisfied by the earnings, dividends, and balance sheet position, even if the market quotation remains disappointingly low. One can think of this as a "central value" concept, with market prices that fluctuate above and below a central or "normal" value as measured by earnings prospects and assets.[3] (For instances of these fluctuations then and now, see the discussion at pages 47–50 of this chapter.)

Guessing the stock market cycle and its turns—what we now call the performance game—they left to speculators. Graham and Dodd thus anticipated, and agreed with, what we now call information-arbitrage or stale-news efficiency, meaning that new developments are reflected quickly in the prices of stocks. In their view too much skill and effort were already devoted to the game of outguessing the market over the near term for one to assume that he could do better than average. (''[T]he current market price already takes into account the consensus of opinion as to [near term] prospects.'')[4]

Their approach was drastically selective. Like the bond houses of the 1890s, they thought it was not possible, and in any event not necessary, to have an opinion on the precise value of all or even most stocks. The analyst should focus on those that are of investment grade (unless selling at distress prices), then look for discrepancies between intrinsic value and market value, and even then act only when the discrepancy provides a substantial margin of safety—in short, apply the same principles that would be used to determine ''value to a private investor.''[5] The approach was not new. Only in the 1920s had investors, or those who thought of themselves as such, begun to ignore the price-value equation and systematically bought ''good'' stocks at bad prices.

Graham and Dodd had a very long view of the investment process and its ability to repeat itself time and again. Before World War I, the major bankers could be counted on to reject poor issues, even at the cost of some underwriting profits. But even the best of the firms had succumbed to the pressures of 1928–1929 and, lacking good securities, begun to sell shoddy ones. It seemed too much to expect that they would not do so again. The Securities Act of 1933 offered much better disclosure but no protection beyond that against the sale of speculative stocks. The investor needed, therefore, either a thoroughgoing knowledge of finance or a good adviser. Both would find in *Security Analysis*—and this remains its almost unique contribution—a rational, highly articulated basis on which to invest in an inefficient, often quite irrational market and thereby to help oneself even while helping the market to function more effectively.

Graham and Dodd also had a very long view of the role of the investor within the corporation. Like Roosevelt, they had an optimistic view of man's ability to better his own condition through intelligence and effort. Not content merely to understand the workings of the market and reduce them to usable principles, from edition to edition they devoted increasing attention to proposals for improvements in accounting and management practices. Their special concerns, however, were the policies of management toward shareholders, espcially dividend policy, and the impact that even public investors could have in monitoring management. Why don't investors behave much as if they were shareholders of a closely held corporation? It simply made no sense in their view for an investor to use all his critical skills in making buy-sell decisions and then to suspend those efforts between times. It also made no sense for a company that was doing poorly, with the prospect of continuing losses, to tell its shareholders—and worse yet for them to acquiesce—that their only option was to follow the Wall Street Rule and liquidate their holdings, often at a substantial loss over what could be realized if the company as a whole were liquidated. This sheeplike behavior perpetuates bad corporate policies even as it aggravates bad market prices.

Most of this material on managerial competence and shareholder relations was dropped or greatly shortened in the fourth (1962) edition. Almost no one was listening. The stock market has always respected Graham and Dodd but never embraced it. The patient, disciplined, but very successful attitudes they sought to inculcate never took root. Why not? The reason is essentially the one supplied by Keynes in the second of our two "wise" books: that security analysis as defined by Graham and Dodd is an exercise that is too painstaking and for many just too boring, as well as quite difficult, more art than science. There is no excitement, no action in watching eggs that take years to come to a boil. A good many money managers say that they are Graham-and-Dodders, but in practice they dilute the recipe and shorten up on their investment horizons. "Value investing" strains too much the patience and independence of the investor, who would need the courage to play against the crowd often under trying circumstances. In 1987, for example, many true Graham-and-Dodders, rightly or wrongly—and as it turned out, rightly—chose to hold a fistful of Treasury bills while a bull market was setting record highs. Unable to find stocks at discounts from long-term values, they decided to sit it out. But that takes courage, and whether in times of boom or bust, there are very few who will stay the course. Informal but very consistent estimates are that no more than about 5 percent of the money invested in stocks is managed on these fundamental, value to a "private owner," principles. The number is only an approximation, but taking it as even roughly accurate, over 90 percent of investors are focusing on the short-term behavior of stock prices or using diversified portfolio techniques to buy a slice of the market as a whole. In either case they are shying away from making price and value decisions, as Graham and Dodd so ardently urged them to do.[6]

Keynes

Is it unfair to insist that all those who claim to have a better than ordinary understanding of securities markets document that fact by demon-

strating better than ordinary success as investors? Perhaps, but the fact
is that, like Graham and Dodd, Keynes had an enviable investment record, both for his own account and for Kings College and the insurance
companies whose portfolios he largely managed. Over a nine-year period,
beginning January 1929—hardly the most propitious moment to begin
keeping score—a Kings College fund that held various British and American securities appreciated by over 150 percent, as compared with the
cumulative losses experienced by all the relevant market indices.[7] His
speeches at the annual meetings of the National Mutual Life Assurance
Society, of which he was chairman, became something of an event in
London financial circles.

But the similarities between Graham and Dodd, on the one hand, and
Keynes, on the other, went far beyond the simple fact of investment
success. The methodology was the same, and that in turn grew out of
a shared view of the role and operation of financial markets. Keynes
agreed that it was not useful to try to outguess the market cycle, by
trying as he once had to buy shares in each leading industry in periods
of slumps and then selling them in booms. After twenty years he abandoned the effort, concluding that while a Kings College fund had done
well by purchasing particular shares at times of greatly depressed prices,
it had not been able to take much advantage of a systematic movement
in and out of stocks at different phases of the cycle. Like Graham and
Dodd, he thus rejected the market-timing or performance game that has
been so costly for current-day money managers, arguing that it is "not
merely fantastic, but destructive of the whole system."[8] Instead he fell
back on the older notion of paying as little attention as possible to stock
market fluctuations, saying that while ignoring them is silly, it is "aw-
fully bad for all of us to be constantly revaluing our investments according to market movements."[9] There is a curious effect, Keynes said, to
this popular preoccupation with market prices. For many investors un-
quoted holdings, such as real estate, do seem safer—and produce less
anxiety—than stocks, because one is not burdened by knowing by how
much their ready-market quotations fluctuate.[10]

Like Graham and Dodd, Keynes rejected the aspect of efficient market
theory that argues that stocks are priced fairly at all times in accordance
with their long-term expectations, as well as the essential aspect of modern portfolio theory that argues for a highly diversified portfolio. (Graham and Dodd had concluded that the market is efficient, but only in
the limited sense that it tends *over time* to correct the extremes of over-

and underpricing.) Instead he opted for the same "value to a private owner" standard as Graham and Dodd, emphasizing the desirability of investing in a few, rather than many stocks, saying that he was "incapable of having adequate knowledge of more than a very limited range of investments." He bought as large a unit as market conditions allow, buying only where the market price was sufficiently cheap in relation to assets and earning power to meet a rigorous "safety-first" test—even though it meant rejecting many classes of securities altogether. He confined his purchases to those few stocks he knew something about and in the management of which he believed.[11] Again, as in Graham and Dodd, there was recognition of the "complete impotence, when things go wrong, of the shareholders, separated from one another, each with only a tiny stake in the concern, and practically incapable of joint action. . . ." There is a need for an institutional proxy to represent them.[12]

INVESTING ON FUNDAMENTALS
VERSUS MODERN FINANCE THEORY
What distinguishes Keynes/Graham and Dodd from most modern financial economists is an eyes-open, explicit recognition that the condition of economic life is one of profound uncertainty. Only their investment experience could have taught them that. By contrast it is widely thought today that there is a strict and *predictable* relationship between the risk and return from stocks. The risk is measurable in precise, arithmetic terms—the so-called *beta*, which is the past history of a company's stock price fluctuations relative to a market basket. The prospective return is then calculated as a direct and proportionate function of the risk, meaning that if you want 20 percent more return, you must pay for it with 20 percent more historic volatility of price fluctuations. Starting from the (arguably) appealing premise that there is no free lunch, that because one would not knowingly accept a greater risk except for a greater return, modern finance theory concludes that there is a linear relationship between the two. All the uncertainty dries up. An essential assumption underlying this modern "capital asset pricing model" (CAPM), as it is called, is that risk is something quantifiable, and the debate among most of the scholars is only how to define or adjust the market basket used as a yardstick for risk. Note that risk is to be measured not by studying companies but by studying the history of their stock prices. Look at the mirror of a company's performance, we are told, not at the company itself.

Except for a small dissenting group, there is no doubt in academia today that risk can be measured in this oblique fashion—only as to how best to do it. Indeed, according to the CAPM, risk is something that can be divided by suitable means into two component parts, the "systematic" portion that is the risk of major events, such as a recession, that affect all issuers, and the "unsystematic" that consists of the risks, such as an important invention, that are peculiar to a given company. Since diversification is thought to eliminate all the unsystematic risk, financial economists reject the selection of individual stocks in the fashion of Keynes in favor of broadly based portfolios—not one or two dozen companies, but literally hundreds. "To suppose that safety-first consists in having a small gamble in a large number of directions" struck Keynes as a travesty of investment policy. The "social object of skilled investment," he said, "should be to defeat the dark forces of time and ignorance which envelop our future." Fund managers with a portfolio of two hundred or more securities, the favorites of the day, try to save themselves the bother.

Risk and uncertainty

The distinction that is lost in modern portfolio theory is the critical one between risk and uncertainty. Risk as used in a dice game or fire insurance business means that, as Keynes and later Frank Knight wrote, one can either conduct a logical, a priori calculation of probability or at least gather statistical evidence of probability based on empirical data.[13] Risk is measurable. Uncertainty is something quite different, meaning the type of problem, such as the prospects of a new business, where, as Keynes said, the basis of the knowledge on which to estimate the likely returns is extremely precarious.[14] (The commercial success of the new computer being designed in your garage depends on the unknowable fact of who else is working in his garage.) Uncertainty of this sort is quite different from a mere probability, such as a train accident. However unlikely, train accidents are part of a sufficiently homogeneous group as to be subject to statistical analysis. No such luck with that computer.

Our knowledge of the likely return from investments, as Keynes said in *The General Theory*, is very slight and often negligible.[15] It is not simply that the calculation would be laborious, but rather that very little rational basis may exist for numerical calculation and comparison of any kind.[16] This overriding sense of an uncertain future, one that resists all but the roughest estimates, was reflected in his insistence on making each investment on a basis of "safety-first," just as it was in Graham and

Dodd's equally firm requirement of a "margin of safety." In Graham's concluding chapter of *The Intelligent Investor*, he described the margin of safety as the central concept of investment. Most speculators believe that they have the odds in their favor, but such claims turn out to be quite subjective. "A true margin of safety," he said, "is one that can be demonstrated by figures, by persuasive reasoning, and by reference to a body of actual experience."[17] No wonder the dropout rate is 95 percent. Warren Buffett, Graham's most successful disciple, tried to capture this same, almost obsessive concern with business uncertainty and ignorance when he said that his first rule is "never lose money" and his second rule is: "Never forget Rule No. 1."

Safety first, a true margin of safety, and never forget rule no. 1. Those "rules" contain more than a faint echo of the strongbox investors of the nineteenth century described in chapter 1. The primary focus of the bankers of that earlier day was to eliminate the weak issues, for any of a variety of reasons. There might be weak management, too much debt, a loss of competitive position. It simply did not matter. By considering the possibility of gain only after a rigorous analysis of weakness, a large number of companies were flatly rejected, regardless of price.

It is fair, then, to ask who is to buy the speculative issues, or are they to be excluded from the capital markets at the time that they most need capital? Where are tomorrow's investment-grade issues to come from? The question can be answered on two levels. First, there seems to be no shortage of people willing to take a flier on the next computer or genetic engineering company. The mystery of discovery and the excitement of being in on the ground floor are difficult to resist. Historically the problem instead has been to create a proper framework for those who fancy themselves as investors but discover only after a time that they had in fact been speculating. On a more profound level, however, the answer usually given in the period that ended shortly after World War I is probably as good today: these start-up, high risk undertakings are best suited for private venture capital groups, who have not only the requisite technical skills but an opportunity to monitor a company's management at close hand. As Dewing wrote in 1920, "the highly speculative enterprise should not be backed by the general public. It requires too much investigation and discrimination. . . ."[18]

Risk and uncertainty are very abstract concepts, and while we can accept risk—and even insure against it, so that it almost ceases to exist— the mind tends to flee from uncertainty. It is such a miserably unsettling, unacceptable state. One gropes in the fog for signposts, and there are no halogen lamps to light the way. Modern financial economists and others talk of uncertainty, but then they lapse into an analytic structure in which they quantify the "uncertainties" in very precise terms and construct elegant graphs of "efficient" portfolios that, for a given level of risk, produce the greatest expected returns.[19]

Uncertainty in business is a state that produces nothing so comforting as an efficient portfolio. Consider oil reserves, for example, which have been the subject of so much takeover activity in recent years. To value Oil Company X, for example, one must make assumptions about the extent and quality of its reserves, the cost to recover them, and the success of future drilling programs. American oil companies are required to publish data on their proven reserves. Even assuming them to be accurate, these reserves will not be taken out of the ground except over a long period, twenty years or more in some cases. Thus the investor needs to make projections about the price of oil five, ten, and more years hence. Those prices will in turn depend on a number of remarkably unpredictable supply-side factors, such as domestic and foreign exploration programs, which have been shrinking recently under the impact of lower prices, but may well revive; on a number of other economic variables, such as improved recovery methods; and on a number of noneconomic factors, such as the politics of the Middle East and the needs of various governments to earn foreign exchange. The demand side is also uncertain, depending as it does on the likelihood of alternative fuel supplies, the impact of conservation measures, the general level of economic activity, and the development of new petrochemical applications that add to the uses of oil.

These estimates would help to establish the value of Company X's proven reserves. Hardy as they may be, however, they do not reflect the value of the company's probable but unproven reserves, for which information is not generally available, and which are often the more valuable of the two. And even that is not the end of the process. Currency exchange rates and discount rates also enter in.

We can now see that if we had decided in 1981 to invest in Oil Company X, the decision was simply too complex and too unique—not like a train accident at all—for any sort of statistical tabulation to have had much value. The oil industry had just benefited from major OPEC-driven price increases and supply constraints. No doubt United States Steel (now USX), DuPont, and the others that acquired oil companies in 1981 made detailed discounted cash flow calculations, but by 1986 it was apparent that these decisions turned on some assumptions (e.g., estimates of future returns) that were unreliable and others (e.g., the discount rate) that were essentially arbitrary. Yet billions of dollars were invested, and perhaps wisely, on the basis of these probability estimates. The error in the capital asset pricing model is not that these estimates should be avoided, but only the sanguine assumption that such estimates, based individually on inescapable ignorance, become wise in the aggregate. This assumption seems reasonable only if one never looks beyond the realm of stock price changes, the mere reflection of a complex underlying reality, making no effort to grapple directly, as Keynes would have us do, with the "dark forces" of ignorance.

Given the uncertainty of long-term expectations, Keynes argued that there is an understandable tendency to fall back on the present state of affairs and to accept it not merely for what it is, but to project it on into the future. The present state is much less relevant, but it is something about which we are much more confident, and that is no small matter. (Something very like this behavior was observed years later in studies of security analysts' projections.)[20] The effect is to produce a working assumption—what might be called the Keynesian convention—that the "existing market valuation, however arrived at, is uniquely correct in relation to our existing knowledge of the facts . . . , and that it will only change in proportion to changes in this knowledge; though, philosophically speaking, it cannot be uniquely correct, since our existing knowledge does not provide a sufficient basis for a calculated mathematical expectation."[21] Lacking a satisfactory basis for an estimate, however, security analysts are in a quandary. Providing *some* estimate of future earnings is what they are paid to do. Too often they simply project a continuation of the past on into the future.

What is remarkable is that this Keynesian convention reads so much like modern finance theory, under which the price of a stock at any time is the best available estimate of long-term values, because it reflects all publicly available information about the firm and its prospects. The price will change, therefore, only when some new bit of information comes to light and the process begins anew. It is as though present-day economists had cribbed from Keynes, even while rejecting his analysis. The difference is that for Keynes the convention was the wages of a state of ignorance and uncertainty—we do not "really believe that the existing state of affairs will continue indefinitely"—while for financial economists it is the happy triumph of high intelligence working on a free flow of information in a world of quantifiable probabilities.

Practical implications of the disagreement

The conflict as to the proper investment approach is almost total. According to modern financial theory, investors seeking higher than market rates of return should not do research about individual companies, but rather should borrow money and leverage their portfolios or buy high *beta* stocks, such as new issues of unseasoned companies. In general, investors should buy the market basket of stocks, not just those few that they understand and regard as offering better value.

The fundamental-value investor disagrees on all points, reserving special scorn for buying on margin. (If you know what you're doing, you don't need to buy on margin; and if you don't know, then it's surely an error.) For a Graham-Dodd investor, the margin-of-safety concept implies that a more than ordinarily successful investment operation depends on an analysis of business, not market, risk and on minimizing risk rather than seeking it out. This is a view consistent with the empirical work recently done by Dennis C. Mueller and others, suggesting that firms with consistently high returns are less, not more, risky investments. (Those businessmen who deliberately take extra risks are often acting out of some urgent need to improve on a presently poor performance.)[22]

THE STOCK MARKET IS NOT AN ORDINARY MARKET.

Keynes's ultimate contribution was his recognition that the stock market, with its ability to make liquid for the individual investor what is a fixed investment for the community, was having the unintended effect of destabilizing our capital markets. This is a critical point. The organized investment markets, in addition to their obvious advantages, had unexpectedly introduced two major weaknesses that were not visible when investments were primarily in private businesses and were, therefore, fixed for the individual as well as the community as a whole. First, the stock market turned out to be an astonishingly liquid one, a market with remarkably high turnover rates. Second, it is an almost wholly secondary market, meaning that the transactions on the exchange consist almost entirely of transfers of existing investments, rather than the creation of new ones or even the elimination of existing units from the supply. The liquidity tends to encourage an emphasis on near-term expectations, because the investor need not concern himself with the uncertainties of

the long term if at any time he has the ability to revise his commitment—
he need only do so before the crowd. The social dilemma, of course, is
that there is liquidity only for the individual, not for the community.
Liquidity
There being no liquidity for the community, why is it not clear to economists and investors alike that risk and reward can be measured only at
the business level, not at the market level? The distributable profits of a
company are the only rewards for the community. There are none other.
A stock is not inherently more valuable because it is marketable. Buffett,
for example, tries to protect against the illusion of liquidity by assuming
it away, by making believe that the stock market is going to close down
the next day. He's not buying stocks, he's buying businesses.

Marketability, the ability to sell on short notice, is relevant to an
avowed trader who intends to close out his position within a few minutes
or days, but it ought not to influence much an investment decision.
The spread between the bid and asked prices—marketability's principal
relevance—is usually less than the penalty exacted for in-and-out trading
or for redeeming mutual fund shares. Yet even sophisticated observers
insist that the same business may be twice as valuable simply because the
shares are actively traded.[23]

A too-active market tends to substitute what Graham and Dodd called
"financial reasoning" for "business reasoning." The stock ticker too
often registers an aggregate valuation for enterprises that is totally unrelated to what a normal appraisal of the underlying business would produce. Just as in 1929–1930, few shareholders of General Electric knew
that the stock price represented a valuation of about $2.7 billion; a short
while later many of them were willing to sell their shares in some otherwise good companies at discounts of as much as 90 percent from the
value that "a single private owner would have unhesitatingly placed
upon [them]."[24] And a few years after that, in 1937–1938, they repeated
the process, sending the price of General Electric down from about 65
to 27.

> It was little short of nonsense for the stock market to say in 1937
> that General Electric Company was worth $1,870,000,000 and almost
> precisely a year later that it was worth only $784,000,000. Certainly
> nothing had happened. . . . To speak of these prices as representing
> "investment values" or the "appraisal of investors" is to do violence
> either to the English language or to common sense, or both.[25]

The more the shares turn, the more certain it becomes that people will think of themselves as owning not a part of a business but as owning some intangible financial instruments, and the more likely that the prices of the shares will bear little relationship to "Main Street" values.

Stock prices fluctuate over so wide a range and with such frequency that investors understandably, if incorrectly, focus on the behavior of prices. In the last edition of *The Intelligent Investor*, Graham illustrated the severity of the price changes for a number of companies. Table 2-1 contains price quotations for McGraw-Hill, a well-known company that enjoyed quite stable earnings. In each of the thirteen years prior to the writing of the fourth revised edition, the price had either advanced or declined over a range of at least three-to-two from one year to the next.

An almost wholly secondary market

The second disquieting factor is that the stock market is largely a market of secondary transactions, a market of derived demands. It is very unlike the wheat market, for example, where the ultimate purchasers do not make their purchases with a view to resale but rather to feed livestock or make flour. No investor ordinarily buys stocks to consume either them or their underlying resources. . . . The latter are, of course, legally inaccessible to the shareholders. Instead, stocks are bought for resale,

Table 2-1

Large Year-to-Year Fluctuations
of McGraw-Hill, 1958–1971[26]

From	To	Advances		Declines	
1958	1959	39	-72		
1959	1960	54	$-109\frac{3}{4}$		
1960	1961	$21\frac{3}{4}$	$-43\frac{1}{8}$		
1961	1962			$43\frac{1}{8}$	$-18\frac{1}{4}$
1962	1963	$18\frac{1}{4}$	$-32\frac{1}{4}$		
1963	1964	$23\frac{3}{8}$	$-38\frac{7}{8}$		
1964	1965	$28\frac{3}{8}$	-61		
1965	1966	$37\frac{1}{2}$	$-79\frac{1}{2}$		
1966	1967	$54\frac{1}{2}$	-112		
1967	1968			$56\frac{1}{4}$	$-37\frac{1}{2}$
1968	1969			$54\frac{5}{8}$	-24
1969	1970			$39\frac{1}{2}$	-10
1970	1971	10	$-24\frac{1}{8}$		

except for such few as are from time to time taken off the market in mergers, liquidations, and stock repurchase programs. From year to year, the great majority simply move from hand to hand, bought by shareholders whose expectations of a return *of* capital and most of the return *on* capital depend entirely on the willingness of others to share such expectations. Except for the current dividend, often a minor factor, there is no current use and enjoyment of stocks as in real estate and many other assets.

The demand for stocks is unusual but not quite unique. It is very much like the demand for gold, which also is consumed in only small quantities relative to the total amount in existence. Both have an indefinite shelf life, and unlike wheat the storage and handling of both stocks and gold are simple and inexpensive.

In the wheat market, unlike that for gold or stocks, traders can focus on the demand for bread, and the weather and other factors affecting supply, and then estimate what they can afford to pay and still turn a profit on the settlement date of their contracts. It is true that only about 3 percent of all future contracts in agricultural commodities are normally settled by actual delivery, the rest being settled in cash by the traders among themselves. But that should not matter, at least so long as those who do produce or consume wheat provide some external, objective discipline to the trading game. In fact, the traders of wheat have little occasion to let their gaze wander from "true value," since it is already a near-term calculation, determined by millers, and bakers and farmers, and not subject to nearly so much uncertainty as the long-term value of the investments in the bricks and mortar that underlie so many common stocks.

That is not to say that wheat or other commodity prices are consistently rational. In any such market, where goods are purchased not just for their own sake but for resale, the current price will reflect not only production and consumption decisions but also the buyer's estimate of the market's own behavior.[27] Bubbles are indeed possible in commodities as well as stocks. This author wrote a few years ago, when wine prices had soared to unrealistic levels:

> While speculative bubbles may occur in the markets for tulips or wine, they seem to do so only when . . . the buyer has changed. For example, it would be very difficult for me to drink a bottle of wine for which I paid $10,000, [and almost] inevitably the only persons who would buy

> it from me are those who would purchase it for "investment" [that
> is, for trading in a purely secondary market].[28]

Such bubbles are, however, less likely in stocks.

Unlike the more usual $5 bottles of wine, however, for most stocks
there are only traders, no "drinkers." The prospective investor suspects
that he ought to do a fundamental valuation of the enterprise. He ought
to be thinking about how the business is doing, much as a traditional
bank lender would analyze a borrower's income statement and financial
policies, because he is looking to the borrower for the return of his
capital. But if you expect merely to resell, you are inescapably drawn to
thinking in terms of the market. Financial statements become merely a
guide to what the *market* will do, rather than a statement of what the
company will do. However confident the investor may be as to the soundness of his valuation, his success depends largely on what measure of
value a prospective buyer a year or two later will adopt—after having
worked *his* way through all the same substantive uncertainties, only to
realize that he, in turn, must come to grips with the fact of being able
to sell only to another trader. The result was captured in Keynes's often
quoted observation that professional investment resembles a newspaper
beauty contest in which the winners are the ones

> whose choice most nearly corresponds to the average preferences of the
> competitors as a whole; so that each competitor has to pick, not those
> faces which he himself finds prettiest, but those which he thinks likeli-
> est to catch the fancy of the other competitors, all of whom are looking
> at the problem from the same point of view. . . . [We] have reached
> the third degree where we devote our intelligences to anticipating what
> average opinion expects the average opinion to be.[29]

While Graham and Dodd did not express it so graphically, they had in
1934 described the stock market in almost precisely the same terms:

> For stock speculation is largely a matter of A trying to decide what B,
> C and D are likely to think—with B, C and D trying to do the same.[30]

This notion of stocks, or gold for that matter, passing from hand to
hand—without the intervention of either new supplies or the elimination
of old ones—leads to some tantalizing fantasies. Imagine, for example,
the creation of what Graham called a "frozen corporation," one whose
charter effectively forbade both the payment of dividends and any liquidation or merger. There is no way to get any money out of the company

itself. The shares would, so far as one can tell, trade forever, with no current return, but on what basis would they be valued? Gardner Ackley has created a similar puzzle expressed in gold by assuming that the existing supply is constant, as is virtually the case, and then asking how one would determine the equilibrium price, if there is no production to lower the price and no consumption to raise it. In the case of the frozen corporation, one can at least calculate the enterprise value, the value if the business could have been sold as a whole. But there are no external constraints, nothing resembling the baker or miller in the wheat market, to translate the enterprise value into share values for trading purposes. The connection with the underlying, "real" values becomes woefully tenuous.

TWO EXAMPLES FIFTY YEARS APART

Graham's *The Intelligent Investor*, is richly annotated with examples in all directions of stock prices that could not be explained on rational grounds. A number of them focused on the extraordinarily wide swings in market price that sometimes accompanied quite modest changes in earnings and prospects. Graham's description of the extreme price changes in the common stock of S. H. Kress, a then well-known variety chain, is illustrative:[31]

> The stability of the annual earnings per share of [S. H. Kress] common stock [for 1924–1945] is extraordinary. In sixteen out of the twenty-two years they varied only between $1.93 and $2.32. In the other six, including the boom and deepest depression years, the range widened only to $1.32–$2.88. It may properly be concluded that this record at no point showed any definite indications of permanent change for either the better or the worse in the company's affairs or prospects. Hence the variations in market price must have been entirely psychological in their origin. They offer a fairly accurate measurement of the breadth of price change ascribable to the mere vagaries of the stock market— while the "article valued" changed its character not at all.

The price fluctuations in the Kress common stock and the earnings per share are shown in Chart 2-1.

This same inconsistency between stock prices and earnings appears in the more recent example of General Foods Corporation. The company's food processing business was, like the variety stores of Kress, rather straightforward. General Foods' earnings per share showed a similarly

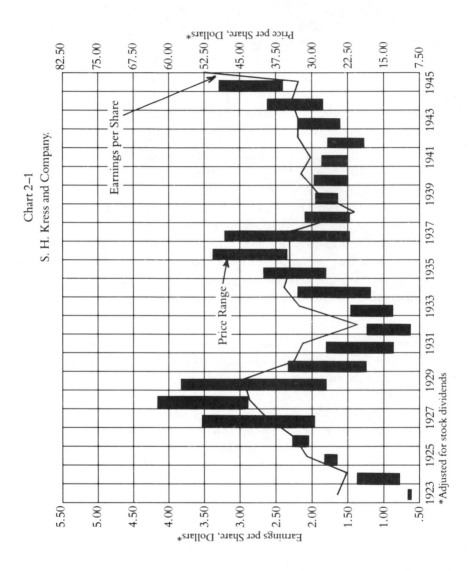

Chart 2–1
S. H. Kress and Company.

consistent pattern, the major difference being that the earnings tended to increase in a steady fashion rather than merely to remain stable. During a thirty-four-year period, 1951–1984, earnings per share of General Foods common stock (adjusted for stock splits) rose from $.57 to $6.61, a compounded annual increase of 7.5 percent, which in light of the substantial dividend payments should have provoked neither very much enthusiasm nor despair. General Foods is a major coffee processor, and given the wide swings in coffee and other commodity prices during the period, the earnings show remarkably steady growth. Earnings declined in only five of those years, declined by as much as 10 percent only twice, and even then quickly recovered.

From 1951 to 1984, the stock price of General Foods increased about ten times, just as the earnings had done. But unlike the earnings, the market prices of General Foods common stock were subject to extraordinarily wide swings that, as in the case of Kress, cannot be explained by anything other than the whims and fashions of the stock market. The following chart sets forth the earnings per share of General Foods common stock and the annual price range of the stock. During the later years there occurred fairly abrupt changes in interest rates that might have affected the value of the common stock, regardless of earnings. The chart therefore includes the "price" of a high-grade bond index derived from Standard & Poor's statistical data. Since bond prices and stock prices both tend to move in a direction opposite to changes in interest rates, it was possible that the General Foods stock price changes were simply a function of interest rate fluctuations. Chart 2-2 makes it quite clear, however, that very little of the wide swings in the stock price can be ascribed to any such rational factors.

RECENT RESEARCH DATA

The reader may be wondering at this point whether Keynes's view of the stock market as one beset by widespread speculation and structural defects has not been overtaken by subsequent events. In the fifty years since he wrote *The General Theory* a great deal of effort has been expended on developing and testing what is called the efficient market theory. This is an issue to which we will return in looking at takeover bids in chapter 5, but given the importance of it, some discussion now should be helpful.

The efficient market theory states in its relevant aspect that competition among sophisticated investors enables the stock market to price stocks consistently in accordance with our best expectations of companies' *long-term* earnings—or dividends, the distinction not being important for our purposes. (The trading by nonprofessionals is said to be random and of no net effect.) All relevant publicly available information is analyzed by investors and any new data, such as an earnings release, are quickly noted, digested and then reflected in the share price. The process takes place almost instantaneously, even in the face of complex data. Efficient market theory does not, of course, claim that stock prices will always turn out to have been correct, but only that they represent the best available estimates and that no systematic method exists for selecting those stocks that will do better and those that will do worse.

A huge number of tests have been run, mostly on the basis of an extensive data base of stock prices at the University of Chicago. Doctoral candidates have earned their degrees by testing almost every conceivable

Chart 2-2
General Foods Corporation
(1950–84)

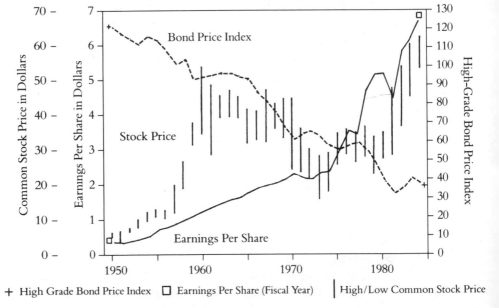

+ High Grade Bond Price Index   ☐ Earnings Per Share (Fiscal Year) | High/Low Common Stock Price

NOTES: 1. Price per share and earnings per share are adjusted for stock dividends and splits.
         2. General Foods was acquired by Philip Morris in 1985. Each share of common stock was converted into $120 cash.

aspect, including such trivia as whether stock prices are more apt to move up than down on Mondays.

Some of these tests tend to reject the efficient market hypothesis. The fluctuations in stock prices are too great to be explained by changes in fundamentals, and the market overprices its favorites by too much and underprices too many others. The extensive research by Professor Robert J. Shiller is particularly interesting, because it explores the social and emotional aspects of stock investing. His studies suggest, for example, that the overpricing that occurs at times for specific companies is the result not so much of a conscious willingness to pay too much and then, as Keynes said, to sell out before the crowd, but rather a tendency to follow the crowd and to buy stocks with cheery prospects but with too little attention to the price. Where Keynes saw a possibly cunning investor, one who capitalizes on a fad or fashion, Shiller's more systematic analysis describes the investor as one who is more likely to be captured by it.

Some other studies also suggest that the market tends to overreact. Sanjoy Basu and then David A. Goodman and John W. Peavy showed that investors can achieve much superior results by buying low price-earnings ratio stocks rather than those with high P/E ratios, reinforcing the suspicion that buyers tend to congregate around the stocks that are then in favor and to neglect those that are not.[32] In a very simple experiment, Werner DeBondt and Richard Thaler demonstrated that buying stocks that have been the biggest losers in the past produces results over time that are much better than buying the recent winners or tracking the market as a whole.[33]

Studies of new stock issues uniformly bear out the Keynesian (and Graham and Dodd) observation that while new issues are surely risky, the returns are not better but *worse* than that of the market generally. That is consistent, of course, with the high sales commissions paid on new issues. They need to be peddled aggressively, which would hardly be the case if the rewards were better than average. Their appeal is more that of a lottery: on average you should expect to lose, but occasionally there is a big "hit."

There are, on the other hand, numbers of studies that are said to support efficient market theory. They tend to fall into a few distinct categories. One such group studies the speed of the market's response to discrete, testable new information, such as an announcement of a stock split, block trade, or earnings release. The tests show that the market does respond to these announcements quickly, so that the market can be said to be efficient in the stale-news or information-arbitrage sense of the term. In short, Wall Street has big ears.

Efficiency in this stale-news sense is a desirable attribute, and there is no disagreement that Wall Street does react quickly to developments. But the concept has important limitations. It makes no statement at all about fundamental-value efficiency—that is, about whether the stock was properly valued before (or after) the announcement. There is confusion on this matter. It ought to be clear, but frequently is not, that because information travels quickly, the decisions based on it are not necessarily correct or wise.

A number of us in the academic community have tried to get others to focus on this, but with little luck and no small amount of frustration. The notion that in the stock market you can "trust prices," as so many textbooks on corporate finance state, has obviously dangerous implications. (The bond market is much easier to trust, because there are many fewer variables to contend with.) It reinforces the already great inclination of analysts and money managers to pursue the favorites of the day, instead of doing fundamental, price-value analysis on a company-by-company basis.

Another important group of tests, one that has captured a good deal of attention, is also said to support efficient market theory.[34] These tests show that market professionals are unable on average to do better than the market as a whole. Indeed, after management fees and other charges, they do worse. One result of these studies has been the creation of a number of so-called index funds that consist of an unchanging portfolio of securities that in some cases simply match, for example, those in the Standard & Poor's 500 Stock Index. After all, why pay for managers who cannot deliver? The question is what these studies tell us about the stock market. According to many financial economists, they provide powerful support for efficient market theory, because if mutual funds cannot outperform the market, it follows that all the varied and detailed information employed by these professional managers is already reflected in the market price. Attempts to pick particular stocks as undervalued are a waste.

While that is a permissible interpretation of those studies, it is certainly not the only one. It depends on what is called the rational expectations hypothesis, meaning that the managers in reality are focusing their attention on fundamental values. If managers are really trying to defeat the "dark forces" of ignorance, if they are true Graham-and-Dodders, and if even they cannot do better than the market averages, then the market prices must be quite wise, or at least as wise as can be. But what if managers are focusing their attention elsewhere? These mutual fund studies are equally consistent with Keynes's view that the market professionals are now, at least as much as they were fifty years ago, retreating from uncertain, difficult long-term projections into the relative safety of following the crowd to the stocks with cheery prospects. Perhaps, as Keynes said, they have more reason to do so, because it is prudent for professionals to show to clients a portfolio that reflects the prevailing wisdom, rather than to risk all by going an independent route. And in that case, market prices would not be very wise at all.

STOCK PRICES ARE ONLY A MIRROR

Stock prices are nothing more than a mirror of reality, and if the reality is that the market is predominantly engaged in playing out a short term, market-timing game, then the mirror will not reflect anything better. All that can be said of these mutual fund studies, therefore, is that by supposing investors to be rational (or not), one can conclude that stock prices are also rational (or not). Just as we do not hesitate to question how the public votes for Congress, or how Congress votes on the budget, we should not hesitate to question how investors vote on stocks. "Don't argue with the market" is about as sensible as putting one's congressman on a permanent pedestal.

Of the recent literature on efficient market theory, one article, written in 1986 by Fischer Black, deserves special attention. Black was an academic economist but is now in Wall Street. He is a leading proponent of modern finance theory, and the article was his presidential address at the American Finance Association. In many respects the article, entitled "Noise," simply restated the conventional view that the stock market is efficient and that it is only differences in information, not opinion, that create the trading. This insistence on there being differences in information is so essential to modern theory because if shades of opinion, perspective, and wisdom were allowed into the picture, it would not be possible to make the assumption that there is a collective, best available set of homogeneous expectations about the future of earnings and dividends. Efficient market theory depends on that assumption, because if opinion and intelligence are factors, if the market is simply a voting or betting machine, the expectations obviously will range all over the lot and so will stock prices. Thus Black reaffirmed the neoclassical belief that "[d]ifferences in beliefs must derive ultimately from differences in information." Trading depends on those differences in information, not differences in opinion or long- versus short-term perspectives.

Black's years in Wall Street had awakened him, however, to a hitherto unnoticed, "arbitrary element," one that he called "noise." Prices were too volatile and too divorced from value. This experience and insight did not, however, lead him to discard the principle of market efficiency, but instead to redefine it in a way that is very revealing. Some of the most violent price swings fall safely within Black's new definition, which it is better to set out than to summarize:

> However, we might define an efficient market as one in which price is within a factor of 2 of value, i.e., the price is more than *half* of value and less than *twice* value. The factor of two is arbitrary, of course. Intuitively, though, it seems reasonable to me, in the light of sources of uncertainty about value and the strength of the forces tending to cause price to return to value. By this definition, I think almost all markets are efficient almost all of the time. "Almost all" means at least 90%.[35]

According to Black, stock prices can drop in half or double and still be "efficient." What is so striking is that the original definition of an efficient market was one in which there was no money to be made in the study of individual stocks and companies, after taking into account the cost of the study itself. In this new, expanded definition, the price of a stock with earnings of $1 per share and a central value of 12 can fluctuate anywhere form 6 to 24 and still be considered efficient. And 10 percent of the time the price discrepancies may be greater still.

In nine trading days in October 1987, the stock of Apple Computer lost over $2 billion in market value. Nothing of that magnitude had happened at the company, and yet according to Black's definition the price was efficient both before and after. For a set of very strict views, efficient market theory seems to require some increasingly flexible assumptions.

The social aspects of investing and financial markets, those that tempt investors to follow the crowd and to overlook price-value equations, should not be defined away so casually. The necessary information is widely available and of remarkably good quality. But it is not the information that changes so rapidly. Although there are quantitative aspects to it, finance is not a physical science. In the business world, as anyone who has spent time there well knows, the attitudes and temperament that managers bring to the process are essential elements of success. Finance is no different.

➤ 3 ➤ The Performance Game

The stock market resembles a huge laundry in which institutions take in large blocks of each other's washing—nowadays to the tune of 30 million shares a day—without true rhyme or reason. But technologically it is remarkably well-organized. (A Conversation with Benjamin Graham, *Fin. An. J.* [Sept./Oct. 1976]: 20)

LOOKING BACK over the years since the New Deal, some very good things have happened to investors. The trading or operating efficiency of the market has greatly increased. Ben Graham was right: the stock market is a technological marvel. Commissions are much lower, and large blocks of stock can be sold with remarkable speed and at prices that change little from the previous transactions. The back-office breakdowns of the late 1960s have been cured, and stocks now trade at volumes twenty times greater without imposing serious strains on the flow of securities, money, and paperwork.

It is not a picture of perfection. The American rules with respect to insider trading are a model for other countries; but there is still too much uncertainty about who is and who is not an insider, and the Supreme Court has been reluctant to give an expansive reading to an already modest legislative mandate. The public continues to pay large commissions, aptly known as "loads," to buy the shares of mutual funds—$4 billion of commissions in 1986—even though there are large numbers of no-load funds with equally good or better records. To bend the brokers' recommendations in favor of this fund or that, the bait includes not just commissions but expensive cars, trips, and jewelry. Under the Securities and Exchange Commission's new rule 12b-1, the advertising and other costs of selling to new customers can be charged to the existing ones instead of to the manager. By imposing a second layer of securities, managers, and fees on top of the first, the funds sometimes increase the pitfalls rather than reduce them. With it all, however, and having in mind a goal of workable, not perfect, rules, the market has achieved a high degree of fairness.

The fundamental-value efficiency of the market, however—its ability to price stocks closely to their real values—has not improved much, or we would not be so sorely beset by boom and bust. The pension funds and other such institutions grew in size and came to dominate the trading and pricing of stocks, but the contributions they might have made somehow slipped away. Instead of the patient, long-term perspectives that one would expect of pension fund managers, instead of using the market rather than being used by it, increasingly they trade in almost seamless fashion round the world and round the clock. Major institutions hold daily briefings, with overseas offices "patching in" electronically, in an atmosphere of urgency that World War II commanders would have understood. The concern for liquidity—that American institution— has become an obsession. It feeds on low commissions and newly created options and other "derived" securities, and it focuses on arbitrage, market timing, and other financial operations divorced from real benefits to the economy. As one mutual fund industry official put it, "it's all market timing today. They're looking for two, three, four switches a year."

The institutions might have stood to one side in all this, but in fact they are among the worst offenders. They regularly take in "each other's washing," as Graham said, at a pace that now surpasses the heady days of 1928–1929. They have fallen victim to the doctrine of "risk management" that prescribes intensive trading, index funds, and a variety of other tactics to stay close to market trends regardless of where those trends may be going. No particular company is looked at very much, matters very much, or matters for very long.

The Institutionalization of the Stock Market

For the past thirty years, the ownership of American public corporations has become increasingly concentrated, thus encouraging hopes that the insurance companies, pension funds, investment companies, and other institutional investors would, by taking an active role, protect not only their own interests but those of shareholders generally. All the ingredients seemed to be there. They own large blocks of stock, some of them as much as $100 million in a single company. They have the staffs and the sophistication. As it has turned out, however, the money managers have contributed almost nothing to the direction or oversight of the companies whose stocks they so briefly hold.

When the Securities Act of 1933 was adopted, institutions owned about 8 percent of the outstanding New York Stock Exchange listed securities.[1] Since the 1950s, the bank-managed trust funds, insurance companies, pension funds and other financial institutions have gradually increased their ownership so that at the end of 1986 they owned about 45 percent of the almost $3 trillion of public company stocks. (The precise amount of institutional ownership is difficult to calculate, in part because of the lack of recent data and in part because of a definition that sometimes, for example, includes bank trust accounts and investment advisory accounts, and sometimes not.) Because the institutions tend to concentrate their investments in the larger capitalization companies that offer better liquidity, the percentage ownership of these companies is often much higher. As early as 1971 the SEC, in its Institutional Investors Study, found that a selected group of 213 major financial institutions owned 40 percent or more of the common shares of 27 companies, and in nine of these they owned 50 percent or more. In 1985, according to a Wharton School study, 82 percent of the stocks held by banks were in companies with a market value of at least $1 billion, although those larger companies represented only 70 percent of the market value of all publicly owned companies.[2]

For ten years now the SEC has required that those who manage more than $100 million report publicly on their holdings. Relying on those data, and looking just at 306 of the companies in the Standard & Poor's 500 Stock Index, Salomon Brothers found that in 1981 institutions owned 40 percent or more of 180 companies—that is, more than half of the companies in their study. The institutions owned 50 percent or more of 101 of these companies and 60 percent or more of 27 of them, and if foreign and intercorporate holdings had been included, the figures would have been higher still. More current data show that banks and other institutions now own, for example, 81 percent of Digital Equipment, 79 percent of K mart, and 72 percent of Citicorp.[3]

Large hopes, but only small results

For sixty years there have been high hopes that the institutions would do something with their stocks besides sitting on them. As early as 1927, Ripley suggested that the investment trusts, competently run, might be able to participate in corporate government in an ''intelligent and entirely helpful way.''[4] In 1938, although the institutions were still a minor factor, the SEC wondered whether, with their research facilities and professional skills, they might serve "not only . . . their own interests but the interests of the other public stockholders."[5] The search was for a group that could wield some of the influence of a J. P. Morgan without the overweening power of a Morgan. As the mutual funds and other financial intermediaries grew in importance during the 1950s and 1960s, so too did the expectations. The SEC's Institutional Investor Study in 1971 expressed the then common view that the "collectivization of otherwise disparate shareholder interests through institutional investment has created the most formidable potential counter-force to corporate managerial hegemony."[6]

The institutions did seem to be crowding out the individual or nonprofessional investor, leading the chairman of the Federal Reserve Board to see "an obvious risk . . . [that institutions] may virtually corner the market in individual stocks."[7] There were some who wondered about the consequences if such powerful institutions now chose to take a more active role in their portfolio companies. Situations might arise in which an employee benefit fund, for example, might pursue the interests of the employees, at the expense of other shareholders. On the bright side, however, it was widely hoped that as the market lost its liquidity, particularly for large investors, the institutions might have no choice but to take a longer view of their interests and act more as owners of their portfolio companies.

The hope that the institutional investors might be locked in died stillborn, because the market developed block trading mechanisms that avoided the threatened loss of liquidity. The institutions never cornered the market, and the very notion of a corner became irrelevant as Salomon, Goldman Sachs, and others created the trading facilities that enabled institutions to get in and out of large positions with remarkable ease. For the month of January 1960 the volume of trading on the New York Stock Exchange was 64 million shares. For January 1980 it was 1,158 million shares. For January 1985 it was 2,674 million shares. The level of trading as a whole increased rapidly, but trading by institutions increased even more rapidly, as Table 3-1 indicates.

Although the buyers and sellers do not of course identify themselves, block trading—trading in units of 10,000 shares or more—is an almost entirely institutional phenomenon. A large proportion even of the trading in blocks as small as 1,000 shares is also institutional, and on any given day only about 10 percent of the total volume on the New York

Stock Exchange is in units of less than 1,000 shares. Estimates are that pension funds, bank trust departments, investment bank trading departments, and other institutions account for about 75 percent of the trading.

The precise figure is not very important. Even at some much lower figure the institutionalization of the market is essentially complete, in the sense that the trading has moved ''upstairs'' to the trading desks of the major trading firms and away from the auction market on the floor of the Exchange. The historic role of the Exchange specialist as a market-maker will continue to diminish, because it makes no sense for a trader seeking to buy 25,000 shares—an average block today—to see if the specialist has 2,000 or 2,500 shares to sell, particularly if in the process the trader has to reveal his own hand.

Mutual funds and other institutions have from time to time acted as owners of a business, rather than stock traders, but the record is very poor. A senior officer at one of the major funds tells of bringing a lawsuit to contest the allegedly unfair buyout of a portfolio company and then bearing litigation expenses of $1 million before settling the case in order to have done with it. It was a classic ''free rider'' problem. The risk, he said, is all yours, but the benefits must be shared. Not worth it, was his conclusion; he'd rather do his public service in some other, more rewarding fashion. Unlike litigation, which they almost uniformly reject, the institutions have of late begun to use their voting rights a bit more energetically, but the effort has been scattered and the response of other investors only lukewarm. In 1986 one large state pension fund solicited proxies against management proposals at a dozen corporations but failed to defeat any of them.

Mutual funds and pension funds perform a real service. Investors and

Table 3-1
Growth in Block Trading[8]

Block Trading	1965	1970	1975	1980	1985
Blocks as a percentage of total activity	3.1%	15.4%	16.6%	29.2%	51.7%
Average number blocks daily	9	68	136	528	2139
Total shares, annual (000,000)	48	451	779	3311	14222

pensioners need advisers and they need a proxy to represent them at shareholder meetings and in the boardroom. It would be so much simpler if only the fund managers felt free to vote the interests of the fund rather than the interests of the manager, but in fact the voting process has been skewed by a variety of distortions. This process is addressed in more detail in chapter 7, where we will think about how best to unskew it. But as the system now functions, there are distortions that must at least be noted. For example, while mutual funds feel fairly free to vote their proxy cards against management, bank trust departments are understandably reluctant to antagonize potential customers of the commercial side of the bank. And those customers are not bashful about making their feelings known. Recently, the CEOs of GTE and a number of other companies submitting antitakeover proposals for shareholder approval wrote to their counterparts at literally hundreds of other companies, urging them in turn to "instruct" their pension fund managers to approve the proposals. The merits of the proposals, some of which were objectionable by almost any standard, were beside the point. Fearing to lose goodwill, if not the account itself, the fund managers were in no position to disregard those instructions. Nor was there much incentive to do so. Retaining old clients and winning new ones depend not on voting success but on market success. Even those hardy souls who do not fear the loss of accounts are constrained by a fear that negative votes will diminish the flow of financial information on which they rely. As a result of these and other pressures, money managers routinely relinquish voting and other rights, contrary to their clients' interests.

Part of the problem lies in the proxy rules which the SEC has interpreted so as to force maximum compliance with the filing and disclosure requirements of the Securities Exchange Act. The key is the definition of the term *solicitation*, which includes any "communication" to ten or more shareholders if it is "reasonably calculated to result in the procurement, witholding, or revocation of a proxy." Thus if a fund manager were to conclude that Company X has made a proposal to shareholders that ought to be defeated, he could not simply call up the "old boy/girl" network to join hands, except by complying with the Commission's procedures. The Batterymarch Financial Management firm has been trying to accomplish the same result without "soliciting" anyone, by the device of simply announcing ten days beforehand how it intends to vote. While useful, that is not as good as a few phone calls and sticking proxy cards in people's hands. Some managers supplement the formal voting process by a series of informal contacts with corporate executives, not just on matters submitted to shareholders for approval but on a whole range of issues. These informal efforts are desirable, but again they are not a substitute for getting out the vote.

The Investor Responsibility Research Center and others have attempted to raise money managers' consciousness of their voting rights. The Center keeps score on the results, and James Heard, until recently its deputy director, has suggested that institutions disclose how they vote, the better to hold them accountable. Others believe that better results would flow if institutional investors were allowed a secret ballot.

But most of the attention of these groups has been devoted to resisting antitakeover defenses, as if nothing else mattered. On other issues the institutions rarely take an interest. For the twelve months ended August 31, 1986, for example, there were only twenty-seven proxy contests for board seats, essentially the same number as twenty years earlier. Sadly enough, the funds seem to be vindicating the criticism so often leveled at them, that they are not so much interested in acting as intelligent long-term owners as they are in making sure that the door stays open for good opportunities to sell out.

In one sense, this apathy is quite puzzling. The institutions own enough stock so that with a few phone calls they could elect their candidates to a number of boards. Yet even the antitakeover provisions continue to win, and the institutions continue to behave very much like supplicants. There are exceptions, notably the two dozen proxy contests waged annually, plus a few threatened ones, such as the one that unseated the management at Allegis (né United Airlines) last year. But why do such large amounts of power remain dormant for so long? Working men in the pits of a West Virginia coal mine are able to organize to achieve common goals, while sophisticated investors in Boston and New York remain a dispersed and very ineffective group.

One reason is that the pace of trading has so quickened in recent years as to leave little time or opportunity for institutional shareholders to be anything but passive. One institutional investor (too) easily replaces another and is no better than another. Some of the contempt expressed by corporate executives for in-and-out investors may be a function of managers' traditional arrogance. But there is more to it than that. Buffett, who is blessed with a better, less transient class of shareholders at Berkshire Hathaway, observed that if much of the stock of many large corporations is owned on a "revolving door" basis by institutions that . . . do not think and behave like owners, it is understandable that managers will not think of them as owners.[9]

The Performance Game

Ours is a very open society, and many subjects that were once taboo are now parlor conversation. For some reason, however, the performance game, in which institutions turn their portfolios at rates that have long passed the point of virtue, is a surprisingly well-kept secret. When people hear that the pace of trading now exceeds that of 1929, or that it may have jumped by ten times or more just since 1960, it comes as a surprise. At the beginning of the 1960s three million shares a day were traded on the New York Stock Exchange. As recently as 1981, an average day's trading was "only" 47 million shares. But now the evening news announces a 160-million-share day as if it were routine, which it is, and as if it were somehow a good thing, particularly if prices rose that day. Except for the brokers, and except for the excitement of watching huge sums of money change hands, what's so good about it?

The performance game is far too expensive to be considered a game and much too focused on market timing to perform well. The extent of the trading is not easy to measure, because so much of it has moved away from the so-called cash markets, to the Chicago Mercantile Exchange and other markets that trade the options and futures that have become a proxy for cash market stocks. In early 1987, for example, the value of the stocks underlying just the trading in stock-index futures was running at an annual rate in excess of $3 trillion, well above the level in the cash market. On the other hand the commissions for trading futures are only about one-tenth those for an equal amount of stock, so that in one respect at least the trading values may overstate the importance of these derived securities. The analysis would also be a good deal easier if the trading could be compartmentalized, with a group of trader-speculators accounting for much of the increased turnover but without much impact on institutional and other "serious" investors. But the speculative side of the market has not been successfully segregated. Institutional investors are right in the middle of the action, aggravating the problem rather than containing it.

We need a financial sedative. In 1960 the turnover of New York Stock Exchange stocks was 12 percent. In 1986 the turnover, including the trading in those stocks that took place off the Exchange, was about 87 percent. It is true that some portion, one-fifth perhaps, of the trading in 1986 represented transactions by market-makers, but they accounted for a substantial part of the trading back in 1960, too. Remember that the trading here is not like that in the wheat market, a process of advancing a commodity from point X in the economy, the farmers, to point Y, the bread bakers. It is, as Keynes noted, an almost wholly secondary market, meaning that the stocks don't go anywhere. Despite all the switching, at the end of the year the institutions as a group own roughly the same stocks as they did at the beginning.

These high turnovers are destructive of all the goals and functions that we have set for investors in the management of their own and their clients' money, in the operation of the market, and in the governance of corporations. They impose an exorbitant tax on the funds that are being churned, currently reducing by about one-sixth the underlying stream of income (see Table 3-4 in this chapter). By encouraging an emphasis on trading rather than investing, they focus the intelligence and energies of the investment community on short-term developments. By disguising the fact that there is liquidity for individuals but not for the community, they divert attention from the business fundamentals that are the market's proper concern. They turn shareholders into traders and investors into gypsies, who could not sensibly have more than a trivial interest in how to vote their shares or otherwise acting as guardians of the corporate store.

Index Funds

Some investors have tried to cope with the dilemma by creating so-called index funds that invest in a broad selection of stocks that mimic an index, such as the Standard & Poor's 500 Stock Index. That reduces their trading costs, and if history is a good indication, they would earn an average compounded annual return of about 10 percent,[10] reduced only by modest fees. A majority of institutionally managed funds have consistently underperformed the market, so that these index funds make a certain sense. But by late 1986 there were about $100 billion of equity funds that were expressly indexed and another $200–300 billion that were "closet-indexed," or invested to track the S&P 500 closely but not exactly.[11] In all they now represent about 30–40 percent of the institutional funds available for stock investment. The catch is that Wall Street has forgotten again that what works for the innovators, and even the first few of the imitators, may not work as the crowd moves in.

There is nothing wrong with a buy-and-hold strategy, but index fund managers have made a calculated judgment to ignore price and value. By leaving the decision to the statisticians at Standard & Poor's, they obligate themselves to buy each new stock as it became a component of the index. The money in these index funds is now so large that it does not simply piggyback the market, it influences it. The stock of Reebok jumped 6 percent, about $70 million, the day its selection as an S&P 500 stock was announced. Seeing that, some funds have begun to lobby with Standard & Poor's to have British Petroleum, for example, added to the index. Others buy stocks such as Nippon Telegraph at 270 times earnings, knowing that it is overpriced, but unable to do otherwise because it constitutes 12 percent of the relevant index. Some funds instruct their brokers to "make the close," meaning that they should execute transactions, not at the best available price but at the close of the day, so as to track the index, which itself is priced at the close. And all of them feel compelled to own both Ford and General Motors, forgetting, as a study has shown, that even if one accepts much of modern finance theory, what scholars call an "optimal" portfolio would probably include one or the other, but not both.[12]

These managers thus contribute nothing to the process by which markets are supposed to maintain their vigor. The manager of an index fund cannot remember the names of 500 companies, much less know much about what they are doing. He has solved the Keynesian dilemma of how to follow closely a great number of companies by following none. Fearful of making the hard choice between Ford and General Motors, fearful of being wrong, fearful of being second-guessed, he seeks the safety of a once-and-for-all decision.

Until recently, there was a great deal of self-congratulation as these "indexers" tracked the S&P 500 while it roughly tripled in five years. Now that there seems to have been a major market turn, what will happen on the down side of the cycle? Such a fund manager is quite prepared to see his clients' worth drop by 30 or 40 percent, or more, so long as the losses are within a fraction of those suffered by others. If the decline continues, will he soon have second thoughts, as he did about the "nifty-fifty" group of growth stocks and other once-upon-a-time, fashionably "safe" choices?

It may help to use again a "Main Street" test, to think of 20 shareholders of local companies, instead of 20,000 or 200,000 of public ones. By eliminating the stock market as an intermediary, by refusing to think of stocks as having some life and value of their own, there is less risk of substituting financial reasoning for business reasoning. Applying this Main Street test, it is very unlikely that those twenty shareholders would play the performance game or adopt indexing. Some might own shares of this or that local business, while others would no doubt reach different conclusions about which—the manufacturer of toasters, the department store, and so on—would be best. But having become shareholders of the department store in January, they would not change their minds in July and again in December. And it is almost inconceivable that they would contract to buy, willy-nilly, shares of each and every company that leased prime space on Main Street (but not on Vine). The puzzle is why, as the number of shareholders increases, those same twenty investors behave so differently.

The Roaring Eighties

We maintain an eerie, almost conspiratorial silence about the perform-ance game. The SEC and others, such as the Investor Responsibility Research Center, have studied the role of institutional investors in the corporate proxy voting process in great detail, but without mentioning how portfolio turnover has soared. (Who has time to think about the voting of shares that may well have been sold before the meeting is held?) Even the *Wall Street Journal* has not kept up. Its "Abreast of the Market" column reports on trading in the cash market, but it has yet to recognize that the cash market is increasingly overshadowed by the burgeoning markets in options, futures, and yes, futures options. These it covers on the "commodities" page, along with pork bellies. If the options and futures markets trade four times the value of the stocks traded in the central market, which is the central market?

In the month of January 1960 total trading on the New York Stock Exchange was 64 million shares. The volume grew to 221 million shares in January 1970, 1,158 million in January 1980, and 3,261 million in January 1987. Table 3-2 shows the annual volume of trading and rate of turnover on the New York Stock Exchange for the indicated years from 1960 to 1986.

The number of registered representatives more than doubled from 196,000 in 1976 to 404,000 in 1986, but what they contributed is not clear. Was the stock market inefficient in 1976? Did it become more efficient in 1986? In chapter 2, it was noted that the balance between investment and speculation is not one that can be resolved in the abstract. Some amount of speculation is arguably useful, to grease the wheels of investment, to maintain liquidity. But it is useful only so long as the traders' short-term focus—all that chatter about "new" money coming into the market, someone shooting the president of country X last night, guessing this week's report on the money supply, and so on—does not distort the impact on prices of those who are trying to think like part owners of a specific business. No one has even attempted to estimate the point at which the grease ceases merely to lubricate and causes the market to skid and lose direction.

The more you look, the worse it gets

While the fivefold increase in annual turnover reflected in Table 3-2, from 12 percent to 64 percent, is serious enough, the actual increase was much steeper. In the first place, the data in Table 3-2 include only the trading on the New York Stock Exchange. Like the usual summary on the evening news, or even the *Wall Street Journal*'s daily column, they do not include the significant trading of those Exchange-listed stocks that now occurs elsewhere, on the regional exchanges, in the over-the-counter market and in foreign markets. The so-called consolidated trading in those stocks in the United States adds another 12 percentage points to the total and, according to the SEC, trading abroad adds 11 points more.[13] Thus the turnover in Exchange-listed stocks for 1986 was about 87 percent, not 64 percent.

Japanese, British, and other foreign markets experienced lower rates of trading in the past, but the gap between those markets and the American market is narrowing. The lower commissions that became effective in Britain after the 1986, "Big Bang" deregulation are narrowing it even further. Table 3-3 sets forth the exchange trading volume in equity shares of domestic companies for several leading foreign markets. (In the case of Japan, a high proportion of the shares are held long-term under inter-

Table 3-2

Annual Trading

New York Stock Exchange

	1960	1965	1970	1975	1980	1986
Shares traded (millions)	767	1556	2937	4693	11532	35680
Annual turnover rate	12%	16%	19%	21%	36%	64%

corporate arrangements or by banks, so that the figures would be much higher if calculated as a percentage of the shares available for trading.)

The Roaring Twenties

A little history may help. Trading on Wall Street was very active in the great bull market of the 1920s. The annual turnover on the New York Stock Exchange in 1927, 1928, and 1929 was 94 percent, 132 percent, and 119 percent, respectively. It then dropped as low as 9 percent in 1942, and was still only 12 percent in 1952 and 1960.

Trading in the 1927–1929 period was, of course, stimulated by the high levels of margin account borrowing. Stocks were purchased on small down payments, with the broker lending the balance. For some years now, Federal Reserve Board regulations have limited margin debt to half the purchase price, but those regulations no longer mean much. Vast new markets have developed in stock options, and in options and futures in various stock indices, that effectively nullify the congressional intent. Even in the 1920s, a margin trader could not speculate in so many ways and at so little cost as now. A Standard & Poor's 500 stock-index future, for example, represented at the beginning of 1987 $130,000 or more of securities, but it required a minimum down payment of only $10,000. (Partly in an effort to ward off legislation, the down payment was increased after the market break of October 1987.) For about eight cents on the dollar, the buyer of the contract could acquire the financial equivalent of ownership of 500 stocks, and unlike a margin account, he paid no interest on the balance. It is true that he owned only a financial interest in those stocks, not a legal or voting interest, because the contract was settled in cash, not securities. But legal rights are not what attract margin buyers. One effect is that the amount of margin debt is no longer a good measure of the overall level of speculation. The speculators have switched to stock-index futures and options, because, as one broker said, "why bother with IBM versus Pfizer versus GM."[14]

Table 3-3

Trading Volume as a Percentage of Market Capitalization[15]

	1975	1982	1985
Germany	20%	21%	47%
Japan	36	35	41
Netherlands	26	19	33
United Kingdom	41	17	22

OPTIONS, FUTURES, AND OTHER PARAPHERNALIA

The trading data in Table 3-2 are, therefore, incomplete for the second reason that they do not reflect the trading in these various "derived" or proxy securities. The growth in stock-index options and futures alone has been astonishing; the values represented thereby now dwarf those in the so-called cash market. Index options differ from futures in the principal respect that the trader pays a premium—about 12 percent of the value of the covered securities—for the option, but except for the premium, which is hardly trivial, he has no risk if the market price moves against his expectation. The index future buyer or seller, on the other hand, may have put down only $10,000, but the entire risk is his.

Some comparisons may help put these new products in perspective. For the two weeks ended November 10, 1986, the average daily face value of the trading in all stock-index futures transactions was $9.65 billion.[16] An additional $8.22 billion of average daily trading took place during that period in stock-index options. The total value of the securities represented by stock-index trading averaged, therefore, almost $18 billion a day. (Even those startling figures quickly became stale. By early 1987, the average daily trading value of stock-index futures alone was over $13 billion.) By contrast, the daily average of all stock trading in the domestic cash market during that same two-week period in November 1986 was "only" $7.25 billion. And the foregoing data do not include the trading in options on individual stocks, which was also large. More options on IBM are routinely traded than are shares of IBM.

The trading in futures and option contracts, while huge by any standard, is difficult to compare with that in the cash market. Stock-index futures are the most like stocks, because the purchaser has the full risk of his bet that prices will move this way or that. If stock prices drop, and the practice is to mark these futures contracts to market on a daily basis, he must either increase the initial payment or see the contract sold out. Indeed, his position is almost indistinguishable from that of someone buying an individual stock on margin, and trading by the latter has always been an integral part of the dynamics of the market as a whole. It is true that the buyer of a stock-index future pays lower commissions and that he has bought a basket of stocks rather than a single one. But the process is very much like the old-fashioned buying on margin, except that, as that broker said, you need no longer "bother with IBM versus Pfizer versus GM." (What a pity; that "bother" is the assurance that money manager is doing the job for which many of his customers hired him and that the market in turn is doing the job for which it was created.

To simplify things a bit, let's ignore all the option trading, whether in stocks or indices. Let's count just those stock-index futures. Simply by adding to the trading in stocks the trading in stock-index futures, the annual rate of turnover would increase from the 1986 domestic cash market rate of 76 percent to a combined rate well over 150 percent. That is a level not seen since the turn of the century, when, as noted in chapter 1, the New York Stock Exchange was a den of rank speculation and the serious investor took his business elsewhere. Now there is no other place for him to go.

The director of market regulation at the SEC, Richard Ketchum, speaks of stock-index futures as "an enormously valuable product [that] provide new and more effective hedging techniques."[17] That sounds fine, but in reality the trading in options and futures is almost purely speculative. The distinction between gambling and investment, it has been said, is that in investments everyone can win. No one "loses," for example, when the owner of an apartment house receives from his tenants a fair market rent. To read some of the promotional literature, one might think that index futures are also a place where everyone can win. Wrong. Futures, like other derived securities, are intrinsically speculative, a form of gambling in which *no one can win unless someone else loses*. It is as if the landlord who built that apartment house did so not to collect rent from a tenant receiving real value, but to bet with a bookie on whether the building would be worth more this week than last. Collectively the only winners in the futures market, as in Jimmy the Greek's Nevada betting parlor, are those who take the bets, not those who place them.

Pension funds and other institutional shareholders, who ought to have left this trading frenzy to others, have instead joined the party. Individual funds often turn over their portfolios at a rate of 150–200 percent. Include the trading of stock-index futures, and the figure is higher still. It was not too many years ago that a broker who turned over a client's portfolio at a 150 percent rate might have had his broker-dealer registration revoked for "churning" the account.[18] Today there is no need to worry. The institutions account for about 75 percent of the total trading, even though by most estimates they own less than half the outstanding shares. They lead the market, but in the wrong direction.

*Why are nice people like pension funds
buying stock-index futures?*

In addition to hyperactive trading in the cash market, institutional investors have begun to make aggressive use of stock-index futures. On the
surface, it is surprising that trusteed employee funds that measure their
obligations in ten- and twenty-year installments would bet against someone on whether the stock market will be higher/lower in 90 or 180 days.
They don't buy stocks on margin; why buy futures? The underlying
explanation can only be one of three: (1) there are speculators who trade
with such a short-term focus as to create from time to time minor pricing
discrepancies on which the funds can capitalize; (2) the funds themselves
have fallen prey to speculative impulses, focusing on the market prices
of stocks rather than the underlying stream of dividends or earnings; and
(3) while trading in futures may not be good for the fund, it may serve
very well the interests of a manager more eager to avoid comparatively
bad results than to produce genuinely good ones. In fact, each of the
three helps to explain at least part of the process.

The institutions that use stock-index futures do so in one or more of
four ways, although others will no doubt be created. (One major banking firm, Goldman Sachs, has offered "synthetic futures," which is
about as synthetic as one can get.) The first of the four is of interest
primarily to managers of index funds. If new funds become available to
a manager, and if the computer determines that the price of a stock-
index future is less than that of the underlying securities, he may decide
to buy the futures contract rather than the stocks. The discounts from
underlying value are rarely as much as 1 percent. But the commissions
on a stock-index future are quite low, approximately $25 per $130,000
contract, so that even assuming that the manager eventually buys the
stocks that comprise the index, there may be an opportunity to commit
new funds at a slight (though short-lived) saving, and to do so quickly.
Transactions of this kind represent no more than a series of one-time
purchases, and so account for only a minor part of the total trading in
stock-index futures.

Locking in profits

Another use that institutional investors make of index futures is to "lock
in" profits, as the expression goes. It used to be that if an investor
thought that a stock was overpriced, he sold his holdings or at least pared
them. That's now "primitive," we are told. The current technique is

to sell a futures contract. In effect the fund manager who may already own a market basket of stocks decides that he is happy to "sell" all or a portion of the portfolio three or six months hence. He is still in the market, but he wants, to some extent, to be out. Under some highly unusual circumstances there may be a rational basis for this strategy. But for the most part, when the door is closed, even partly, something has been locked out—potential profit—just as much as something else has been locked in. What the portfolio manager has done is to confess that he thinks the "market" is high and so should lessen his exposure, but is afraid to be caught on the sidelines if it moves still higher. In other words, he has not only abdicated responsibility for "having to bother with IBM versus Pfizer versus GM," he has decided not to take responsibility even for the grosser, overall value of his highly diversified portfolio.

Program trading

A third use is so-called program trading, sometimes called index arbitrage, in which computers are again used, this time to find and "arbitrage" the minor but sometimes financially significant discrepancies between index futures and the (500) covered stocks. These index arbitrages, whether by institutions or others, have accounted at times for as much as 20 percent of the trading in stocks, and the unwinding of them near the contract settlement dates may cause brief but sharp market fluctuations. Otherwise—at least in normal markets—they are little more than a classic case of a zero-sum game being played out for the sole benefit of the brokers and for whatever entertainment value they may have. One enthusiastic booster explained it well:

> People can trade anything. They could trade futures on the exact population of the United States as determined by the census bureau at the end of each year, or the size of the federal debt, or the number of people killed each month in automobile accidents in the United States.[19]

In the immediate wake of the October 1987 market break, it was thought that program trading was a major factor causing the huge decline on Monday, October 19. But that seems unlikely. Such trading consists almost entirely of selling futures and buying stocks, but with prices falling so rapidly an arbitrageur would have been foolish to have predicted at what prices the shares could be bought. The other potential arbitrage—buy futures and sell stocks—was even less likely, because of long-standing restrictions on short sales of stocks in declining markets.

Stock-index futures have been promoted so heavily that the public has begun to believe that the Standard & Poor's 500 Stock Index has some intrinsic meaning—something more than just guessing the population—and that there is a value to insuring that this synthetic product, this abstraction, trades at prices close to the real thing. What risk is being insured against? The only "risk" is that while $13 + billion of stock-index futures are being traded daily, primarily by speculators intent on guessing the next market turn, someone could from time to time find a 0.5 percent mismatch. Who cares?

Portfolio insurance

The fourth, and the most important, institutional use of index futures is portfolio insurance, which is surely a very attractive sounding concept. It is a misnomer. There is no insurance, only a product or program in which the money manager, or the pension manager to whom several money managers in turn report, *begins* to sell index futures not when they believe the fundamental prospects are poor, not after the market has risen, but rather after the market as a whole has *dropped* by some designated percentage, e.g., 3 percent or 5 percent. If the market then starts to rise, the "insured" fund begins to buy futures. As one broker said in a moment of candor, this selling on the way down and buying on the way up sounds like the reverse of what he or we would do. He was right.

By mid-1987 about $80 billion of pension funds were covered by portfolio insurance, and the market was still growing. But the concept seems seriously flawed. First, it is very costly. The costs are difficult to estimate, because they include not just commissions but also the slippage that is likely to occur from selling index futures in what by definition are falling markets and buying in rising ones. According to those who sell these "insurance" programs, they cost anywhere from $2\frac{1}{2}$ to 4 percent a year. If maintained year in, year out, such a program would be a very heavy anchor to carry, particularly when, as in early 1987, that same S&P 500 was earning less than 6 percent on its market value. Whatever may be the point of running an index fund, it is lost if one gives back 40 percent or so of the underlying income stream. If in order to hold down the cost the program is not maintained consistently, the pension manager must decide when to insure and when not. In other words he is right back in the slippery business of guessing market turns that he had sought to escape.

The second major flaw is that a sharp market decline may or may not indicate the likelihood of further, sharp declines. The trigger point is wholly arbitrary, whether fixed at 3 percent, 5 percent, or 10 percent. There is no more reason to pick one than another, and no reason to believe that stocks will then continue to decline rather than move up.

Why do respected academic economists lend themselves to this essentially shabby enterprise? Nothing in modern finance has been better demonstrated than that the stock market is a random walk in the sense that the history and pattern of stock prices do not contain any useful information about future prices. Scholars agree on very little in finance, but they do agree that all the chatter about the market having reached a "bottom," all the reading of charts by technical analysts, are a waste. Yet financial economists who wrote, or at least approved, those good studies in the 1970s have been employed by Wall Street in the 1980s to write and sell portfolio insurance programs based on the notion that it is not a random walk, that declines of 3 percent or 5 percent, or whatever, are valid signals about when to sell stock-index futures. How remarkable. One of the brokerage firms has had the good taste at least not to call it insurance, using instead the term "dynamic hedging strategies," whatever that means.

The third flaw seemed to be only a potential one until that fateful Monday, October 19, but then there were revealed again the inadequacies of trading mechanisms that even if rational for an individual investor can be quite irrational for a crowd. The purpose of portfolio insurance is to protect against a severe market decline. If there are too many of these programs, however, they may aggravate dramatically the very decline against which they are designed to protect. One of the exchanges had taken steps to limit the daily price movement in its stock-index future contracts, but these insurance programs are designed to sell on a major decline and *to keep on selling so long as the decline continues.* Which is what happened on "Black Monday." When, as in 1985, only $5 billion were committed to portfolio insurance, they could respond to the market without in turn affecting the market. At the time this book was begun, in 1986, there were $35 billion. By mid-October 1987, there was said to be $80 billion. As their popularity grew, so too did the risks of a snowball effect. The likelihood of any such calamity was remote, but it was no more remote than the possibility of a financial panic, and while panics are rare, they do sometimes happen. As with some of the other new financial instruments, we had created a device that may reallocate risk, but cannot reduce it for the community and may even increase it in times of stress.

One way to look at portfolio insurance and some of these other products is that, first, Wall Street persuaded the customers to play a market-timing game in which they would become preoccupied with the short-term behavior of stock prices. (Financial economists gave it an intellectual cachet by arguing that day-to-day price fluctuations are an important test of investment risk.) The inevitable result was to emphasize price volatility, since the customers took their eyes off earnings and other fundamentals, which tend to remain relatively stable. Having helped produce the disease—high turnover in the cash market—the brokers then packaged an expensive "remedy" that aggravates the problem. It's a bit like asking for a bandage from a mugger and, of course, getting hit again.

Buyers and sellers of stock-index futures are together betting over $26 billion a day—$13 billion betting stocks up, $13 billion betting stocks down—on the over 100,000 contracts being written at about $130,000 a contract. All of the ostensibly productive uses together account for no more than a minor part—about 20 percent—of the total trading. Wall Street has always tried to put an elegant face on even the most speculative aspects of its business, hence the use of highly trained economists to market portfolio insurance programs. Jimmy the Greek is more forthright.

The heavy transaction costs are a self-imposed tax on those who manage their own moneys, but they are a hidden tax on those whose money is in mutual funds or employee benefit programs. Portfolio insurance, for example, is increasingly used in defined contribution plans where the costs are borne by the employees, not the company. In booming markets, the costs are overshadowed by the increases in stock prices. But when the stock market flattens out, the turnover tax will become painful, and painfully clear.

SPECULATION IS INCREASINGLY WIDESPREAD.
We seem to have become expert at the trading of a variety of financial assets, not just stocks. Debt instruments now trade at rates far above their historic patterns. According to Albert Wojnilower, the average holding period of over-ten-year Treasury bonds, measured by the amount outstanding divided by trading volume at the major dealers, which used to be calculated in years, has shortened to about twenty days. We should be concerned that, like the sardines that are bought for trading only, corporate bonds are being treated simply as a device for speculation on

interest rates, with little regard for the credit-worthiness of the borrower. Similarly disturbing patterns have emerged in the marketing of mutual funds. The primary purposes of an investment company are to provide for small investors a degree of diversification and the benefits of professional research and analysis. Increasingly, however, the fund managers are exhorting investors to buy shares of the new "sector" funds, many of which in turn are indexed, so that the investors can easily and frequently switch their money from one industry to the next. Stores and phone lines have been added to facilitate the process. What happened to the role of the manager?

Modern financial theory rests on the cornerstone that investors reach a thoughtful consensus about the *long-term* profit expectations of various industries and companies, and that it is on the basis of this consensus that prices are set so efficiently. High turnovers, however, are a serious distraction from any such patient endeavors. Worse yet are the futures and options that, as Goldman Sachs claims, allow an "equity investor . . . to establish . . . market positions quickly and with less capital."[20]

> *Item*: A well-known stock trader reports that Wall Street has become much more short-term oriented, and while the brightest people used to be making twenty-year forecasts of McDonald's, the heroes now are the arbitrageurs and corporate raiders. He, for one, finds it "a disadvantage to take fundamentals into account. . . . It is good to have a sense of what is supposed to be going on in an industry. . . . But fundamental research—since you are dealing in very, very short terms, the two are basically in conflict."[21]
>
> *Item*: An informal survey of 1,400 money managers discloses that only 8 percent worry about the amount of debt on a balance sheet.[22]

In an effort to substantiate these speculative patterns, John Pound and Robert J. Shiller studied a group of institutional investors who held stocks that had both risen sharply in price and enjoyed high price-earnings ratios.[23] Compared to a control group, these institutions showed much higher turnover rates. Pound and Shiller went on to find that, as the anecdotal items suggest, these high turnover, enthusiastic institutions were not thinking much about fundamental values or about the prices they paid.[24] Very few of them, only 12%, bothered even to compare the price of the stock to either current or future earnings or prospects.

Index funds simply change the shape of the problem. The necessary choices between Ford and General Motors—or between the two of them and IBM—are abandoned in favor of a process that buys or sells them all with equal, and equally undiscerning, enthusiasm.

INVESTMENT RISK VERSUS MARKET RISK

Too bad that we cannot, like a politician, go out and by "pressing the flesh" capture a sense of what it means when people trade in a single day 200 million shares, plus $13 billion in stock-index futures. The Chicago School economists and finance teachers speak of efficient markets, but it is an abstract analysis, devoid of any richness of detail or context.

One retail brokerage firm instructs its security analysts to make a recommendation every day, as if the world changes each time the sun comes up. A major money manager convenes its top people worldwide for an hour every day, the assumption being that something is happening every 24 hours and that there is some urgency to the process. Shift money to this sector, underweight the oils, buy interest-sensitive stocks . . . and do it now. There is nothing in the business world, nothing on such a scale, that corresponds to the frenetic pace and rhythm of Wall Street. Businessmen circulate memoranda, they exchange comments, and eventually there are meetings to (dis)approve a capital project. At a supermarket chain, for example, the closest analogy are the weekly pricing sessions and the changes to meet the competition. But the policies that shape those decisions, and the capital invested in them, change only slowly. If, as claimed, Wall Street is a true picture of Main Street, then somehow the video tape is running on "fast forward."

For those trying to conduct an investment operation, rather than a trading or speculative one, the performance game is not simply a bad way to play. It is the wrong kind of game. Shiller has amply demonstrated that stock price fluctuations are much too large to be explained by changes in the underlying stream of dividends.[25] The swings in stock market prices exceed by too much what should have occurred, far too much to be explained by swings in dividend or even interest rates. Price increases in bull markets greatly exceed the subsequent changes in dividends, and in bear markets prices fall too far.

The sound and fury of a 200-million share day should be of concern only to those who dwell on short-term price fluctuations and who measure investment risk by the volatility of day-to-day changes. Eventually

the market prices do coincide with long-term values. Indeed, if they did
not, there would be no room for an investment operation of any kind.
But it takes the sort of patient inquiry that is not found among in-and-
outers or those who buy Reebok without studying it.

Of the managers who have enjoyed outstanding results over a long
period, a highly disproportionate number have been those who grew up
and learned their lessons in "Graham-and-Doddsville."[26] Some bought
a few stocks; some held very diversified portfolios; some bought large
capitalization stocks; some bought primarily stocks of quite small companies. Yet a group of Graham-and-Dodders, despite often substantial
management fees, outperformed the market over periods of thirteen to
twenty-eight years by an average of about 11 percentage points annually.

In thinking about turnover, it is notable that all but one of the Graham-
and-Dodders in the study experienced three or more *consecutive* years in
which they significantly underperformed the market.[27] The Sequoia
Fund, for example, enjoyed an average annual return more than twice
that of the market, even though for one three-year period it underperformed the market by over 20 percent. The explanation lies in the fact
that while the market returns to its central values over longer periods,
it can be held in thrall to its recurring manic-depressive moods for quite
a time. Yet *Forbes* and all the others who follow the funds insist on
keeping score on a calendar year basis. There are two rules to remember.
If a silly season sets in, (1) it will end eventually, it is true, but (2) it is
nowhere written that it will end by Christmas.

The compound annual rate of return, with income reinvested, for the
stocks comprising the Standard & Poor's 500 Stock Index over the sixty-
year period 1926–1985 was 9.8 percent. That is consistent with most
investors' expectations that common stocks do better than bonds and at
least on a long-term basis are a satisfactory hedge against inflation. During that same period the Consumer Price Index rose at a compounded
annual rate of 3.1 percent and the compound annual rate of return on
corporate bonds was 4.8 percent. No one held his stocks for sixty years,
of course, but the process for those who jumped in and out was very
different from the process for those who bought for investment. The
following Chart 3-1 compares the total returns of the Standard & Poor's
500, including dividends, over one-year and five-year periods for the years
1946–1985.[28] On a moving five-year basis, the fluctuations are quite
modest, with only one year showing a decline of more than 1 percent.
In fact, the pattern is very similar to that of the earnings of the S&P

500, when calculated on a moving five-year basis. Not so the year-to-year changes in the one-year returns, which are very volatile. In one ten-year period, from 1953 to 1963, the annual percentage changes in the one-year returns showed the following pattern:

–1.0 +52.6 +31.6 +6.6 –10.8 +43.4 +12.0 +0.5 +26.8 –8.7 +22.7

In seven of those years, the year-to-year change was at least 25 percentage points, and many of the years swing from positive to negative or back again. Still, the institutional crowd has chosen to be myopic. Brokers currently speak of those who hold for a year as having a "long-term outlook," and with portfolio turnover of 100 percent and more, many institutions have an attention span that is much shorter.

The institutions have engaged in a frenzy of activity to protect them-selves against what is uniquely a market risk, not investment risk. On a short-term basis, as measured by the one-year returns in Chart 3-1, the market is volatile. *But that is a risk only for those who choose to accept it.* The distinction is between investment risk, i.e., a decline in the intrinsic

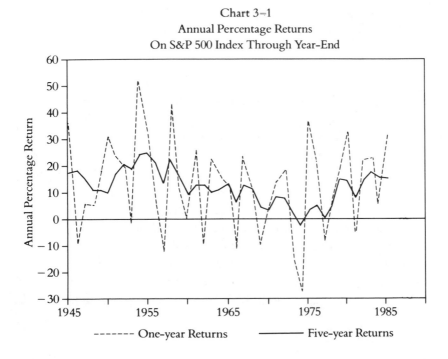

Chart 3–1
Annual Percentage Returns
On S&P 500 Index Through Year-End

------ One-year Returns　　——— Five-year Returns

value of an enterprise, and mere quotational risk. Those who understand the difference are highly visible among the successful managers, and those who do not fall prey to economists selling expensive portfolio insurance.

SOCIAL COSTS

One purpose of financial markets is to insure or hedge against a range of contingencies, so that risks are borne by those best suited. James Tobin suggested that financial markets should by now have developed an array of inflation-indexed instruments, thus shifting the major monetary risk that most of us are poorly equipped to bear. That has yet to happen. By comparison, what is the risk that we would like to see reallocated with a dozen different option contracts for IBM common stock, all of which expire in a few months' time, but which in the aggregate attract more trading than the stock itself? Thus far, as Tobin said, the market has produced only:

> options and futures contracts [that] do not stretch very far into the future. They serve mainly to allow greater leverage to short-term specu- lators and arbitrageurs, and to limit losses in one direction or another. Collectively they contain considerable redundancy. Every financial mar- ket absorbs private resources to operate, and government resources to police. The country cannot afford all the markets that enthusiasts may dream up.[29]

The costs of all this activity are very heavy. In the first months of 1987 trading in stocks was at an annual rate of about $2.8 trillion, equal to an annual turnover rate of almost 100 percent. The trading in stock- index futures, which in 1986 totaled about $2.5 trillion, was also at a record level. The principal single purpose of the stock market is to pro- vide an after-market for those who buy new stock issues. The stock market mobilizes savings and (hopefully) allocates them to their most profitable uses. But no one would sensibly design a machine that creates so much noise and burns so much energy when only $25–30 billion of new common stocks are sold for cash annually.

It so happens that the value of these new issues is roughly matched by the cost of trading the old ones. Although precise numbers are elusive, total trading costs are also about $25–30 billion annually. Few new stocks come into the market or are withdrawn, and institutional investors sell principally to reinvest. Each cash trade typically represents, therefore, both a purchase and a sale by an investor. For large investors, each side of the trade costs about one-half of 1 percent of the transaction's value, if there are included not only the commissions but the larger, although less visible effects of the trade on the market price, or the spreads between the bid and asked, and the effect on custodial and other fees and expenses.[30] (The major trading firms make a living from institutions asking to sell 300,000 shares and willing to take a half-point under the market.) Money managers who try to internalize the costs of block trading incur substantial back-office expenses in equipping and staffing a trading desk, bookkeeping, and the like. And those are only the costs of trading in stocks. The commissions on the trading in stock-index futures, for example, run about $6 million a day, or about $1 billion a year.

Liquidity is a good thing, but we are drowning in it. Perhaps the social waste is missed because the securities we trade are intangibles, mere pieces of paper or computer entries. Perhaps it helps to think instead of buying and selling houses. Consider the town of Mamaroneck, New York, having (let us assume) four villages, each with about five hundred single-family homes, in which life proceeds normally—until the year 19??, when instead of the usual ninety houses changing hands, almost everyone in town sold his house and many sold their next house as well. At the end of the year, the real estate brokers had earned commissions of over $25 million, even after aggressive discounting, and some twenty-nine-year-old brokers had earned $1 million or more. Brokers' commissions and other moving expenses exceeded the town budget. Voting in village elections, never vigorous, became quite desultory, because those who lived in one of the four villages often found themselves in another a few months later. People bought houses without inspecting the cellars. (As one of the more active buyers put it, "As a trader, I think it is a disadvantage to take fundamentals [like cellars] into account.") Others entered into contracts to buy houses, or even groups of houses, with no intention other than to see if the price would go up. But most remarkably, when the year was over and the census taken, only twenty new houses—the same as the year before—had been built. And 96 percent of those who had lived somewhere in town at the beginning of the year were still there at the end of the year. No one knew why folks had exchanged houses so much, and inquiries of the brokers brought only the response that in an "efficient" market like Mamaroneck, a house could be sold quickly.

Oh well, a mere fantasy. But it is not a fantasy that for over 25 years now the volume of trading has risen in almost unbroken fashion. The annual stock turnover "tax" roughly equals the value of the new stocks issued each year for cash, which is the primary reason for having a stock market at all.

Trading costs are consuming the profits

For some time now, the earnings of American industry have been essentially flat, with the obvious consequence that they have been shrinking in relation to stock prices (see line [3] in Table 3-4). In the meantime, however, trading costs have been growing relative to the outstanding float of stocks, because turnover (including the impact of options and futures trading) has increased so rapidly, more than offsetting even the sharp drop in commission costs since the "May Day" 1975 deregulation (see line [4] in the table). The combined effect of these two trends, relatively *increased* trading and relatively *decreased* earnings—relative in each case to the value of the stock float—is that trading costs (inexorably) consume a larger and larger share of the underlying stream of corporate income (see line [5]). With the Standard & Poor's 500 recently earning less than 6 percent on its market value, the annual trading costs, which now equal almost 1 percent of market value, are consuming about one-sixth of the earnings that are the continuing source—the only such source—of corporate wealth.

The following Table 3-4 sets forth for each of the years 1980–1986 the year-end price of the Standard & Poor's 500 Stock Index, the per share earnings of the index for the year then ended, the ratio of those earnings to market price expressed as a percentage, and the estimated transaction costs at a combined one percent for both sides of the trading in New York Stock Exchange listed companies, based on the average number of shares listed and the reported consolidated tape volume. (The 1 percent figure may be thought of as a reasonable proxy for all trading costs, direct and indirect, in derived securities as well as in the primary market, although in the earlier years covered by the table the figure was probably higher.) Similar data are shown for the first quarter of 1987, based on the preliminary earnings for the year then ended and the annualized turnover during the first quarter of 1987. Finally the table shows the percentage of earnings consumed by trading costs.

Table 3–4

S&P 500, Ratio of Trading Costs to Earnings, 1980–1987

| | Year ended 12/31 | | | | | | | Year ended 3/31 |
	1980	1981	1982	1983	1984	1985	1986	1987
(1) Market value S&P 500	135.76	122.58	140.64	164.93	167.24	211.28	242.17	291.7
(2) S&P 500 earnings	14.82	15.36	12.64	14.03	16.64	14.61	14.48	15.17
(3) Earnings as a percentage of market value (line 2 divided by line 1)	10.9%	12.5%	9.0%	8.5%	9.9%	6.9%	6.0%	5.2%
(4) Estimated trading costs as a percentage of market value	0.4%	0.4%	0.5%	0.6%	0.6%	0.6%	0.8%	0.9%
(5) Trading costs as a percentage of earnings (line 4 divided by line 3)	3.7%	3.0%	5.5%	7.0%	5.9%	9.4%	12.7%	17.6%

By early 1987, as line (5) of the table shows, trading expenses, which are pretax costs for some investors but after-tax for others, were consuming 17.6 percent of corporate earnings. Expenses had risen almost fivefold since 1980, when they accounted for only 3.7 percent of the underlying earnings. Rising stock prices enabled us to hide from this reality but could not change it. No Congress could have imposed on us, in good times and bad, so heavy a tax.

Chart 3-2 shows graphically the impact of these changes over the years 1980–1987. Relative to stock prices, stock trading was up, but corporate earnings declined, so that trading ultimately accounted for over 17 percent of the earnings.

The fact that trading costs, the gross receipts of the stock brokerage business, are very large might not seem remarkable. After all, the same could be said for the gross receipts of the energy industry. In 1985 the revenues of Exxon and Mobil alone exceeded $140 billion. Even in energy, however, we try to distinguish between utility and waste. Tax subsidies were used to encourage the installation of energy-saving devices in the home, and Congress ordered the automobile industry to produce more fuel-efficient cars. By contrast, we have many more doubts as to

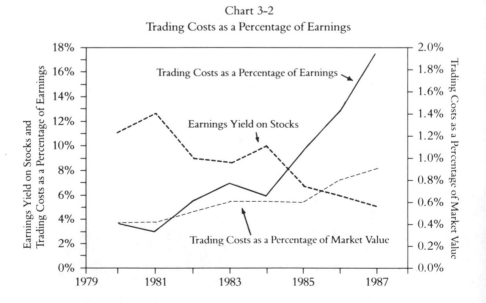

Chart 3-2
Trading Costs as a Percentage of Earnings

the value of financial trading, and yet no one has considered even roughly at what point the process ceased to be desirable.

The Indifference of the
Securities and Exchange Commission

Keynes proposed that we consider a tax on stock turnovers to force investors to adopt a longer-term horizon. So has Felix Rohatyn. The SEC, which ought at least to have shown some interest, has not. The explanation lies partly in the history of the Commission, which has been one of seeking accommodation with Wall Street, not confrontation, and partly in its staffing. The chairman during most of the 1980s was himself a broker but no doubt spoke from conviction when he referred to the "benefits" of active trading. The agency's chief economist for much of that time also believed that high turnovers are conducive to efficiency. Two other commissioners are also unabashed free-marketers. Indeed one of the two, looking forward to the day when retirees would speculate in options, went so far as to express the hope that

> as access opens to the small investor, and as pensioners and others come to understand the benefits of futures and options markets, . . . support for futures and options trading will build.[31]

Buffett and Tobin are two who have recently addressed the liquidity issue from a better perspective. Buffett reminded the shareholders of Berkshire Hathaway in the 1983 annual report that

> [days] when the market trades 100 million shares . . . are a curse for owners, not a blessing—for they mean that owners are paying twice as much to change chairs as they are on a 50-million share day. . . . These expensive activities may decide who eats the pie, but they don't enlarge it.

Buffett, seeing that hyperactive stock markets shrink the pie, was for a time a source of concern to neoclassical financial economists, because he was beating the market by too much, too consistently. It raised concerns that investing by fundamentals might, after all, be valid, and that stock prices were not so efficient. The problem was neatly solved, however, by a rush to label him a "five-star event," meaning that he is unique, someone who can be admired but has no more bearing on the behavior of markets and mankind generally than a circus freak.

No one has tried to dismiss Tobin, a Nobel economist, as a five-star event. Instead, the SEC and its neoclassical supporters have ignored Tobin's 1984 lecture on waste in the financial system. Too bad, but, as Tobin acknowledged, his views run against the "current tides [of his] profession's intellectual admiration for the efficiency of financial markets."[32] Tobin asked whether we are dissipating our talents, whether we are not:

> throwing more and more of our resources, including the cream of our youth, into financial activities remote from the production of goods and services, into activities that generate high private rewards disproportionate to their social productivity. I suspect that the immense power of the computer is being harnessed to this "paper economy," not to do the same transactions more economically but to balloon the quantity and variety of financial exchanges. . . . I fear that, as Keynes saw even in his day, the advantages of the liquidity and negotiability of financial instruments come at the cost of facilitating nth-degree speculation which is short-sighted and inefficient.[33]

Over half (52 percent) of the 1986 graduates of the Columbia School of Business went to work at investment and commercial banking firms, not to mention those who went to business corporations to work on the same transactions. The leading law schools reflect the same influences. The major metropolitan law firms—the ones working on these financial matters—have, over the last ten years, quadrupled the number of law school graduates they seek to hire. Allowing for the completion of judicial clerkships, they currently hire over 85 percent of Columbia Law School graduates. We seem to forget that corporate finance is, or at least ought to be, a relatively minor pursuit, one whose principal purpose is simply to see that those who design, produce and distribute goods and services have sufficient capital.

WHAT TO DO ABOUT IT?

The problems are too deep-rooted just to disappear as the market's mood changes. Keynes and others have from time to time suggested the possibility of a turnover tax, but Buffett has now outlined one. His proposal, quite simply, is to tax at 100 percent all gains from the sale of stocks or derived securities held for less than a year, including gains by pension funds and other tax-exempt entities. The investor could get his money back at any time, if he sold above cost, but "there would be no profit to you from your capital-allocation decisions unless they had a time horizon of at least one year."

Buffett's one-year, 100 percent tax has an elegant simplicity. Essentially it is a nontax tax, which, like the short-swing trading rules under the Securities Exchange Act, is designed to change behavior rather than to exact a penalty or tax. The proposal is easy to understand and relatively easy to implement. Yet it would correct a wide-ranging set of abuses, particularly among the arbitrageurs and greenmailers who populate so much of the market in takeovers. It does raise some questions—for example, as to whether a merger or other "forced" sale would trigger the tax, and if not whether selling into a tender offer should produce a different result. A number of exemptions would be needed, e.g., for stock exchange specialists and other market-makers. But these are not very substantial matters. If a major purpose of financial markets is to direct real investment in physical and human capital to its socially more productive uses, and if short-term speculation drives a wedge between personal and social gains, then why not eliminate the rewards of such behavior?

The one-year, 100 percent tax would virtually end the trading in stock-index futures and other derived securities as it now exists. If not, or if the brokers work their way around the tax, as they might, we should then consider what else to do. These synthetic products are at best a parasite and at worst a cancer on the stream of useful activity. There is no social value in encouraging either quick decisions or cheap decisions—and the two are not very different—about how to allocate the nation's financial capital.

Pushing out the investment horizon a year is not, however, a panacea. Even when shareholders turned their portfolios at a more modest 12 percent annual rate, they contributed little to the management of the companies whose stocks they owned. The Wall Street Rule—love 'em or leave 'em—is older than the performance game. In chapter 7, we will look at the Buffett proposal again.

～ 4 ～ Investors as Owners
of a Business

If shareholders didn't exist, we would need to invent them

T HE BUSINESS of the modern American corporation is, as
an historian has said, to "deliver the goods." Judged by that
standard, it is a very successful institution.

In the current period of increasing foreign competition, large negative
trade balances, and a reallocation of resources from the older, iron-bend-
ing industries to the newer, mind-bending ones, American corporations
may not always seem so successful. And yet the Fortune 500 corporations
as a group continue to earn as much as ever on shareholders' capital—
12–13 percent after taxes—suggesting that we are witnessing the decline
of individual firms and the rise of others, rather than a decline of the
institution. The pension funds and other professional investors, who
could as easily invest in real estate or other assets, continue to increase
their holdings of domestic common stocks. Stocks are the principal vehicle of personal wealth-holding; and while partnerships and trusts are useful in some situations, corporations continue to account for over 80 percent of total business receipts.[1] There is vigorous demand for the shares of
old, established corporations and new, emerging ones. Many institutional
investors, holding widely diversified portfolios, own what is in effect a
slice of the whole pie. It would be difficult to think of a more tangible
vote of confidence.

Maybe that's why we like to tinker with the design of the corporation.
Because it is successful, there is a temptation to fine-tune the corporation,
to let it carry other burdens as well. There was, for a time in the 1970s,

an energetic debate as to the proper goals of the corporation, with some arguing that merely being profitable was not enough. Social goals, however those might be defined, also needed to be considered. Boards of directors should, it was suggested, include representatives of labor and public interest groups. In effect, some commentators were saying that being large as well as successful, perhaps the business corporation could deliver the goods and a lot more, too.

The corporation is vulnerable to tinkering. Except for an occasional Lee Iacocca, presidents and chairmen tend to be private figures with little taste, and perhaps little talent, for dealing with the public. They get more attention when they fire hundreds than when they hire hundreds. Who are these people and by what right do they exercise such power? What is known about executives personally is often little more than the SEC-mandated disclosures of their compensation, which is the highest in the world by far, probably too high by any standard, and recently made more so by golden parachutes. The public seems to find more heroes in locker rooms than boardrooms.

Granting that attitudes toward big business and corporate power may reflect some sloppy thinking, there remain good reasons to tinker. The prestigious American Law Institute has been engaged for several years in an important and provocative effort to define the basic principles by which corporations should be governed. The state statutes under which corporations are chartered have been more concerned with facilitating growth, by clearing away obstacles and ambiguities, than with any concern for rationalizing the overall scheme. There may not be much debate at the moment about the view that the principal goal of the corporation is to maximize long-term profits, but there are plenty of other major issues: how much discretion the managers and other insiders should have in going-private transactions or in resisting takeovers, to what extent shareholder voting rights should remain inviolate, and generally what checks and balances are needed if the corporation is to ''deliver the goods'' efficiently and fairly.

THE SHAREHOLDER IN PRIVATE
AND PUBLIC CORPORATIONS
One of the most troublesome issues has been the role of the public investor, which is the central concern of this book—his role as an investor of his own or his clients' money, as a force in the functioning of the stock market, and of course as the part owner of various businesses.

In the private, closely held corporation, the issue of the shareholder's role as an owner of the business barely exists. Many of the shareholders are active in management and are, therefore, well informed. Each of them is likely to own an appreciable portion of the stock, and many of them are likely to live in the area where the corporation operates. None of these apply to the public corporation, but for reasons that are more to be found in history than good sense or conscious design, we based our corporation laws largely on the model of the private corporation. The result is that the law treats the public shareholder of Federated Department Stores as if he, too, were the owner of a business in the same primal sense as the family owners of a local dry-goods store—and with no attempt to differentiate their roles, their ability to participate in decision-making, their need for information about the business, and so on. Even the Model Business Corporation Act, on which the American Bar Association has energetically labored, still tries to encompass in one statute these two very different sets of firms and problems.

We've known for over fifty years, at least since Berle and Means wrote *The Modern Corporation and Private Property* in 1932, that it was anachronistic to use small-town images to describe investments created and traded in impersonal transactions on Wall Street. The owners of the family dry-goods store elect the directors, who in turn hire the managers, and that's the process described by the corporation laws. But in the large public corporation, the shareholders are little more than transients. Typically they have no direct dealings with the company and individually their stakes are too small to warrant taking an active interest. Who's hiring whom? It would be more accurate to say that the operating management has hired the shareholders' capital, just as it has selected the directors for whom the shareholders vote. The typical election, with only a single slate of candidates that routinely wins over 90 percent of the votes, is closer to the Polish state model than the American. The shareholders may own the corporation, but they do not control it.

AN ACT OF MAGIC

Images of transient shareholders participating in Polish-style elections suggest criticism, but the arrangement is basically sensible. The liquidity of the stock market permits the large aggregations of capital that are required by modern industrial and financial enterprises. Collectively the public's investment is committed indefinitely, as it should be. The public, invited to invest, does not need to seek a repayment or return of its capital from the corporation. In lieu of a promise to repay, such as it would give to a lender, the corporation can simply point the shareholder to the market. The stock market provides the investor with not only a mechanism for the return of his capital but a degree of liquidity that the corporation could not hope to match. It performs what William J. Baumol has called "an act of magic":

> [I]t permits long-term investments to be financed by funds provided by individuals, many of whom wish to make them available for only a very limited period, or who wish to be able to withdraw them at will. Thus it . . . [transforms] "what are short-term credits from the private viewpoint into long-term savings from the social viewpoint . . . to the fullest extent."[2]

Stocks, Baumol was saying, are almost like cash. When he was writing in 1965, the process was still relatively sleepy. But today the commissions are much lower, and an investor can switch out of one stock fund and into another or into a money market fund—which is the equivalent of cash—by a phone call, or while at his personal computer, at almost any hour of the day.

THE WALL STREET RULE

Just because markets are highly liquid, it need not necessarily follow that public shareholders, at least the larger ones, should cease to act like owners of a business and become mere gypsies, without any long-term interest or involvement in the underlying enterprise. Institutional investors often make very considered judgments about the operating management of a corporation before buying shares; and having bought them, they could, if they chose, exert considerable influence without getting enmeshed in day-to-day operations. But with a few exceptions—names such as Buffett, Singleton, and Tisch come to mind—they seem to suspend their critical faculties once they have committed their funds, except when it comes time to sell. They implicitly praise or criticize management, by buying or selling, but seldom get involved more directly, even to the extent of a phone call. There is almost no dissent from the Wall Street Rule, which says that a shareholder who is not pleased with a company is better off selling the shares than trying to change or influence its direction. That particular shareholder may indeed be better off, but what is good for the shareholder may not be good for the corporation—or for the community of shareholders, which of course cannot sell.

How can it be that shareholders, even the skilled, professional share-holders, can behave in ways that are rational for them individually but not for the group? Mancur Olson explained in *The Logic of Collective Action*[3] that large groups such as public shareholders behave very differently from small ones. The differences are not merely quantitative. It is true that public shareholders rarely hold any particular stock for long, selling in November what they bought in February, so there is no point in investing much time in overseeing the management. But even when the turnover was less, the Wall Street Rule still applied.

On the one hand, the benefits of belonging to a large group (whether shareholders, union members, or taxpayers)—a liberal dividend policy, higher pay scales, or a good fire department—are available to everyone in the group if they are available to any. As economists say, these are "collective" or "public" goods. On the other hand, being a good fellow, paying one's dues, taxes, or whatever, doesn't improve the benefits. Cheat on your taxes, and the sanitation department still picks up the garbage. The individual member's interests, therefore, are best served by nonparticipation—as, for example, by a Wall Street Rule that says to enjoy whatever benefits are already available but never, never contribute to improvements. The result is that a labor organization, for example, will function effectively, if at all, only (a) with some degree of coercion, e.g., a union shop so that workers must join up, or (b) with some separate, selective inducement for the leaders of the group. The cases where shareholders actively attempt to overthrow management are almost uniquely those where the insurgents seek to take control *for themselves*. Any others who did so would probably be dismissed as gadflies or cranks.

The usual way of expressing the dilemma in the corporate context is to say that the shareholders have the ownership but managers have the control. In effect there is a void at the highest level of power. Those who have been hired to run the business on behalf of the owners largely control the process by which they are hired. Without accountability to someone, it is not clear whether the power is legitimately held.

To some extent this separation of ownership and control is inescapable. An investor cannot fully enjoy the benefits of liquidity if at the same time he is burdened with continuing responsibilities. The shares, Berle and Means concluded, should move freely from hand to hand, "impersonal—like Iago's purse" ("'twas mine, 'tis his, and has been slave to thousands").[4] While that is no doubt true, all it means is that the shareholders of a large public corporation cannot be counted on to participate in business decisions to the same extent as would the shareholders of a family-owned business. It is the directors and particularly the managers who conduct the corporation's day-to-day affairs and provide the necessary continuity.

That still leaves a lot of room to fashion a role for the shareholder that would be consistent with his status as a Big Board rather than small company shareholder. Rights to information, rights to approve fundamental changes in the capital structure or the character of the enterprise, rights to participate in the election of directors and other matters on a basis that would be meaningful in the few cases where it needs to be meaningful—these and other rights would enable the shareholders to keep management under check.

HOW IMPORTANT IS SHAREHOLDER POWER?

Some argue that a self-perpetuating management, one not accountable directly to shareholders, is not so foolish a notion as to be rejected out of hand. The Roman Catholic Church, our oldest universities, and many hospitals have long functioned without the consent of the governed or of their members, and most of them have developed mechanisms for renewal and for the maintenance of excellence that have been sustained over long periods. Called managerialism, this school of thought proceeds from an odd combination of cynicism or realism on the one hand and idealism on the other. The argument is that since shareholders' control is a fiction, their votes might as well be scrapped, and that corporate officers, freed of the myth and constraints of "shareholder democracy," will respond primarily to social and economic interests rather than to selfish ones. There is a good deal to be said for their position, at least the part that contends that shareholders are, for whatever reasons, very apathetic voters on whom we should not waste much effort. And the reasons why they are so apathetic will occupy our attention throughout the book.

Some financial economists have reached a conclusion similar to that of the managerialists, although from a quite different perspective. The failure of shareholders to hold managers more strictly accountable is not for them a defect but rather an arrangement sanctioned by the workings of the marketplace. There is no reason to intervene, they say, even in the face of managerial shirking or the diversion of assets to personal ends, because these are no more than the inevitable costs of a flexible, "efficient" bargain that shareholders have struck with their agents, the executives. Several different versions of this market-based analysis have been suggested, but underlying them all is a reliance on market transactions, either to act as a constraint against excessive inefficiency and self-dealing or to imply a degree of consent. Thus one version is that, regardless of how much discretion managers enjoy, it is no more than what shareholders approved when the company first issued stock or they first bought it. It is part of an implied contract, and if shareholders were unhappy with the arrangement they would long ago have taken their investment funds elsewhere.

A second such version is that there are markets at work at various levels within the corporation that effectively and sufficiently monitor managers. The executive officers, for example, are working for and may seem to control the corporation, but they are also working in, and will be judged by, a larger managerial market that will follow them through-out their careers.[5] They cannot, therefore, afford to think of these jobs as a one-time, make-the-most-of-it opportunity. (In the long run we are not, as Keynes said, all dead; we are simply back in the market.) The same is said to be true of directors, who if they do not monitor the officers vigorously, will also see the market for their services dry up.

Still a third version of this market-based analysis is that corporate directors and executives are not merely competing for their jobs but they and the corporations they control are competing in capital markets that would not tolerate for long arrangements in which investors perceived that they were at too great risk because of inefficient or unfair rules. There is thus no need to legislate against the current rash of dual class voting stocks, which at some companies are being used by insiders to seize effective voting control, once and forever. If necessary, it is said, the marketplace, in this case the stock market, would in due course raise the cost of capital for such firms and thereby eliminate the abuses, if indeed they be such, or at least reduce them to a minimal level.[6] (In the perfect markets that are assumed to exist, the producer has no choice but to raise prices to reflect added costs but competition will not permit him to do so.) The burden of abuse is thus imposed not on those who are wronged, but rather on the wrong-doer.

These market-based views of the shareholder's role currently command a considerable following and, if accepted, have important implications. Even the once firm prohibition against stripping the public of its voting rights could be bargained away, if we believe that investors are "contract-ing" on equal terms. These are issues to which we will return. Two aspects of the argument are striking, however. First, this tendency of shareholders to act as no more than a rubber stamp is turned into a consensual sword to be used against them. At the time they purchase their shares, when the "contract" is first written, they are deemed to have had an adequate opportunity to negotiate, much as if it were a more normal, bilateral agreement between parties of roughly equal strength. And the bargain is said to be binding even with respect to remote possibilities, such as going-private transactions, not contemplated or even discussed at the time the shares were purchased.

The other striking aspect of this market-based model is the insistence on analyzing the issues through the single lens of a market mechanism—principally the buying and selling of shares—and an exclusive reliance on that same single mechanism for maintaining managerial vigor and integrity. These Chicago School economists, who believe for example that "[o]utside directors are . . . disciplined by the market for their services"[7] in monitoring managers, seem to have found there and elsewhere markets that no one else has discovered. (To the extent that there is such a market, why would it not reward directors who are compliant rather than diligent, since it is the managers who control so much of the selection?) Worse yet, the corporate structure, the paths along which information and power flow, and social aspirations and pressures are all irrelevant, except insofar as they respond to or can be translated into the prices of goods, stocks, or services. Or if not wholly irrelevant, the necessary institutional structures, the rights and remedies of shareholders, will spring into being solely as a result of market forces.

SHAREHOLDERS AS WATCHDOGS

In any event, the more widely held view—the one reflected, for example, in the federal securities laws—has been that managers should also be held accountable to the shareholders within the corporate framework. Market constraints are useful, but not so perfect that we should rely on them to the exclusion of all else. That consensus rests primarily on two different notions: (1) that managers, like the rest of us, need to account in some direct fashion to someone other than themselves, and (2) that the shareholders—or more precisely the common shareholders—are better suited for the task than anyone else because, as Ray Garrett said, they are "the ultimate beneficiaries of corporate growth and profit and the ultimate losers from the opposite."[8]

This consensus rests largely on pragmatic grounds. The holders of the common shares enjoy important voting, informational/reporting, and

litigation rights and remedies, and rightly so. But not because they are
so-called investors. After all, bondholders are that, and they rarely get
votes or anything more than the strictly construed terms of their bond
contract. And not even because they are owner-shareholders, as distinguished from mere lenders. Under the law, preferred shareholders are
that, and they tend to have even fewer protections than bondholders.
The management should be held accountable to the common shareholders, because there is a deeply rooted fear of unaccountable power, because
shareholder interests coincide best with society's interest in efficiency,
and because, potentially at least, they make the best monitors.

Don't expect too much of shareholders. They are at best a watchdog
of last resort, a recuperative device that comes into play only when various others have failed. Product markets, where the company sells its
goods, are the primary mechanism for disciplining poor managers. Lower
sales mean lower profits, so that earnings and capital are promptly redi-
rected to more efficient firms. Banks and other lenders also play a major
role. And even within the corporation, while the independent, outside
directors too often fail to live up to our expectations, still any experienced
corporate lawyer or banker can recount cases where, with no publicity (it
would be counterproductive), directors have forced changes in business
plans, unseated "entrenched" managements, and put their corporations
back on the track. Better good directors than good public shareholders.

While product markets and these other constraints are useful, they
have important limitations. There is still a need for vigilant shareholders.
A large public corporation can drift along for years while living on the
fat of earlier periods or on the reduced profits of its current operations.
If there were perfect competition in the product market, the penalty for
sloth would be swift and sure, but there is not. In a perfect world,
competition is by price alone, and the invisible-hand-of-the-market theorem works wells. But our product markets are not perfect. Brand loyalties and various oligopolistic factors blunt and slow down the impact of
a manager's mediocre performance. Capital markets also work slowly.
Banks continue to lend even to less efficient producers because the burden
of reduced profitability falls in the first instance not on them but on
stock prices. These falling stock prices, in theory, should raise the cost
of capital, as economists have suggested. For companies with capital requirements too huge to be financed internally or with debt, such as the
public utilities were for many years, that discipline may work well. But
for most companies, the equity markets are not an effective constraint,

because the decision to issue new shares is usually one that can be delayed almost indefinitely. Consider, for example, that the value of new common shares issued publicly for cash each year does not amount to more than about 1 percent of the value of the shares already outstanding. Where's the discipline? These new equity issues do not account for more than a minor portion of even the externally financed investment.

The ability of directors to monitor management is also uneven, hampered often by directors' lack of independence, lack of time, or lack of information. Winthrop Knowlton and Ira M. Millstein, drawing on years of board experience, summarized the problem well:

> Directors have some information but not enough. Besides, most of them have other things on their minds. Inside directors work full-time for particular parts of the company, and the great majority of outside directors have other jobs. The outside director has many reasons—practical, philosophical, emotional—for playing a more passive role than the one we espouse. It is easier to be a permissive parent than a disciplined one. And in their permissive and passive stance, most boards . . . have a tendency (1) not to appraise the performance of CEOs critically enough; (2) to overestimate the ability of managers to manage different kinds of businesses well; (3) to allow managers to build enterprises that may be too large and diversified for anyone to manage well; and (4) to wait too long to respond to ongoing political, social, and economic change.[9]

It is true, of course, that we do not have a well-defined or quantifiable sense of how useful it is to have shareholders as watchdogs. Even though they are a potential factor in many corporations, they are an immediately credible one in only a few. And there are costs involved. It is, for example, understandable that managements do not like to submit transactions for shareholder approval, not even those so radical as to turn a can company, i.e., American Can, into one engaged in almost anything but making cans. There are out-of-pocket expenses and there are the indirect but potentially larger costs of delaying or perhaps losing a presumably attractive opportunity. The CEO already "knows" that it's a good deal, and the shareholders are likely, indeed almost certain, to approve the management proposal. Instances of rejection are virtually unknown. The problem is that the usual risk/reward analysis doesn't work when speaking of shareholder approval. The risks or costs may be fairly obvious, but the benefits are almost inescapably unquantifiable. Without a shareholder vote and the detailed, federally mandated disclosures that otherwise could be avoided, we can only guess how many ill-advised projects would have moved ahead.

MANAGERS DO NEED TO BE WATCHED.

If one looks at any issue long enough and hard enough, it becomes a larger issue, then a problem, and finally it may become a crisis. In short, while there are problems, they need to be seen in institutional terms— the inherent conflicts between those who operate or govern an organization and the stockholders or members of it—rather than as a criticism of managers as a class. In this respect, the governance of corporations is not different from that of the Republic.

And there are important, unavoidable conflicts, precisely because of the need to give management broad discretion. Assuming that most managements are competent, still some are not, and they may not be able to correct or even recognize their own deficiencies. Or they may be quite competent but less zealous than if they were using their own, not hired, capital. There is a well-recognized tendency to have some degree of slack in the organization, to achieve "satisfactory" rather than maximum profits. Or if both competent and zealous, the managers may still not deal fairly with the public shareholders. They may skim off too much of the profits for themselves, although blatant self-dealing is rare. Much more likely, they simply will not make adequate dividend or other distributions. There are enormous temptations to keep the money, to let the company grow, and thereby to respond to their own and their colleagues' desire for stability, security, running a bigger business, creating new job opportunities and a sense of excitement. There's a lot of recognition in being the president of a Fortune 500 company, even if the ranking is by sales, not profits.

Warren Buffett, chairman of Berkshire Hathaway Inc., noted that CEOs "behave a little differently" with the shareholders' money:

> "[W]ith corporate aircraft . . . I happen to know what the habits of many CEOs are. They've explained them to me, and . . . I think they probably buy a little different kind of corporate aircraft than they might if they were buying with their own money. And I think they probably maybe even eat a little differently when they're eating on the company.
>
> And I also notice that when they eat companies they behave a little differently. . . . You see, the equation of the CEO is frequently very different than the shareholders' equation. . . . My personal equation in owning the *Wall Street Journal* at 15 times earnings, 20 times earnings,

30 times earnings—if I own practically zero percent of my company stock, it's very clear I become much more significant in life and price becomes no object.[10]

Such problems exist, of course, in corporations with declining capital, as well as those with money to burn. Like Winston Churchill contemplating the fate of the British Empire at the close of World War II, few managers are willing to preside over the liquidation or contraction of a company that for so long has meant so much to so many—in this case its employees and officers. And just as a large enterprise usually means enhanced prestige and salaries, so too does a smaller one force painful decisions about personal pay and perquisites. Yet if the investors' money is not to be frittered away, if the corporation is to operate efficiently, liquidations and reductions in scale are a necessary part of the process.

Corporate officers need monitoring. According to a study by Henry G. Grabowski and Dennis C. Mueller, among others like it, management-controlled firms are less profitable than those where ownership and control are not separated. Management-controlled firms retain a higher percentage of earnings, and the returns on these "plowed back" earnings are far below those on money raised by newly issued debt or equity.[11] Like the rest of us, managers are not always on their best behavior and are sometimes on their worst. They have a private agenda, it seems, to maximize the size of the corporation rather than the per share value of its stock. (If you keep your eye mostly on corporate wealth, you might well buy the *Wall Street Journal* at thirty times earnings, but it's doubtful that the shareholders would thank you for it.) Constraints are needed to bring that private agenda back into line.

SHAREHOLDERS AS MONITORS:
THE FAILURE OF THE LEGAL STRUCTURE

While managers may need watching, what reason is there to think that shareholders are well equipped to do the job? They have never shown much interest in it. Partly the answer may be the dilemma of thousands of dispersed shareholders, each with only a small interest in the company, so that it becomes economically "irrational" for any one of them to take an interest. But there is obviously more to it than that. As we have already seen, the modern American shareholders are in many respects an unattractive group, one for whom it is difficult to have much respect. Institutions, in particular, trade stocks at a frightening pace, trying to decide whether it is in the fall of this year rather than the spring of next that GM's stock will have its best rise. Or they buy an index-basket of stocks, not caring what's in it. Not behaving like owners of a business, having put nothing back into the corporate pot, they then come whining about their "rights."

We will have a good deal more, if not much good, to say about these professional shareholders. But the effort to make something socially useful out of this wimpy lot does not depend on how much we like them or how much they deserve our attention. Assume for the moment that they can be induced to take a more active interest in the businesses they own, that somehow money managers with $1 trillion at stake are not wholly beyond redemption. (In chapter 7, we will have some suggestions for making born-again investors out of these stock market sinners.) Even so, there would still remain serious problems of how power is distributed within the corporation and the absence of adequate mechanisms by which even a vigilant shareholder body could make its presence felt.

The state corporation laws

The corporate form of organization has developed over a long time, beginning early in the country's history when each corporation was specially chartered to embark on a particular venture, typically with strict limitations. By the end of the nineteenth century, however, the process had changed. The states began to write general corporation laws that enabled managements to operate with minimal interference from the state and also with increasing internal flexibility. For the most part, these "enabling" statutes were useful. The nation's business was expanding rapidly, and it was necessary to eliminate restraints born of an earlier period when corporate charters were still considered an act of grace. It was appropriate, on the one hand, that corporations be chartered for longer periods and for broader purposes, and, on the other, that they be authorized to change their line of business with something less than unanimous approval of the shareholders. Much less certain is whether it was also appropriate that corporate officers be given the freedom to do business *with* and not just *for* the company, i.e., to engage in self-dealing. But the legislatures' interest seems to have stopped at the point of "enabling" these conflict of interest transactions, although at an earlier time they had been categorically prohibited. Basic questions, such as whether self-dealing is valid only if the terms are fair to the corporation, were left for another day.

These enabling laws were speeded up by a competition among the states, led at first by New Jersey and then—and still—by Delaware, to induce corporations to use the local law even if their business and offices were largely or wholly elsewhere. A business physically located in Indiana must comply with the environmental laws of Indiana. But with minor exceptions, the rule in the United States has been that the *internal affairs* of a corporation, including the rights of shareholders located anywhere, are determined by the law of the state of incorporation, even if there is no other contact. While the rule simplifies the determination of the applicable law in situations where a corporation does business, and has shareholders, in a number of states, it opens up a competition for charters that knows few restraints and has continued almost without letup since the turn of the century.

This pattern accelerated during the 1920s. The nation's business, it was said, was business, but some of the practices had more to do with increasing personal control than increasing corporate profits. The right to vote by proxy, which was first designed as a simple convenience to enable absent shareholders to exercise their franchise, became the "blind" proxy by which shareholders were disenfranchised. Proxies were issued in blank form, enabling the managers, bankers, or promoters to vote them on issues that had not been mentioned and for directors who had not been identified.

There also appeared a rash of classified common stocks, with one of the classes having sole voting rights. The most celebrated instance was Dodge Brothers Motor Car Company, in 1925. The investment bankers, Dillon Read, having purchased the company, resold it to the public for about $130 million. However, they kept all the Class B shares, the sole voting stock, at a cost of about $2 million.[12] At the close of the nineteenth century, the issuance of common stock with no voting rights whatever would not have been permitted, but one by one, state legislatures—including Delaware and New York—had made the necessary changes. Assuming that there are not what economists call market imperfections or failures, competition among the producers of goods and services produce benefits for society. But competition among lawgivers and regulators can produce, for rather obvious reasons, the reverse effect.

The New York Stock Exchange

The one bright spot was the New York Stock Exchange. Having a monopoly in the trading of the larger, more profitable public companies, the Exchange was able to use its power to list and delist stocks to set minimum standards of disclosure and fairness that were well above those of the state laws. No meaningful competition affected its policies. New York, for example, had amended out of its laws even what modest requirements for financial disclosure had once existed. The Exchange, however, gradually imposed requirements for financial disclosure of commendable breadth, first as part of the listing application and then as part of a process of continuous disclosure. While the Exchange rules did not reach all corporations, they reached the most important and most visible ones and set a standard for the rest.

The Exchange's rules, it is true, did not go as they might have. They required, for example, an annual report to shareholders with financial statements certified by independent accountants, but they did not require disclosure of even so elementary an item as the corporation's total sales, and almost 40 percent of those listed chose not to provide it.[13] Financial statements were required, but the degree of disclosure and the choice of accounting principles were largely within the issuer's discretion. The reports to shareholders often failed to consolidate the financial accounts of major subsidiaries. Electric Light and Power Corporation, for example, reported that it had no funded debt, even though the subsidiaries that produced all its income had $140 million of debt.[14]

THE GREAT CRASH:
A TIME OF MISERY AND OF OPPORTUNITY
At least until recently, we had largely forgotten about the crash of 1929. There had been stock market failures before, and of course banking panics and failures. But this one time the process seemed interminable. When the worst appeared to be over, the worst had yet to happen. Of $50 billion of securities sold to the American public from 1920 to 1933, approximately one-half had become absolutely worthless by 1933. By 1934 almost half of the foreign securities sold to American investors in the seven years 1923–1930 were in default. Nor was it just a matter of new issues. The aggregate value of the stocks listed on the New York Stock Exchange on September 1, 1929, was $89 billion. Less than three years later, in 1932, their total value was only $15 billion. And these were the best of companies, the blue chips. During the 1920s the "large, new army of investors" predicted by Charles E. Mitchell had been drawn into the stock market. Many of them who had by 1932 lost their jobs and their bank accounts, or at least seen the accounts frozen, had also lost 83 percent of their investments in the stocks of New York Stock Exchange companies, measured from the peak.[15] Some of the bluest chips—General

Electric, U. S. Steel and Sears, Roebuck—lost over 90 percent of their value.[16]

But adversity is also a time of opportunity, and the early years of the Roosevelt administration were an unprecedented occasion to rethink and refashion the modern public corporation. It was clear that remedial action would be taken, that only action at the federal level would do, and that the Great Depression and the disclosures of financial exploitation by financiers and others in privileged places created broad popular support for reform.

As Congress looked to see what had gone wrong, it was Wall Street that captured most of the attention. Men like Mitchell, J. P. Morgan, and Richard Whitney, president of the New York Stock Exchange, were mythical figures in American life. Cast almost exclusively from a single, genteel eastern mold, they were, as John Brooks later wrote, "unabashedly preoccupied with money and never dreamed of trying to disguise the fact . . . ; they had no ambitions except to become richer and more socially prominent."[17] Yet despite these remarkably narrow interests, they became folk heroes. A well-known advertising man, Bruce Barton, suggested that Jesus of Nazareth might best be described as "the founder of modern business."[18] A Princeton economist commented that upon the stage of the Stock Exchange "can be discovered the aristocracy of American intelligence."[19]

The fall from grace was all the greater. The causes of the crisis were many and complex, but Wall Street was where the stinking bodies lay. Mitchell, the "genius of the New Economic Era,"[20] had created the new National City Bank that joined commercial and investment banking under one roof, but he was no Jesus. Under his prodding, National City had participated aggressively in the underwriting of over $90 million of Peruvian bonds, despite extensive data in its files that Peru would almost certainly default—which it did. The bank traded in its own shares and manipulated its financial statements in order to drive up the price. The bank bribed officers of other companies in order to win the right to sell new issues. Mitchell and his fellow officers purchased from the bank underwritten securities at prices almost 50 percent below the price at which they would shortly be sold to the public. In 1929 they borrowed $2 million from the bank without interest or collateral to help cushion the impact of the stock market crash, a year that Mitchell also received a bonus of over $1 million.[21]

Politically the most vulnerable targets were on Wall Street, not Main

Street, and that is where the congressional committees did their digging. Mitchell was indicted. The president of the Chase National Bank, who had sold short his own bank's stock, lied about it. J. P. Morgan, the son, publicly observed that the leisure class was the heart of American life, and then had the bad luck to define the leisure class as being the "twenty-five or thirty million families" who had servants, although at the time there were but two million servants in the whole country. Samuel Insull, who kept thirty-six bodyguards more or less busy while he scrambled in vain to preserve his investment trusts and the empire of 150 utilities and other companies that they controlled, fled to Turkey, only to be brought back and indicted.[22]

Even when those tainted by the hearings were industrialists or businessmen rather than bankers or promoters, the disclosures related principally to their sale and trading of securities—their own or someone else's—in the market, and not to the day-to-day operations of their steel mills or other "real" businesses. A pool created by a brokerage firm to pump up the shares of RCA showed a profit—matched, of course, by other people's losses—of almost $5 million in a single week, and the participants included the wife of the company's chief executive, David Sarnoff, as well as a Chrysler, a Rockefeller, and the national chairman of the Democratic Party.[23] It was fraud of the most primitive character. But still it was outside the company's normal operations.

The Federal Securities laws:

a modest first installment

Beginning with the Securities Act of 1933 and ending with the Investment Company Act of 1940, Congress passed in all six statutes. Fraud and manipulation in the securities markets were the principal diseases. Disclosure was to be the pervasive remedy. The Securities Act of 1933, proposed by President Roosevelt immediately after taking office and promptly enacted, required full disclosure in the sale of new securities, and it broadened the civil remedies of injured investors. The Securities Act was useful, but its effects were limited. Felix Frankfurter, still at Harvard, who had played a major role in the drafting and passage of the Act, described it as "a belated and conservative attempt to curb the recurrence of old abuses. . . . " It was, he wrote, "a modest first installment . . . strong insofar as publicity is potent; it is weak insofar as publicity is not enough."[24]

What the Securities Act of 1933 did for the new issue market, the Securities Exchange Act of 1934 did for the trading market. With respect to the extension of margin credit, the stock exchanges, and broker-dealers, the Exchange Act established wholly new standards and a framework of self-regulation coupled with administrative oversight. But these were provisions for the stock market, intended to cure speculative excesses and to raise standards. For the industrial and commercial companies whose shares are traded on the exchanges, rather than those that do the trading, the 1934 Act's impact was, like that of the 1933 Act, relatively modest. The Exchange Act required disclosure on a continuing basis, as compared to the one-time, prospectus requirements of the 1933 Act. It also prohibited fraud in securities trading, and by an ingenious new device intended to avoid the always slippery problems of defining and proving fraud, it forbade all short-swing trading, i.e., buy-and-sell (or sell-and-buy) stock trades completed in less than six months, by corporate insiders.

Disclosure, the primary achievement of those statutes, is one of those remarkable tools that accomplishes so much with so little. Disclosure is a cure for fraud in the sale and trading of securities; the two cannot coexist. Disclosure keeps markets fair and is a necessary condition if securities, or indeed any other products, are to be priced correctly in accordance with their economic value. Without reasonably correct pricing—"efficient" pricing in the jargon of economists—capital will not be directed to its most profitable uses. And if investors perceive the market as a whole to have been skewed against them by the "smart" money, by those with inside information, they will eventually leave and the cost of capital for all of us will go up. In short, disclosure is important if we are to treat investors fairly and also if they in turn are to fulfill their economic function.

For other purposes, too, not just in securities transactions, disclosure is a powerful device. It discourages self-dealing and other conflicts of interest with which a CEO might feel comfortable if only the "details" did not have to be published. Disclosure helps to influence behavior and set minimum standards by bringing to bear the values and ethics of the community. The 1933 and 1934 securities laws have accomplished what law does best, which is to act as a catalyst for the community's attitudes. There is not much argument that corporate executives are much more honest and loyal today than they were sixty years ago. True, there is still some argument from Chicagoans who believe that market forces alone are enough to compel management to make available all the relevant information, and that the SEC regulations are an unnecessary burden.

But there is convincing evidence, and most observers agree, that the case for disclosure is quite strong not just as a matter of equity but on grounds of economic efficiency.[25]

A small dose of federal corporation law:
the proxy rules

But information does not by itself suffice to create an institutional framework or the pathways of power by which the information can be put to good use. Valuable as it is, the availability of information leads only to the second-tier inquiry, information to be utilized in what ways and for what end? In the 1934 Act, for better or worse, beyond disclosure and the regulation of insider trading, Congress made only a single, limited contribution to corporate law reform, and that was the proxy rules. Section 14(a) of the 1934 Act imposed a very thin federal overlay on the state corporation laws that regulate shareholder meetings and voting procedures. The Section 14(a) proxy rules, which apply to any ''solicitation'' of proxies or similar consents, require, for example, that all matters to be voted upon at shareholders' meetings be fully described in a proxy statement and that the shareholders be given the opportunity on the proxy card to choose between approval and disapproval of each agenda item. But in all other respects, such as whether the management can effect fundamental changes in the company's business—e.g., switching from the manufacture of cans to financial services—wholly on its own authority, without the need to call a shareholder meeting, or if there is a meeting, whether the public should be legally entitled to vote, the authority of the states was left intact.

It is easy to see why Roosevelt, Frankfurter, and Sam Rayburn, then the chairman of the House Commerce Committee, adopted disclosure as the keystone of the federal securities laws. They were anxious to move swiftly and to capitalize on the public outrage growing out of the congressional hearings, but even in the dark days of 1933 they had a remarkable confidence in the resilience of the private system, even if that resilience was not then much in evidence. There was a striking contrast between these progressive politicians, on the one hand, and those, such as Professors Berle, Douglas, and Tugwell, on the other, who contemplated a marriage or at least a partnership of industry and government to regulate what they saw as a failed and unresponsive economic system. Finding too little competition, they despaired of reviving it. So far as the securities business and corporate governance were concerned, however, these advisers were looking at problems different from those addressed by Roosevelt. The president was concerned primarily with fraud and speculative excesses, and, as Brandeis had said and Roosevelt often repeated, for fraud, overreaching, and other such abuses, "[s]unlight is the best of disinfectants."

This conservative response did not save Roosevelt from bitter criticism. America was a class-conscious society in 1933, more so than today. The mood among corporate managers and in Wall Street, among the bankers and brokers, seems to have been not so much repentance—which is rare in any case and usually confined to temples other than those of the money changers—but anger that Roosevelt, one of their own kind, could have so fully and openly betrayed them. Seen through the dry air of history, these fears clearly were misplaced. The federal securities laws were intended to save investment banking and brokerage and the existing pattern of investor-owned, privately controlled corporations, not to destroy them. Congress sought only to make them clean up their act.

In effect Roosevelt elected to protect shareholders in their access to a free and more honest marketplace, rather than in their access to the levers of corporate power, at the workplace. The economy had all but closed down; there were hungry children in the homes and angry men in the streets. The Gross National Product, in a fall much more serious than that of the Dow, had dropped in three years from $104 billion to $41 billion. Allowing for price changes, roughly half of the nation's production of shoes, steel and light bulbs had dried up. Roosevelt's first act as president, even before proposing the Securities Act, was to declare a four-day banking holiday. By then the governors of almost half the states had already closed or were closing their banks, $37 million of gold was being withdrawn from the system daily, and in the single two-day period before the inauguration, over $500 million of currency had been taken out of the banking system.[26]

Roosevelt was willing, as he said time and again, to experiment and to improvise. In the early twentieth century, Presidents Theodore Roosevelt, Taft, and Wilson had all suggested the need for a federal incorporation or licensing statute, and these proposals now resurfaced. But priorities had to be set, and Roosevelt, like others, believed that "unregulated speculation in securities . . . had so much to do with the terrible conditions in the years following 1929."[27] The primary goal of the 1934 Act was to create the Securities and Exchange Commission and to regulate the New York Stock Exchange—that "perfect institution," according to its president, Richard Whitney, who would in time go off to jail but in 1934 was still a powerful figure to reckon with—and the fight was very bitter. It was reasonable to hope that if Wall Street could be decontaminated, then the corporations on Main Street, given a strong dose of disclosure salts and a mild dose of shareholder democracy, would be more responsive to the interests of their shareholders.

SHAREHOLDER VOTING:

AN EMPTY RITUAL

Out of thousands of public companies, the number of proxy contests still averages only about twenty-five a year. The figure could hardly be lower. Except in rare cases, there is no one but management for whom it makes pocketbook sense to solicit proxies. In the end, it is fair to say that Congress, in adopting the proxy rules, did not achieve the enfranchisement of shareholders in any meaningful sense. It did, however, use such meetings of shareholders as do occur as the occasion and lever for requiring remarkably full and fair disclosure, not just of the specific business to be transacted but also of the overall conduct of the corporation's business and affairs. Like the 1933 Act, the proxy rules were strong insofar as publicity is potent. Insofar as the proxy soliciting machinery remained the almost personal property of management, insofar as nonvoting stock and other devices for disenfranchising shareholders have been allowed to proliferate, insofar as public shareholders continue in any event to show little interest in exercising their franchise, nothing much else happened.

Perhaps it was just as well that nothing more was attempted. The outlook for the private industrial system seemed so bleak that we can at least speculate whether a more ambitious program might have been along the fascist or socialist lines that Douglas and others envisaged as the only workable solution.[28] Roosevelt and the Senate Banking Committee, among others, mentioned the possibility of a broader federal statute,[29] but what it would have contained we do not know, because nothing came of it. All during the New Deal years there was interest in the federal chartering of corporations. Even Roosevelt talked at times of a federal licensing bill, although much of the emphasis was on antitrust. In the end, he did not push even the modest proposal by Douglas, by then chairman of the SEC, to bring over-the-counter companies under the proxy rules and disclosure provisions of the Securities Exchange Act. Hearings were held from time to time on the issue of corporate accountability, but nothing came of them.

AFTER THE NEW DEAL

Once the New Deal closed down, the impetus for change in the structure of the public corporation all but dried up. A half-century later, the problems that were visible in the early 1930s are still unresolved, and in many respects ground has been lost, not gained. Part of the explanation is the lack of a coherent view of how corporations should be governed, but much of it is a simple exercise of power. We have long known that large, dispersed groups are difficult to mobilize. Corporations lobby, their lawyers lobby, shareholders do not lobby. (In the December 1986 SEC hearings on the issue of whether to permit the New York Stock Exchange to list shares with less than full voting rights, institutional investors testified in unusually large numbers. Perhaps that represents a change, and if so, it is a welcome one.)

William L. Cary wrote a celebrated article in 1974 describing how the Empress Delaware had no clothes, and indeed was being paid to take them off.[30] Cary, who had been chairman of the SEC in the early years of the Kennedy administration and was widely respected, did not uncover anything that was not already well known. But Cary was uncharacteristically blunt in his criticism of this "race for the bottom"[31] in which

> a pygmy among the 50 states prescribes . . . and indeed denigrates national corporate policy . . . to encourage incorporation within its borders. . . .[32]

Cary was, he later said, called in Delaware everything but a lesbian.[33] It's one thing to discover a wrong, far worse to remind people of the wrongs of which they already know and in which they have acquiesced.

The dilemma resembles Gresham's Law. Just as bad money drives out the good, so too does the pandering by one state force the others to cheapen their currency, all of them searching for the lowest common denominator. It is partly a problem of what economists call externalities. The transaction between Delaware and those incorporating there has costs that are borne at a later time by the shareholders, who—being dispersed and wholly unorganized—failed to demand a place at the bargaining table. If these were local businesses with local shareholders, Delaware would have local interests to protect, but with few exceptions the major corporations are physically based elsewhere. Shareholders are a product of securities markets that are national and international in scope, with no local ties worth mentioning. Delaware's only concern is the $120 million, about 12 percent of its budget, that it receives annually from franchise taxes, plus perhaps the welfare of a large and skilled body of local lawyers.

The Report of the Corporation Law Revision Commission of New Jersey in 1968 was quite direct:

> It is clear that the major protections to investors, creditors, employees, customers, and the general public have come, and must continue to come, from Federal legislation and not from state corporation acts. . . . Any attempt to provide such regulations in the public interest through state incorporation acts and similar legislation would only drive corporations out of the state to more hospitable jurisdictions.[34]

Many of the states have adopted uniform laws, such as the Uniform Commercial Code, to achieve consistency across state lines in business and financial transactions. There is even a uniform law regulating the sale of securities. But no one seems to have suggested that a uniform corporation law commission be created to consider the necessary "major protections to investors."

Cary proposed a federal minimum standards act, which would leave the states free to compete as to fees and as to a variety of substantive terms, but not as to certain basic protections. His bill of particulars is instructive, because it was so very modest. It did not propose much that was not already reflected either in the regulations of the New York Stock Exchange—hardly a radical group—or the federal securities laws. Cary suggested, for example, restrictions on nonvoting shares, a prescribed and exclusive standard for the indemnification out of corporate funds of liabilities incurred by directors and officers personally, more frequent shareholder approval of major corporate transactions, and limitations on the number of shares issuable by directors without specific authorization by shareholders. That is still a worthwhile agenda, one on which there has been retreat not progress since 1974. It is an agenda to which we will return in chapter 7.

Cary was not the only one to see the need to reexamine the corporate structure, although he was a wonderful catalyst. The 1970s were a period of increasing attention to the "myth," as Myles Mace called it, that directors were adequately directing the business or holding to account the officers who did. In 1970 the Penn Central had collapsed in a sea of debt, while the directors continued to pay dividends. As one of them said, "[t]hey took their fees and they didn't do anything. . . . They didn't know the factual picture and they didn't try to find out."[35] Penn

Central was not typical, but it was a chilling reminder that the impact of many boards is negligible. Too many of even the nominally independent directors are bankers, lawyers, and others selling services to the company, and the rest often lack the information or the encouragement to set standards of accountability. (The bigger the boardroom table, the more the directors, the quicker everyone goes to lunch.) It does happen, directors do sometimes speak up, but too often it takes courage, and the system should not depend on that.

The legislative process in New York and Delaware is corrupt, not technically but in the sense that it does not address shareholder interests. In 1967 Delaware revised its corporation statute by the device of a hand-picked group that drafted the new law, held no hearings, and saw the bill through the legislature without discussion or comment. One of the participants acknowledged that the drafting was "aimed at the interests of the corporations themselves."[36] The one member of the drafting group who represented the plaintiff's bar hoped that the law would help solidify "Delaware's position as a 'good' State in which to incorporate."[37] It did. A corrupt process bred a corrupt result.

In the more than fifty years since the passage of the federal securities laws, almost no state—California is an exception—has required that corporations with some substantial number of shareholders distribute audited financial statements. What could be more basic than a periodic report on management's stewardship? For most of that time, there existed literally thousands of public corporations that, not being listed on an exchange, were subject to inadequate federal disclosure requirements. And there are still a good lot of them that have less than the five hundred shareholders necessary to bring them under federal law.

Protections for directors rather than shareholders

By contrast, there was a prompt and urgent response in Delaware and elsewhere to the 1985 decision in *Smith v. Van Gorkom.*[38] In the *Smith* case, the Delaware Supreme Court held directors liable for having approved a merger/sale of their company on the most casual basis, without consulting outside counsel, without seeing the terms of the merger agreement, and without consulting the company's banker or otherwise testing the fairness of the price. (It's true that the directors left a small window open for seeking higher bids later, even though this deal had been signed and announced, but on balance it was about as clear-cut a failure to exercise due diligence as one is likely to see.) The problem of the *Smith* decision was not so much that directors would henceforth be held to a strict standard of care. The number of times that directors have been held personally liable for a failure to act with reasonable diligence, without some element of self-dealing, fades almost to the point of nonexistence. But a "cornerstone of the boardroom culture is the near fanatical concern for 'the liability of today's director,'" described by James D. Cox and Harry L. Munsinger,[39] a fear fed by a steady flow of exhortations in executive trade publications that, since the *Smith* decision, almost invariably feature the word "crisis." What gave this "crisis" the necessary sense of reality was the fact that directors and officers liability insurance, once commonplace, had become more difficult to obtain, largely because the market for liability insurance of any kind had become very tight. Directors and officers were accustomed to being protected, and as one well-known Delaware lawyer put it, legislation was required to enable directors to operate with inadequate coverage or even to "go bare."[40]

Delaware and a number of other states quickly adopted provisions effectively insulating directors from any responsibility for their own negligence. Liability remains a possibility only in cases of bad faith and self-dealing. Except for Virginia, none of the states acted on the proposal then being considered by the American Law Institute, that directors continue to be responsible for violations of the business judgment rule, in effect for gross negligence, but that the damages be limited in amount.[41] That proposal would allow directors to act boldly in takeover contests, where huge sums are at stake—without eliminating all standards of diligence, however. Instead we have the almost mocking picture of a corporation, Burroughs, telling its shareholders in a proxy statement that their directors have a fiduciary duty to exercise their business judgment, even while it proposes a charter provision that expressly exculpates directors when they violate that duty.[42] The statutes will still be on the books, and the Burroughs charter provision will still be there, when the insurance crisis has come and gone, as it has already begun to do.

The race for the bottom, the process by which corporations can play one state against another, is as much at work today as in 1974 when Cary so successfully dramatized it. The memorandum in support of the governor's 1986 Program Bill in New York to deal with the issues raised by the *Smith* decision in Delaware spoke of the need to correct a situation in which New York "has lagged behind other states." In addition to providing a more lenient statutory test for indemnification, the New York statute adopted an important part of the Delaware statute by permitting dissatisfied companies to go one step better and write provisions of their own. Eager to improve on the 1986 legislation, the director of the Committee on Corporations, Authorities and Commissions of the New York State Senate met in May 1987 with representatives of the governor and the Assembly, major bar associations, and the Business Council, hoping to "proceed promptly" on a bill—eventually adopted—extending New York's provisions for exculpation of directors and officers. At the conclusion of the meeting, the preparation of the next draft, one that would deal with the still unresolved issues, was turned over to the general counsel of International Paper Company.[43] Where were the shareholders' lawyers?

In defense of Delaware

Every system has its defenders, and this one is no exception. Admittedly, corporations and corporation lawyers control the choice of the state of incorporation. The defense is that in making that choice, corporations are heavily influenced by the wishes of the shareholders, because otherwise the latter would sell off their shares (or refuse to buy), thus increasing the cost of capital and also the risk of a takeover bid. Thus if Delaware were actually a state in which shareholders lacked essential protections, it would be the least popular state, not the most popular one. The failure of such a trend to develop, according to (now) Judge Ralph Winter, "suggests that investors . . . believe they do better under Delaware law than under the laws of others states."[44]

The substance of this analysis is that the shareholder has contracted with management on a wide variety of terms, including the state of incorporation. When investors buy shares, either on the open market or particularly as part of an initial public offering, they are said to have "consented"—implicitly rather than explicitly, of course—to all the possibilities embedded in the corporation statutes and case law of the state in question. That is quite a mouthful, considering that the corporate law is frequently ambiguous and varies from state to state and within any state from time to time. Applying what in effect is an extreme version of the efficient market hypothesis, the defense argues that investors, in buying shares, go far beyond even the usual business factors that affect such decisions. They also consider the state of the law with respect to what at the moment are only remote possibilities, such as a sale of the business. While no such sale is then contemplated, investors are thought to price the shares up or down depending, for example, on a state's appraisal remedy in the event that (a) there is a sale and (b) the terms of the sale are not to their liking. Such "rationality," Herbert Simon wrote, "implies a complete, and unattainable, knowledge of the consequences of each choice."[45] Such perfect information rarely exists in actual behavior, and stock picking is an unlikely exception. (Simon's insight is confirmed by the managers of several respected mutual funds, all of whom report that they never think of the state of incorporation in picking stocks and that they never heard of anyone who does.)

Nonetheless there is research that is said to endorse or validate the permissiveness of Delaware. The study most often cited is one that measured the impact on stock prices of announcements that companies planned to reincorporate in Delaware. Finding that the stock prices were not affected, the authors rejected Cary's "stockholder exploitation hypothesis."[46] Judging from the Delaware law and the large numbers of companies that incorporate there, it would seem, therefore, that shareholders actually prefer not receiving an annual report and other protections! In reality, the authors had not bothered to see if investors, in picking stocks, take into account the state of incorporation. And the very real possibility that Delaware, while leading the race, is not all that far ahead of the pack, was also ignored.

The authors of that research, and others of like mind,[47] rely on these event studies as a far-reaching license for a laissez-faire policy. Inhabiting a world of perfect competition, they believe that competition is almost solely by price and that the prices reflect essentially all potentialities, however remote. Investors who don't pay for protections they don't receive have no cause to complain. Indeed, the implication is that the shareholders prefer a "flexible," exploitative arrangement to all others. In effect, anything goes.

THE ROLE AND THE RIGHTS OF SHAREHOLDERS:
A SUMMARY

Stepping back a bit, looking at the process as a whole, it has always been a good deal easier to develop a rational framework to protect shareholders in the purchase and sale of securities than in the internal workings of the corporation. Until after World War I, that dilemma of corporate control was solved reasonably well by the ability to rely on investment bankers as intermediaries, and the bankers in turn—at least the more prestigious of them—accepted the responsibility in the same sense that any of us values his reputation. This history strongly suggests that only when bankers or other professionals take the lead, acting as proxies for the rest of us, are shareholders likely to be vigilant. In any event, by the 1920s, as the shareholder body began to shift and become more dispersed, as bankers ceased to act as surrogates for shareholders, there developed an increasing potential for abuse and a need for more formal accountability.

There have been numerous studies and conferences on corporate governance, most quite thoughtful, but they tend to focus on the roles of officers and directors, which are troublesome enough, rather than that of shareholders. Seven years after the first drafts of the American Law Institute's Principles of Corporate Governance Project appeared, nothing has been circulated with respect to voting, informational, or a number of other gaps in the rights of shareholders. This is so even while the chapters with respect to the duties of directors and the structure of the board have been submitted, revised, and revised again.

The SEC has tinkered from time to time with the proxy rules, principally by permitting shareholders to insert a limited range of proposals of their own in management's proxy material, but the impact has been very minor. These Rule 14a-8 shareholder proposals rarely attract much support, partly because of shareholder indifference, partly because of the rule's severe limitations on the substance and form of the proposals, and partly because of a tendency by some shareholders to politicize and trivialize the process. This shareholder indifference to their voting rights is, of course, obvious to all, and the real issue is whether it reflects, as Judge Winter has suggested, a state of contentment or whether other, more complex forces are at work. It is an issue to which we will return in Chapter 7, after looking at takeover bids, the device that is sometimes said to have all but eliminated the need for the more routine forms of shareholder participation.

The SEC might perhaps have done more tinkering than it did. A reasonable argument can be made that the Commission has authority under the proxy rules to go well beyond the disclosure requirements with which it has largely contented itself.[48] At one point, in the 1940s, the SEC did propose that the management proxy statement be open on some basis for nominations of directors by shareholders as well as by management. But it did not go ahead.[49] For a time, too, the SEC acted as if a federal corporation law could be built on the base of Rule 10b-5, the antifraud rule. But that would have meant distorting the federal law out of all shape to achieve a result that Congress could hardly have intended, and the Supreme Court ultimately and rightly put those notions to rest.

There have also been some gains (as well as losses) at both the federal and state levels in the rights of shareholders to bring derivative and class actions, but the usefulness of these remedies has been stifled by a realistic fear of strike suits on the one hand and collusive settlements on the other. In any event, litigation can assure only honest, not competent, management.

Sad to say, there has been almost no progress in defining the role of the shareholder, not even with respect to such elementary issues as the right to receive fully voting shares or, for companies not under the federal umbrella, the right to an annual report. The British began to deal with the information issue one hundred years ago, and they have come to grips with some of the implications of nonvoting stock. Delaware has yet to start. Comparing the Delaware law today and in 1929, one quickly sees that the state corporation statute, originally written for an owner-managed business, has simply not addressed the major monitoring issues of a publicly owned corporation. (Omissions that continue this long should hardly be thought of as casual.) Yes, the mechanics of holding meetings and voting—the right to hold directors' meetings by telephone or a written consent, rather than in person—have been made more flexible. The plumbing works quite well, but it is only the plumbing that does.

It need not have been so sterile a period. Admittedly, the problems are difficult. But the Bankruptcy Act of 1938 and the Investment Company Act of 1940, to name just two, created a role for the SEC as a proxy or surrogate for shareholders in reorganizations and conflict of interest transactions. The Bankruptcy Act also set a floor under the reorganization bargaining process, precisely because it was recognized that disparate, dispersed groups of shareholders—and bondholders, too—might not otherwise be represented adequately.

The issues are not just those of shareholder rights or democracy, although those are important. It is not enough to say that the shareholders "own" the corporation and should be able to deal with it as they wish. Power is an attribute of responsibility. Shareholder rights are just one aspect of the larger dilemma of fashioning a role for shareholders that recognizes not only the limited opportunity but the limited capability and interest of a trading public to contribute to the governance process. The states are both sponsors and victims, in Cary's words, of a process that for generations has borne no fruit worthy of mention. The legislatures didn't respond, but then the shareholders never lobbied. They seemed to accept whatever Delaware and New York dished out.

This apathy, we know, was "rational" for each of the shareholders acting alone, even though collectively it was clearly against their best interests. The problem is known by a number of terms, such as "rational apathy," the "tyranny of small decisions," and the dilemma of "collective action." The small special interest group, in this case corporate managers, almost always wins out over a large and dispersed group of shareholders, unless that "latent" group is first mobilized by coercion or some form of selective inducement to potential leaders. Indeed, the shareholder case is an extreme of sorts. It is not just that investors are dispersed and diverse, but each of the major investors in turn usually holds a highly diversified portfolio in which no one company matters much and in any event is not likely to be in the portfolio for long. Or they have altogether stopped thinking about individual companies and have created index funds. They are buying indiscriminately chosen market baskets of stocks, the names of which they can barely identify. (Which way the portfolio companies go is not so important to an index fund manager as the fact that whichever way it is, he will be along for the ride.) In political action terms, the situation is utterly chaotic.

One response would be to recognize the existence and roots of this apathy and to adjust the corporate structure to compensate. Melvin A. Eisenberg, for example, has urged that we tilt the balance of power on the board decisively in favor of the independent directors and that shareholders be given a greater opportunity to approve fundamental changes in the business or capital structure. Whether such changes are appropriate or sufficient is open to question, but Eisenberg at least seeks to redress the balance.

A very different response comes from those for whom markets work so well that no other monitoring mechanisms are needed. Chicagoans ignore the deficiencies of the process and the obvious disinterest of the electorate. That is bad enough. They go a step further, however, and use the votes, explicit and otherwise, that are a product of this defective mechanism to argue that the shareholders have knowingly accepted the nonvoting stock and other paraphernalia that have appeared in recent years.

There is a simple test for this bit of sophistry, one already used in this book. Would the proposal have been approved if there were only 20,

mostly nonmanagement shareholders, having approximately equal holdings and living in easy communication of each other, instead of 20,000
scattered ones? The 20 shareholders of a local company would almost
certainly insist that if, for example, the CEO sought to buy the company
from them, they should have the right to a full and free auction, or at
least to know what others would be willing to pay. By contrast, the fact
that the 20,000 shareholders of a public company might approve a
management buyout, allowing executives to take the company ''private''
even when others have not been given a fair opportunity to bid, suggests
that there is a need to reexamine the process and not just to praise it.

Hostile Takeovers:
A Remedy of First Resort
or Last Resort?

Mergers and acquisitions can play a significant role in the workings of
the market mechanism, but the question nags insistently whether we
have not become too dependent on them as means of securing improvement in underperforming companies. (David A. Walker, executive director, Bank of England, *Bank of England Quarterly Bulletin* [May 1987]:
247, 250.)

INSOFAR AS THE FEDERAL securities laws adopted in
the 1930s were intended to foster shareholder participation in the
government of public corporations, not much came of them. To be
sure, there was little other encouragement either from the states or from
management. But then again, neither did shareholders show much interest. Institutional investors were rapidly increasing their share ownership
of the leading corporations, but beyond that, few of them did much to
make their presence felt. The Wall Street Rule reigned. Institutional
investors began to change their stock holdings about as freely, and almost
as often, as their socks. Better, it was said, to deal with (the inevitable)
problems of a business by selling off the shares than by contributing to
the solution. As with the weather, plenty of people complained about
this "rule," but no one did anything about it.

A New Disciplinary Tool

When, therefore, in the early 1960s the hostile tender offer first began
to occur in significant numbers, it was enthusiastically welcomed. A
tender offer is an offer to buy, i.e., a bid for the shareholders of the
target company to *tender*, all or a portion of their shares. Unlike mergers
and other business acquisitions, which require prior approval by the
board of directors of the target, the distinctive genius of the tender offer
is that it can also be hostile, meaning that the target management may

not have approved it. The bidder may choose to circumvent the target's board and deal directly—and only—with the target's shareholders. Tender offers were soon seen, therefore, as a lively new way to reinvigorate those companies that most needed it. Best of all, they were taking shape in the marketplace without a palace revolution in Wilmington and without federal legislation. In fact it was taking place without the intervention of anyone, except a handful of "raiders" willing to confront the target companies, which at the time were typically small and quite removed from the business establishment.

The welcome was warm, indeed. Robin Marris, writing in 1963 in England, where takeovers were already well known, was the first of the scholars to see this potential.[1] Others soon followed here. Henry G. Manne wrote that the tender offer was almost the only scheme for assuring some degree of competitive efficiency among corporate managers. It would give to shareholders, he said, "both power and protection commensurate with their interest in corporate affairs."[2] Judge Henry Friendly later referred to the takeover bid as "the sharpest blade for the improvement of corporate management."[3] Ben Graham wrote that while his efforts to stimulate more intelligent action by the great body of shareholders had produced almost nothing, the cause had ultimately "been rescued by an extraneous development—known as take-overs. . . . "[4]

This enthusiasm was easy to explain. If poor managements produce poor share prices, a turnaround profit potential exists for entrepreneurial investors. Writing in 1973, Graham concluded that the premium prices being paid in these acquisitions usually brought them "within the range of the value of the enterprise under reasonably competent management."[5] The happy result was that even while public shareholders remained passive, they were being bailed out by a few enterprising individuals. Only a handful of companies actually became targets, of course, but others were given notice that they, too, should mend their ways. Many of them had built up cash and other reserves at a time when they were already adequately financed. Sometimes the money went into acquisitions of new businesses, sometimes to gold plate existing ones, and sometimes it just sat there. Shareholders had no way to pry it loose. Then along came the corporate raiders. It was lovely to see. The dilemma of large groups of previously voiceless shareholders was being solved effectively, by holding out the special inducement of corporate control to those willing to step forward.

The early tender offers were regarded much like proxy contests, except that the referendum on management was conducted not by proxy cards but by tenders of stock certificates. The shareholders would, in effect, vote for the "Christians" by keeping their shares and for the "lions" by selling. Right through the 1960s, tender offers and proxy contests seemed to serve the same purposes. The tactics were similar. This was still the period when shareholders relied heavily on the advice of corporate insiders when a control fight erupted. Managements sent letters to shareholders extolling their own records, assuring them that the directors did not intend to tender their own shares, and criticizing the records and intentions of the bidders. Dividends might be raised, the stock split, or favorable earnings news rushed to the press. Because the tender offer was seen as a battle for the confidence of the shareholders, rather than the simple bidding contest that it later became, these defenses often succeeded.

The analogy to proxy contests eventually failed. Proxy contests are waged by those who do not have the necessary votes in hand and are unwilling to pay the price to purchase them. Proxy contests are typically waged by individuals, not by large corporations or others with access to ample financing. The argument in a proxy contest is usually about the privilege of managing someone else's money—the shareholders'. By the mid-1970s, however, with minor exceptions, the usual tender offer was no longer a contest for control, except as a brief, intermediate step toward a complete acquisition of the underlying business and properties. In 1974 the first of the major investment banking firms, Morgan Stanley, abandoned the hitherto strict, although unwritten rule against acting as banker for a hostile bidder. The others followed, except for Goldman Sachs, which continued to take the position—not entirely without its rewards—that it would represent only targets. With the added respectability and access to much larger pools of capital, a new class of bidders emerged. Changing management was no longer the objective, and the advertisements that praised or rebuked them began to dry up.

TARGET COMPANIES:
WHO'S IN CHARGE HERE?
As tender offers gathered steam, they became bidding contests with almost nothing for the shareholders to think about, except to compare the competing bids. Since they were invariably cash offers, that didn't take long. Better yet, the premiums paid by the successful bidders jumped to an average of 80 percent over the market price before the announcement

of the initial offer. Faced with prices so high, the shareholders of a target company lose all interest in a referendum on management. The only question is the address of the banker's window.

In truth, the talk about a referendum on the quality of management had always been somewhat naive. In the absence of any mechanism for collective bargaining or other joint decision-making, each of the share-holders of the target company is faced with the dilemma—one that re-sembles the prisoner's dilemma of game theory[6]—of tendering his own shares, or if not, of seeing the other shareholders (faced with the same dilemma) tender theirs. In the latter case, he is left with stock that has usually lost both value and liquidity. With minor exceptions, therefore, each of them tenders. (In the prisoner's dilemma, there are two prisoners, both of whom could escape with trivial sentences if neither "talks." If either confesses, the other will receive a severe sentence and the confessor will get one that is shorter, but still substantial. Their collective interest is clearly not to talk. But because they cannot discuss their predicament, each—fearing that the other will confess to save his skin—tries to save something of his own. Both confess, both get substantial sentences.)

In this respect a statutory merger is quite different from a tender offer. The required procedure for a merger calls for a shareholder vote on the proposal. Even if a given shareholder votes with a losing minority, he is not frozen out of whatever benefits accrue to the majority if it happens that the merger is approved. His shares will be exchanged at the merger price along with all the rest. The votes are cast individually, but the result is collective.

The history of the various corporation laws makes it clear enough that the tender offer began as something of an accident, arguably a happy one, but an accident nonetheless. No one had ever sat down in Delaware or elsewhere and said: "Let's design a mechanism for the sale of public corporations that does not require a meeting of either the directors or the shareholders." For decades the shareholders seemed not to have any right whatever to sell off the business and assets of the corporation. At least that was the general understanding. It was only the board in most states that could initiate the statutory process of a merger, consolidation or sale of the business. Public policy discussions for the most part focused on whether the public shareholders could participate in the process at all, or whether the board should be free to act alone. As early as 1932, in *The Modern Corporation*, Berle and Means observed that liquidity for public investors carried with it as a necessary corollary that they relinquish any direct participation in the company's operations and that the right of disposition—the *jus disponendi*—of the corporation's assets "ceases to be in the owner of the [shares]."[7]

While that was the common view, the codification of it fell victim to the haphazard way in which the corporation laws grew by accretion over the years. Delaware and the other states undertook almost no systematic overview of the law (except as part of their competitive struggle to win new charters), nor did they try to produce a statute for public corporations that would adequately distinguish them from closely held, private ones. If they had, they would have observed what one British scholar had observed,[8] that hostile tender offers required no change in the rules, only a change in the culture. (There is, perhaps, some poetic justice in the fact that those who had controlled the legislative process so effectively were later hoisted on their own oversights.) True, there had been hostile bids in the nineteenth century, notably for railroads, but then they stopped. Whereas the British had for many years seen one company acquire another by an unfriendly acquisition of its shares, hostile takeovers did not begin to reappear in America until about 1960.

Power had passed not to, but through, the shareholders, and it all began without any conscious legislative thought to the process. In Britain, even forty years ago bidders were encouraged to make tender offers for all the outstanding shares, rather than only a part, by provisions that entitled a remaining minority to be bought out.[9] In the United States, however, none of the myriad issues affecting tender offers had been addressed. No one had thought about how much disclosure ought to be required, whether bidders should be allowed to coerce target company shareholders by offering to buy on a first-come, first-served basis or for what minimum time an offer ought to remain open to encourage competitive bidding.

The most important of these "unconscious choices" was that the power to initiate a sale of the business had been taken from management and given not to the shareholders but to whichever persons *outside* the corporation decided to make a bid. The president's Council of Economic Advisers and some courts have suggested that a tender offer is a latter-day form of town meeting.[10] Not so. While the shareholders have a common interest, they are in no position to negotiate or bargain with a bidder. Their only bargaining agent is the very management that the tender offer is designed to circumvent. The result is a void. Once a company has been "put into play," meaning that a bid has been made or seems likely, and arbitrageurs have bought up much of the stock, the odds are about four to one that the company will be sold to someone, whether a (hostile) black knight, white knight, or something in between. Lions win.

There is a "for sale" sign hanging on the door of American industry, and no one inside the shop has the power to take it down. The situation is unique. Other organizations and institutions simply do not cede the power to liquidate the venture to those who have no prior role or stake in it.

THE EFFECTS OF TAKEOVERS ON CORPORATE EFFICIENCY

Once the role—actually the nonrole—of the shareholder is recognized, the principal questions are whether tender offers (a) focus with some precision on those companies whose resources have been underutilized and (b) transfer control to those who could utilize them better. As Judge Friendly's metaphor of the "sharpest blade" intimates, the tender offer has all the appeal of quick and radical surgery. No matter how bad the company, there is a solution. If several bidders emerge, so much the better, because the business will then be sold to the one for whom it presumably has the highest value. Shareholders win, and economic efficiency wins. Thus it no longer matters that the shareholders have been excluded from any direct role in the process, because all the necessary judgments are being made in the marketplace.

The pruning deadwood thesis

Why, then, has the once large consensus in favor of tender offers been replaced by an increasingly sharp debate? There is general agreement that tender offers should be judged primarily by their effects on corporate productivity. But beyond that the agreement breaks down. Much of the conflict grows out of different views of the stock market and its own inherent efficiency. Financial economists, starting from the assumption that the market determines the value of stocks correctly, i.e., efficiently, believe that the premium price offered in a tender offer *necessarily* signals that real productivity gains are in prospect. The premium price is said to tell us that the assets of the target company will be better utilized thereafter, because in an efficient stock market no other explanation is thought to be possible. Some of the proponents, such as Judge Frank Easterbrook and Daniel Fischel, speak of the improvements as coming almost entirely from the displacement of bad managers. Others, including the Council of Economic Advisers, go beyond merely bad managers and speak in more general, less disparaging terms of improving efficiency by the "transfer of scarce resources to higher valued uses. . . ."[11]

The implications of this point of view are, of course, quite sweeping. No eyebrows are raised as the pace of takeovers accelerates. Companies should be bought and sold, it is said, "like apples." To encourage the process, the Williams Act should be rescinded, thus eliminating such restrictions on bidders as the requirement that if an offer is oversubscribed, those who did tender are entitled to have their shares picked up on a pro rata basis. Before the Williams Act, bidders were able to shape their offers in any fashion they chose. Shares were usually accepted on a first-come, first-served basis, producing a rush to tender.[12] Professional investors were able to beat out individuals, and of course there was no opportunity for a target to seek out other offers.

For those financial economists who believe that it is best to maximize the number of bids, fairness takes a backseat. Even classical economics takes a backseat. Not wanting the auctions that would produce for target company shareholders the best price, that is, the *market price* that willing buyers would pay, Manne and others have been critical of any legislation, federal or state, that requires that a bid remain open long enough for an auction to take place. For those who are less sure about the real gains from takeovers, however, the fairness with which they are conducted is a major consideration.

The populists

The debate about tender offers has important implications for shareholders, and some institutional investors and their trade associations have been increasingly vocal. In general, they agree with the neoclassicists that tender offers are a necessary and useful discipline. In addition, however, there has appeared what might be called a "populist" group, who argue that it does not much matter whether or not the bidders have good motives or whether they are potentially better managers. The shareholders are the owners of the target company, by gosh, and they are entitled to receive any offer that will increase the value of their shares. A profit is a profit, they are saying, and what's wrong with that?

When a CEO tried to make the point that these issues affect all of society, our best known and richest populist, T. Boone Pickens, the chairman of Mesa Petroleum, who has made many a hostile bid, responded with unmistakable clarity:

That's pure crap . . . the shareholders own the company. If you operate
under a free market, the shareholders decide. That's all there is to it.[13]

Nor is that point of view taken just by Pickens, for whom it has obviously self-serving qualities. Professor John C. Coffee, Jr., has also asked why the shareholders are not entitled to take the money and run:

[W]hen one asserts that market forces pressure managers to concentrate
on the short-run, the obvious retort is: why shouldn't they do so if
this is what shareholders want? . . . If shareholders today demand a
higher discount rate or simply have a shorter time horizon in an inflationary world, a critic must explain why this change is not as much
within the shareholders' prerogative as it is to shift their political preference from Democrat to Republican.[14]

Pickens and Coffee are making an important point. Is the simple fact
that the shares are selling well below the price that a single buyer would
pay for the company as a whole all that we need to know? The debate
about corporate governance has for more than fifty years been framed
largely in terms of the conflict between shareholders and managers, with
the assumption that if managers served shareholders' needs, then they
would also be serving society's needs. Various models were created to
describe or deal with the tension between shareholders and managers,
but almost always on the premise that the shareholders' desire for maximum profit is a valid proxy for society's desire for maximum economic
vigor.

The tender offer is unique, because it is the shareholders' only opportunity to disinvest not just by selling off their shares, at whatever price the
stock market offers, but by selling off the whole company, at whatever
price it will bring—and to do so without the approval of the board. If
the tender offer is the "sharpest blade for the improvement of corporate
management" over the long pull, then there is no conflict between the
interests of the shareholders and of society. But if not, if something else
is going on, if the blade too often excises healthy rather than diseased
tissue, then there is a novel and terrible dilemma.

Even a well-run business might be sold, of course, if the price were
high enough. The usually useful test of how the 20 shareholders of a
closely held company—rather than the 20,000 of a public company—
might behave doesn't yield easy answers here. The 20 shareholders might
not sell out at one price (one and one-half times market?) but might do
so at another (two times market?). Or they might have made a commit-

ment to management that transcends price. That is a quite plausible commitment for passive shareholders to have given, as a means of hiring, retaining, and motivating managers. There is no sure response.

The problem is aggravated by the popularity of high turnover, "performance" investing, and by the rapid growth of index funds that buy stocks of five hundred different companies at a time. In neither case is there likely to be a commitment to any specific company in the portfolio, nor are many of the money managers likely to have made the painstaking analysis on which such a commitment might have been based. As we saw in chapter 2, even well-run companies sell from time to time at deep discounts from fundamental values, leaving ample opportunity for a hostile bid at a sufficient premium over market to put the target into play. With 20,000 shareholders it is not possible, of course, to make a commitment to management that "transcends price," because there is no collective voice through which to act. But in today's investment climate, there would in any event be no inclination to do so. The question then is whether we want systematically to dismantle enterprises simply because of these seemingly inevitable market fluctuations. Does the continuity of the venture depend on the ability of the management to maintain at all times a market price at or above its breakup value?

We know that weak managements explain some of the tender offers and potential synergies explain still others. But the question is whether, taken together, these opportunities for improved productivity are just one of many explanations. A number of others have been suggested, and these will be examined shortly. The bankers and lawyers, for example, tell lots of deal-stories about how the tax system has sometimes been manipulated to produce tax savings so large as to explain all or most of the premium portion of the price. More important, some believe that the Chicago School analysis rests almost entirely on the unstated and untested assumption that there is a single, seamless market that covers both the trading in stocks and the trading in whole companies, rather than two distinct markets. These dissenters contend that there is, first, a day-to-day trading market for shares, with the payoff in future share prices, and second, a market with a different class of buyers who are seeking whole companies and are able to price on the basis of cash flows, asset values, tax savings, and other rewards that do not depend on share prices. The bidder in a tender offer, therefore, may be simply arbitraging across markets for reasons having little to do with good industrial policy.

THE SURGE IN TAKEOVERS

These are not easy issues. One way to start is just to remember how much the tender offer game has changed. Initially, in the 1960s, takeovers seemed to operate at the periphery of the corporate system. The targets were small, and many of them were indeed poorly run. The premiums being paid were modest, often no more than 15–20 percent over the preannouncement price, and, we have seen, the tender offer prices seemed just about right. The first $100 million hostile takeover did not take place until the 1970s.

Once the genie was out of the bottle, however, an intense wave of merger activity developed. Announced mergers and acquisitions have grown from $12 billion in 1975 to $44 billion in 1979, to $83 billion in 1981, and to $180 billion in 1985. They remained at about that level during 1986 and the first half of 1987.[15] Over sixty-six of the transactions that closed in 1985–1986 were valued at $1 billion or more. The competition for target companies became so intense that the average premium over market for a large number of hostile bids in the late 1970s and early 1980s was 80 percent.

Hostile bids are the key to all this merger and acquisition activity. In addition to those bids that are avowedly "unsolicited," many management buyouts begin as a response to a threat, or a rumor of a threat, of a hostile bid. And even many of the ostensibly friendly, negotiated mergers are, on analysis, defensive in character. Hostile tender offers do not account for all of this surge in activity, but they have been the major engine driving it. The question, then, is whether this fifteenfold increase in mergers can be attributed primarily to any one cause, such as a search for productivity gains.

The businesses sold in 1985 alone were worth 10 percent of the aggregate average value of the stocks then listed on the New York Stock Exchange and almost 9 percent of the value of all stocks. Buyers have been paying prices almost two times the market price. According to one study of hostile takeovers in the 1970s and early 1980s, bidders were acquiring targets at an average price-earnings ratio of 17, compared to the 8.9 average of the Standard & Poor's 500 Stock Index during the relevant years.[16]

Even the approximately $180 billion of annual merger activity of recent years does not fully reflect the impact of what is happening. Union Carbide, Phillips Petroleum, Carter Hawley Hale, and many others, eager to avoid becoming next month's acquisition, "restructured" themselves by selling businesses and buying back shares. Retirements of stock (net of new issues) by nonfinancial corporations averaged over $60 billion annually in the 1984–1986 period.[17] In 1986, twenty-six of the repurchases were worth at least $500 million.[18]

Let us think for a moment of American industry with one-half being managed demonstrably better than average and the other half worse. At the rate at which acquisitions were being consummated in the mid-1980s, it would take only a few years' time for the overachievers to acquire all the underachievers. (These are in addition to the onlookers who escape being targets only by taking the restructuring or other medicine.) The financial economists' so-called "pruning deadwood" thesis assumes, in fact, that there is some such sharp separation between the winners and losers, even if it is not precisely half on one side and half on the other. The claim is that one group of companies has systematically discovered others whose assets are so shockingly underutilized as to justify an *average* premium of 80 percent. And the supply of skilled bidders able to capitalize on these opportunities seems to grow from year to year.

TESTING THE EFFECTS OF TAKEOVERS

If takeovers are pruning deadwood so wondrously, the beneficent impact of so wide-ranging a process should have begun to show up in a variety of ways. With activity at such an intense level, the University of Chicago and Rochester financial economists, who have produced so much of the empirical research, might have looked for some early effects in the economy as a whole. (So far the benefits would be difficult to find. The increases in business productivity in the United States in the 1980s have been no better than the inadequate 1.5 percent annual rates of the 1970s and lag behind those of our industrialized trading partners.)[19] Or they might have analyzed the profit performance of the acquiring and acquired companies to see if the acquiring companies had been the more successful of the two and to determine the effects of takeovers on acquiring companies. (A number of such profitability studies had previously been made with respect to mergers generally, rather than hostile takeovers in particular. The results were decidedly inconsistent with the notion of high-performing bidders acquiring limping-dog targets.)[20] Or they might have talked to some of the participants. (In a survey of more than two hundred corporate directors, 84 percent said that excellent management was a major plus in assessing potential targets, and 91 percent said that poor management was either no attraction [69 percent] or a minor one [22 percent].)[21]

Stock price studies

What the researchers did was to rely entirely on studies of the changes in the stock prices of the bidders and targets around the "event" of the takeover announcement. The stock prices of the targets rise, as indeed they must, given the large premiums being paid by the bidders. (No premium, no bid.) On the other hand, the stock prices of the bidders rise little, if at all, thus interrupting the substantial and "above-normal" stock price increases they had been enjoying for several years *before* the acquisition of the target companies. The data thus suggest that it may have been the bidders' fat pocketbooks that prompted the takeovers, which they could now afford, rather than any transferable skills. Indeed, some studies show significant declines in the bidders' stock prices relative to other stocks the longer the period after the acquisition.[22] To find in these various studies evidence for the pruning deadwood thesis, it is essential to focus on the bidders' stock price changes for a very brief period before and after the event. Ellen B. Magenheim and Dennis C. Mueller, for example, found that if one waits until three years after a tender offer or other merger, the acquiring company "shareholders are significantly worse off than they would have been had their companies continued to perform in the [three year] post-event period as they had [for three years] prior to the event. . . . "[23] The same pattern, they concluded, could be observed in several of the studies.

The slim pickings of these so-called event studies are what so many of the financial economists insist on calling the "scientific evidence" that hostile takeovers are not only good for the target company shareholders but for the economy. While they are unable to identify the particular sources of the gains,[24] they are sure that the gains do exist. The argument is based on the "neoclassical notion," in Michael Bradley's words, "that there are mutual gains from voluntary trade—that through the process of voluntary exchange, resources will flow to their highest valued use."[25] In this case part of the gains are immediately visible, the large and well-documented gains that go to target company shareholders. These stock profits are ultimately a proxy for real gains in efficiency.

What we see here is a very intense, unshakable reliance on efficient market theory. It is used, first, to explain the takeover phenomenon. The prices are "correct" not only for groups of companies taken as a whole, but for any individual company in an actively traded market.

Because there are no undervalued stocks to be discovered by research or analysis, the only significant opportunities that exist are those companies with undermanaged, underutilized resources. But then the researchers have come forward only with data that assume the critical premise of their argument, namely that stock prices accurately and continuously mirror the profits and prospects of the underlying business. In this simplified view of the world, one that sees everything through the single lens of stock price changes, very short-term stock price changes—some of the studies covered no more than a few days' time—tell us all that we need to know about the motivations and long-term effects of complex events. It is an unchanging, static explanation that is good for all seasons, one that explains tender offers in the 1960s, when they were few in number and premiums were modest, as well as in the 1980s, after dramatic changes had occurred.

Premiums of 80 percent over market, instead of the earlier premiums of 20 percent, should have evoked from these economists something more than unbroken applause. Is it really possible that bidders expect to find *on average* efficiency gains that enable them to pay almost two times the market price for acquired companies? And if so, if they are willing to accept such large risks, how does it happen that they keep little, if any, of the benefits for their own shareholders? Alternative tests, such as studies of the profitability of the targets and bidders—which ought at least to validate the notion of underperforming targets—were not run. "[M]ost financial economists," as two of them (Bradley and Jarrell) have said, "would argue that stockmarket (sic) data are far superior to accounting data in assessing the economic effects of corporate events."[26] But they tend to take account only of that portion of the stock market data that is congenial to their conclusions. Profit and loss data are ignored entirely, even though it is on the basis of such data that the much-admired bidders, and the bankers for the bidders, have based *their* calculations.

PROFITABILITY STUDIES OF TARGETS AND BIDDERS

Struck by the incompleteness of this research, Edward S. Herman of the Wharton School and this author undertook a study (the H & L Study)[27] more in line with traditional techniques. Prior to the current wave of takeovers, most of those who studied the impact of mergers looked at the pre- and post-merger earnings and returns of the merging companies. While they had not looked at hostile takeovers as such, they did uniformly conclude that the effects were either negative or neutral, meaning that the acquired company's profitability either declined or remained flat. The H & L Study sought to fill the gap in the analysis of hostile tender offers left by the reliance on stock price "event" studies. We looked at data for the targets and successful bidders in 56 hostile takeovers that began during the years 1975–1983, using the published financial data of the 112 companies.[28] Published financial data should be a useful analytic tool, because they are the only financial data about the target that are generally available to a hostile bidder. In effect, the study closely tracked the process by which bidders themselves identified potential targets and determined what price to pay.

The 56 targets in the H & L Study were typically large companies from a broad cross-section of industries. The mean total assets of the targets for the year before the bid were over $900 million, almost half that of the bidders, and over the period covered by the study they grew rapidly. For the years 1981–1983 they had mean total assets of $1.5 billion. The average premium over the preannouncement market price was also large—80 percent.[29] Casual marriages of convenience were unlikely. According to the prevailing theory, the superior bidders should have experienced higher returns on capital than the targets. It's like the fabled story that Buffett tells of the toads waiting to be turned into princes by princesses with magic kisses. If these bidders are not bona fide princesses, we are left with some very high-priced toads.

We calculated profitability by the commonly used tests of return on equity (ROE) and return on total capital (ROC). (It is no good, of course, to say simply that one company earns more money than another, without looking to see how much was invested in each.) Return on equity measures the after-tax earnings as a percentage of a company's equity capital, which are the funds that the shareholders have contributed to, or left in, the business. Return on total capital uses the broader capital base of shareholders' equity plus borrowed money, with the income calculated before deducting income taxes and interest charges. The ROC test is particularly useful for those companies that might show an excellent return on equity only because of excessive debt. By eliminating the tax and interest deductions, which can vary for a variety of reasons, ROC also describes more directly the efficiency of operations.

If target companies offer unusual opportunities for improved operations, then they should show distinctly lower profitability rates for a dollar of invested capital than other companies, particularly those in the same industry. That is not what we found, however. The 56 targets in the study showed returns that compared favorably with all other groups: (a) the bidders that acquired them, (b) other companies in the same industries that were selected as "control" companies for the study, and (c) American industry generally. Table 5-1 sets forth for each of five years before the year of the announcement of the bid (years B minus 5 to B minus 1) the ROC for all of the targets and bidders and for the target control companies.

What we see in Table 5-1 is that in each of the five years before the announcement of the bid, the target companies were at least as profitable as the bidders who eventually acquired them. Compared to the control companies, the targets also had good records, performing in some years less well but in others better. The differences between the targets and the control companies were not substantial. What is significant is that on average the targets performed *no less well* than comparable companies in their respective industries. The relatively poor performance implied in the arguments of the (Chicago School) financial economists does not show up.

When the performance of the targets was measured by returns on equity (ROE) rather than returns on capital (ROC), the results were substantially the same. (The ROE data appear in Table 5-2 in the appendix to this chapter.) For example, from the fifth year before the announcement of the bid to the year immediately before, the targets' weighted ROE increased from 13.1 to 16.4 percent, while the control companies increased theirs from 12.9 to 16.8 percent.

These data cast a serious shadow on the conventional wisdom that takeovers are revitalizing American industry. Industrial companies have historically earned about 12–13 percent on their shareholders' equity. The

Table 5-1
Return on total capital (ROC), targets,
bidders, and target-controls
(one to five years before the bid)
(weighted basis)[30]

	B-5	B-4	B-3	B-2	B-1
targets	19.2%	18.3%	20.0%	25.2%	27.6%
bidders	15.2	15.9	19.8	22.0	21.3
target-controls	18.7	19.7	21.2	24.4	21.7

targets in the H & L Study earned as a group slightly better than that in the third, fourth and fifth years before the announcement of the bid, but then in the two years immediately preceding the bid they earned 16–17 percent on equity. Those are exceptionally high returns, a fact that surely was not lost on the bidders.

Particularly striking is the fact that the targets became substantially more profitable, not less, as the date of the bid approached, not at all what we had been led to expect. What the bidders saw were target managements who were doing well, not poorly, and judging from the target-control companies, the relevant industries were also doing well. Financially speaking, the bidders must have been licking their chops. Here were opportunities to acquire companies that in bottom-line terms were performing better than most, better than their own, and better as time went on.

None of this really should surprise us. Prospective acquirers do not often walk into the offices of their investment bankers and ask for a list of badly run companies. They seldom do that in any case, but in hostile tender offers there is the special reason that bidders rarely seek companies in their own industries—what lawyers and economists call horizontal mergers—because of potential antitrust defenses. (While the Department of Justice may not care much about mergers these days, a hostile bid for a competitor gives to the target company a ready-made, viable lawsuit. Even if the bidder wins the litigation, by the time it is unwound someone else will probably have made off with the prize.) More often, therefore, like U. S. Steel (now USX) and DuPont in acquiring oil companies Marathon and Conoco, they go outside their own industries and expertise so that there is added incentive to seek not only good assets but good managers. And to look at industries that are doing well, not poorly. The truly failing companies, such as Lockheed and Chrysler, are like as not left for Congress to bail out, or as in the case of International Harvester and Storage Technology, for informal or formal reorganization.

The tendency to think of takeovers primarily in terms of poorly managed, underutilized resources dies hard. Early on, in the 1960s, it was easy to find potential targets that could be bought with their own money, so to speak, because they had large cash reserves or excess borrowing capacity. Eventually, however, the likely victims learned the lesson that, like driving an old car, your company was less likely to be "stolen" if it looked poor rather than rich. They used their excess capital, and even some that was not excess, to expand existing businesses and to buy others. Marshall Field, Kennecott, and many other companies, unable to manage one business well, spent or borrowed heavily to "defend" themselves by buying still others. Or they restructured, as did Union Carbide and others, borrowing heavily and selling off *good* businesses to pay debts or make themselves unattractive. In case after case, the Golden Rule might have been rephrased to read "Do unto yourself as others would do unto you."

It is still common to hear commentators speak of the typical target as having excess, i.e., underutilized, borrowing capacity.[31] The notion is, first, that the company has not used its resources to the fullest and, second, that a buyer of the company can use the untapped borrowing power to pay a good part of the purchase price. That is not what we found, however. (See Table 5-3 in the appendix to this chapter.) On the contrary, the targets had already tapped their borrowing capacity quite substantially. And the proportion of debt to equity—a common measure of liquidity—was increasing rather than dropping as the year of the bid approached. The targets' debt:equity ratios exceeded those of the bidders and roughly matched those of the control group.[32] A recent study by the Investor Responsibility Research Center showed similar results.[33]

Averages can be deceptive, so in addition to looking at the 56 bidders and 56 targets as a group, the H & L Study broke down each of the two groups, comparing the early, mid-1970s events with the later, 1980s ones. That comparison, it turned out, was a key to some important findings, because the early and late targets, for example, had very different characteristics. A decade ago, in the mid-1970s, there did exist targets apparently ripe for picking. The pruning deadwood thesis seems to have been working then, and working quite well, at least according to our study. For the 21 targets of bids first announced in 1975–1978, the mean return on equity on a weighted basis was a not very good 9 percent for the five years before the bid. Many of those targets seem to have represented attractive turnaround opportunities.

But a few years later, as the volume of takeovers mushroomed, the game changed. For the 25 targets of hostile bids begun in the years 1981–1983, the mean weighted return on equity for the five years before the bid was 16 percent, almost twice the 9 percent of the earlier group. And for the two years immediately before the bid, the return averaged over 18 percent. These later, 1980s targets were performing about as well as any group of companies in America, as well as the control companies, and much better than the bidders. (The results appear in Table 5-4 in the appendix to this chapter.)

Other studies have produced generally similar results. One, by David J. Ravenscraft and F. M. Scherer[34] found that the targets of an earlier period, the 1960–1970s, enjoyed returns on assets not significantly different from those of other manufacturing companies. The second study, by the Investor Responsibility Research Center, looking at the prebid profitability of a number of targets of hostile bids in the years 1979–1984, found that the targets' performance had been ''neither exceptionally good nor exceptionally bad by market standards.''[35] W. T. Grimm and Company, which keeps a detailed, street-smart score on mergers, concluded that many of the targets enjoyed strong market positions and were well managed.

What happened to the bidders?

Turning from targets to bidders, the H & L Study found that the bidders as a group had profitability rates before the bid that were also quite good. On average, however, they were no better than those of the targets.[36] But more significant than the average, overall results was the difference between the bids in the 1970s and those in the 1980s. While the bidders in 1975–1978 were able to find targets with relatively poor operating histories, there are no such good marks for the later, 1981–1983 takeovers. These 1980s bids seem in all respects to have been much more speculative. The bidders sought out targets that were relatively larger, and even more to the point, targets with already excellent profit histories and (at least by industry yardsticks) with little unused debt capacity. It was difficult to see what contribution the bidders could make. Still they persisted in paying almost two times the market price.

One of the recurring patterns in corporate finance is the rapid exploitation of a new opportunity, with the originators enjoying considerable success, but with the imitators close behind. The opportunities dry up, and yet the game continues. Some such pattern was at work here. The bidders in the early years, 1975–1978, found targets with lower rates of return than their own. But as the data in Table 5-5 in the appendix to this chapter show, they achieved for the combined operations of the two companies profitability rates that quickly exceeded even their own good results in the years before the bid. For example, their returns on equity rose from a very acceptable 13.9 percent in the year immediately before the announcement of the bid to an even better 14.8 percent in the first full year after completion of the takeover, and a remarkably good 15.3 percent in the second full year.

No such good marks were earned by the 1981–1983 transactions, which were on average much larger in size. Returns on equity for the bidders dropped from 14.1 percent in the year before the bid to less than 9 percent in the first three years after the takeover. (See Table 5-5 in the appendix to this chapter.) *In short, after the takeover, the bidders performed well below the level of either the bidders or their targets during the years before the bid.*

The data for the years after the takeover possibly were influenced by some extraneous events. The recession during the years 1982–1983, for example, surely depressed profitability rates, regardless of acquisitions. To filter out these effects, the H & L Study used as control companies for the targets a group of one hundred companies selected from the same industries and of approximately the same size. For the bidders the problem was made more difficult by the fact that they and their targets typically were operating in quite different lines of business. A steel company acquired an oil company, an engineering company acquired a nonferrous metals company, and so on. For the bidders, therefore, the Standard & Poor's 400 Industrials Index was used as a control group. While the overall conclusions remained unaffected, the comparisons with the control group did mute somewhat the otherwise sharp contrast between the successful early bids and the much less successful later ones.

Other recent profitability studies

One limitation of this sort of study needs to be noted. Our analysis was based on data for each of the bidders on a companywide basis, rather than separate, segmented data for the businesses they had purchased. Although these were relatively large acquisitions, the fact remains that the success of them could be measured only from their impact on the bidders' overall operating results. The measurement was therefore diluted by the bidders' income from other businesses.

Ravenscraft and Scherer overcame that obstacle by using line-of-business data from the Federal Trade Commission, thus permitting them to follow the acquired companies even after the takeover. They, too, however, found no improvements in operating efficiencies that might justify the acquisition premiums. The only other recent and similar study is one by Stephen A. Rhoades, a staff member of the board of governors of the Federal Reserve System. Having compiled extensive data on the operating performance of banks acquired during the period from 1968–1978, Rhoades concluded that bank mergers do not tend to rid the system of poorly performing companies or to improve the operating performance of the acquired banks.[37]

TAKEOVERS:

TOO COMPLEX FOR ANY ONE EXPLANATION

More data would no doubt be useful. But the contention that the rational pursuit of improved operations is the major explanation of takeovers has ceased to be persuasive. According to the Ravenscraft and Scherer study, it was never persuasive. The H & L Study suggests that it was once a useful explanation, but later failed. Both studies, however, are thoroughly consistent with Mueller's recent conclusion that the dominant effect of mergers on profitability is one of averaging.[38] (Companies with either above-normal or below-normal profits all move toward the average after mergers, not just onward and upward as predicted by the pruning deadwood thesis.)

The process is simply too complex and dynamic for any one explanation. The supply of cash-rich, poorly performing targets dried up, and yet the bidders continued to pay prices far above market. In time the bidders changed, too. At first they were largely entrepreneurial individuals, seeking to buy just enough shares to win control. Later they were operating companies seeking to own and operate the targets as divisions of their own corporations. The market offered unprecedented opportunities to buy major companies with strong market positions—companies such as Otis Elevator, Coca-Cola Bottling Company of Los Angeles, Seven-Up, Sunbeam, Hobart, Garfinckel-Brooks Brothers, Richardson-Vicks, Allied Stores, General Foods, and Marathon Oil. These were businesses that theretofore had not been for sale on any basis. Later still there emerged a much more speculative group of bidders, those who played the game for the profits of the game itself and were as willing to be bought off—to take greenmail and arbitrage profits—as to buy in. Many of them had never run businesses; many of them never would. They profited as if they were successful businessmen, but without having to operate a business. The game itself brought sufficient rewards.

There are still cases where the opportunity for productivity gains explains the premium price. But no one interpretation will do. Too bad. What we have instead is a rather long list of other forces that are at work, some more important, some less, some arguably desirable, some distinctly undesirable. To wit:

1. Bargain pricing

Almost every company sells at one time or another in the day-to-day trading market at a discount from the price it would fetch if sold as a whole—good companies and bad ones, it doesn't matter. As Yogi Berra said, "you can observe a lot just by watching." For years, Exxon sold at less than $3 per barrel of its proven reserves, with everything else thrown in for nothing, at a time when everyone knew that Exxon as a whole would go for two or three times that price. According to Buffett, two of the best-managed companies, Capital Cities and Washington Post, were in excellent businesses and yet their shares sold in the mid-1970s at discounts of 75–80 percent from their values to a private owner.[39] As this author has written, the takeover opportunity therefore is frequently a market phenomenon rather than a business phenomenon, because the stock market:

> systematically produces a group of out-of-favor companies. With al-most 10,000 publicly traded securities to choose from, we should expect to find in almost any season takeover candidates in substantial numbers. It is like fishing in a well-stocked pond. A competent bidder should catch his supper. . . . True, the price for success may be high, but fishing in a stocked pond was never cheap. On the other hand, the price for failure is not high; only the lawyers and bankers need be paid.[40]

Just as they can help to produce opportunities, these swings in market sentiment should at times reduce them. In the summer of 1987, the Standard & Poor's 400 index was valuing $1 of earnings at $20, so that stock market prices exceeded those being paid in mergers a few years earlier only after hotly contested bidding. Takeover activity should have dried up. Nonetheless it continued at the same high levels as during the 1985–1986 period. In order to offer the obligatory premium price, bidders began to pay as much as twenty-five times the targets' current earnings. (One wonders on what untapped values these bidders hoped to feed.) In fact, takeovers continued at a record rate right until Black Monday, October 19, when the financing dried up. The lesson seems to have been that no price is too high if it is payable with other people's money.

2. Arbitraging across two different markets

Takeover opportunities also exist because there is not a single, seamless market here, but rather two quite different ones. In the trading market the buyers have a very short term horizon, and—as we saw in chapter 3—it is getting shorter all the time. In that market, one in which the shares simply move from hand to hand, it is easy to be influenced by other investors. They are the ones to whom you eventually must sell. On that marvelous day, January 23, 1987, when over 300 million shares traded in stocks of New York Stock Exchange companies, there was no hard news, just the scurrying around of so-called investors frantically seeking to find out what everyone else was doing so they could do it too. One financial journal called it "Crazy Friday," but it was only an exaggerated example of many Fridays . . . and Tuesdays, too.

The negotiated, whole-company market is quite different. As you would expect, the negotiated market tends to be more stable. The buyers generally are not buying for immediate resale, and the payoff will be calculated in terms of discounted cash flows and a variety of other factors that are only modestly influenced by stock market pricing. The current stock market multiplier, the price-earnings ratio, is much less of a factor.

As distinct from these private owners, Wall Street tends to oversimplify the valuation process. Graham and Dodd wrote in 1951 that while the private owner of a business would never value it at less than its liquidation value, the reasoning of the stock market is that liquidating value is of no importance in the typical case:

> Let us call these the "Wall Street approach" and the "Main Street approach." On Main Street the idea that a business is worth much less than you could auction it off for would seem preposterous; but in Wall Street, people think of themselves as owning not a part of a business but shares of stock in a business. These shares may be valued, bought and sold on a basis that bears little relationship to a normal appraisal of the business entity on which they have their ownership claim.[41]

The Wall Street approach values companies almost entirely by their (current) earnings. Real estate companies, therefore, with their large cash flows but small reported earnings, tend to be undervalued on Wall Street. The Main Street approach says that cable television companies are worth about $1,500 or so per subscriber, even if not yet profitable. Casualty insurance companies frequently trade in the stock market near or below book value, but it is an almost inflexible rule that the price for the whole company is roughly 175 percent of book. And there are similar Main Street yardsticks for railroad tank car companies, life insurance companies, and others. For the buyer of a whole company, the totality often equals much more than the sum of its shares. One of the attractions of owning an insurance company, as distinct from mere shares of one, is the ability to invest the policyholders' money until they (or their heirs) are paid. It is a marvelous device for running what is in effect an investment company without being subject to the burdensome federal rules that restrict the usual investment companies. Control of these insurance company portfolios has thus attracted a long list of entrepreneurial investors, including not just Lord Keynes but Warren Buffett, Harold Geneen, Henry Singleton, Saul Steinberg, and Laurence Tisch.

Main Street and Wall Street: two different markets, with different types of buyers and different measures of value.

3. Taxes stimulated some takeovers

Taxes help explain the pricing of many of the deals, if not the existence of them. Leveraged buyouts, in which a publicly owned company sells out to a private group that usually includes the senior management of the public company, often represent for a threatened target an attractive alternative to a takeover. The executives keep their jobs and are typically offered the opportunity to own a substantial percentage of the stock at bargain prices. Tax factors have played a particularly large role in these transactions, because with no public investors, and with everyone free to focus on cash flow rather than "accounting" earnings, there is no obstacle to maximizing tax benefits.

At least until recently, a tender offer or other takeover was sufficient to produce some very important tax savings. The buyer was permitted to write up the assets to current values and then, particularly after the Economic Recovery Tax Act of 1981, to write them off for tax purposes over very short periods of time. The inflation of the 1970s had created a large gap between the current market values of corporate assets and their historic cost (tax basis). Chart 5-1 shows the growing difference between the value of nonfinancial corporate plant and equipment on a current (or reproduction) cost basis and on a depreciated historic cost basis.[42] Current cost can be considered an approximation of market value and historic cost an approximation of the tax basis.

While the values in the chart are rough, they do show the potential step-up in basis available for plant and equipment, a potential that was at one time a nearly $1 trillion magnet for the deal makers. Congress, in adopting the 1981 tax act, had expressed concern that its very generous depreciation schedules might be used for existing plants and equipment rather than to stimulate more productive new investments and modernization. And with almost $1 trillion of step-ups waiting to be captured, that is largely what happened. Too often a company stayed in business, with the same management, the same workers, and the same assets. Only the control and the tax deductions had changed.

The large premium prices in some of these mergers and acquisitions could be explained entirely, or almost so, by tax savings. There was no great mystery to the process. For a few dollars, one could attend a conference and receive a three-hundred-page handbook on the subject. At least until the Tax Reform Act of 1986, which changed a good many of the rules, one could find cases where, as in Raymond International, there was created an *annual* tax deduction of $1 for every $5 of the purchase

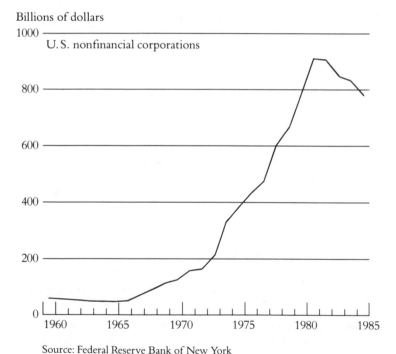

Chart 5–1
Fixed Reproducible Tangible Assets
Current cost less historic cost

Source: Federal Reserve Bank of New York
Quarterly Review, Autumn 1986

price. In the $2.6 billion acquisition of Electronic Data Systems, General Motors claimed a $2 billion write-up of intangible assets that would produce a write-down of $400 million annually for five years. In the Dan River buyout, various tax deductions, plus the premature liquidation of pension plans and other nonoperating sources, accounted for two-thirds of the $150 million purchase price. No one of the deductions was novel, but in varying mixes it was often possible for a business to operate tax-free for five or six years.

Chicago School scholars, eager to show that the market is driven by positive motives, argue that most of the tax savings in theory could have been obtained without the bother of a takeover.[43] But some could not, either because the law precluded them, as in the General Motors case, or because financial conventions for public companies precluded them. It is all well and good to say that any company can choose to account for inventories on a last-in, first-out basis, thus reducing its taxes in an inflationary environment, but public companies have been demonstrably reluctant to reduce taxes at the ''expense'' of reducing income as reported to shareholders. If nothing else, takeovers created the opportunities for bringing various tax savings together in convenient, marketable form.

The tax impact, of course, was never entirely positive. The shareholders of the target typically paid capital gains taxes, and in some cases there was a substantial ''recapture'' of the depreciation allowances that had been enjoyed by the seller. But on balance the Treasury was a heavy loser, often for reasons that Congress had neither anticipated nor intended.

The 1986 Tax Reform Act has eliminated many of these subsidies. There will still be an incentive to substitute debt for equity—substituting tax-deductible interest payments for nondeductible dividends—but the new lower corporate income tax rate of 34 percent reduces even that. And some of the other tax incentives have been reduced or even eliminated. It used to be the rule that even though the buyer wrote up the acquired assets in order to enjoy larger depreciation deductions, the selling corporation paid no tax on the appreciated value of the assets it had sold. By rescinding that rule, known as the *General Utilities* doctrine, Congress now hopes to tax those gains. Also many of the selling stockholders of a target company will be paying capital gains taxes at the new 28 percent maximum average rate, not 20 percent. In addition, while the buyer can still write up, and then write off, a variety of acquired assets, it can no longer do so on quite the same accelerated basis.

How these changes will affect the number of takeovers is not clear. Because of the tax benefits, there has been greater interest in employee stock ownership plans as a financing device. One possibility is that the bidders will in time decline to pay the same large premiums. Another is that bidders will substitute stock for cash as takeover currency in order to make the transactions tax-free, thereby avoiding the impact of both the higher capital gains tax on selling stockholders and the repeal of the *General Utilities* doctrine.[44]

4. The junk bond factor

Ultimately, as each merger wave gains momentum, as prices inflate, buyers are forced to substitute something else—what might be called "funny money"—for hard cash or other forms of "serious" money. It has to happen. There isn't enough serious money to keep the game going. The buyer either runs out of cash or out of sources of investment-grade (serious) loans. An investment-grade lender usually looks for $4 or more of earnings for each $1 of interest on *all* of the borrowers' debt, and an acquisitive CEO quickly strains these limits. One alternative is to issue additional shares of common stock, the supply of which is constrained by little except the capacity of the printing press, but that too has limitations. For one thing, it is rare that the buyer can use common stock to pay two times market for a company without diluting the earnings, and the value, of its own common stock, which by definition is selling at one times market—at least not if the targets are almost half the size of the bidders, as is the case in the current wave of hostile bids.

Almost any security can qualify as funny money, depending on what else is happening in the market. Usually it takes the form of senior securities, either bonds or preferred stock. While it has been said that nothing really new ever happens in corporate finance, it is also true that the same elves reappear in different garb. In the 1960s, funny money often took the form of preferred stocks convertible into common. The common stocks of many companies, particularly conglomerates, were selling at very high price-earnings ratios, which enabled those companies to use their inflated currency to pay high "prices." In effect they could pay $800 for a cat because they were buying them with $900 dogs. What made convertible preferred stocks particularly attractive was the ability to issue what was in substance common stock without diluting the issuer's own reported earnings per share. (Under the then accounting rules, the dilutive effects of these preferred stocks did not have to be reported until they were in fact converted.)

The present merger wave, with announced deals up from $12 billion in 1975 to $173 billion in 1986, is a product largely of an active tender offer market. And tender offers, which require speed, must be made in cash, rather than securities that would be subject to registration under the federal securities laws. Even though the prices have soared, cash remains the coin of tender offers.[45]

Enter the junk bond to be issued by the bidder, not directly to the target shareholders, but rather to third-party investors who, as in the Pantry Pride bid for Revlon, provide much of the cash that will be paid to the target company shareholders. Or, as in the case of Scovill and Metromedia, the cash is first borrowed from banks, and only after the takeover does the junk bond financing take place. (The proceeds are used to pay back the banks.) Elaborate networks have sprung up in the junk bond market, permitting the investment bankers to issue the written assurance that they are "highly confident" the money will be forthcoming, without which the bid would lack credibility. Over $125 billion of junk bonds are outstanding, and commercial banks, under increasing competitive pressure to make high interest loans, own even more of what might be called junk notes. Being less visible than publicly issued bonds, these low-grade bank loans have attracted less attention, but they are no less troubling.

Cheap money, whether from banks or investors, has been a major factor driving takeovers. Ted Turner, using zero-coupon junk bond financing, boasted that he didn't bargain over price when he bought MGM. (He probably didn't realize it, but he was expressing the economics textbook "moral hazard" that no risks are too large if the money is not your own.) Those zero-coupon bonds, where no interest is payable until the bond matures years later, were originally created as a device for investing in United States Treasury bonds, where the credit is unimpeachable. Later they became the preferred vehicle in cases such as Turner Broadcasting, where the earnings shortfall was so large that it was necessary to recognize it from the outset. In effect, the worse the credit, the longer the investors are willing to wait for their money.

Managers have a strong preference for low dividends and little, if any, debt, much preferring the warmth of a debt-free balance sheet. The new preference for debt, therefore, might have been acceptable if the borrowers and lenders had shown some restraint. But as the managers of the Sequoia Fund aptly noted, we seem to have

> arrived at the point where Ben Graham's time-tested "margin of safety" approach to fixed income investment has not only been cashiered but has, in remarkably short order, been replaced by the market's acceptance of a "margin of peril." Instead of calculating the degree to which free cash flow can decline from historic levels and still comfortably service the debt, the question has become how much must cash flow *increase* from historic levels in order to just scrape by [emphasis added].

Turner Broadcasting, Allied Stores, Metromedia, and Scovill Manufacturing, to name just a few, sold bonds on the basis of operating income that fell far short of the level required simply to cover interest payments. These bonds are subject to a major risk of capital loss, but unlike the common stock they in fact resemble, there is no possibility of a major gain.

Most of these securities, and others like them, have been issued in the past three or four years. The bankers are sure to raise enough money to cover the first few years' interest charges, and the issuers have yet to be tested by a full business cycle. We haven't seen such leveraged companies—a debt:equity ratio of 100:1 in Metromedia—since the pyramidal holding companies of the 1920s. The Federal Reserve Board, acting in the face of considerable opposition and with only limited powers, has taken very modest, essentially ineffective steps under the margin rules to curb junk bond financing of hostile tender offers.[46] (This also is reminiscent of the 1920s, when the Federal Reserve Board jawboned around the question of soaring margin debt.) The financial markets are in one of those occasionally recurring, bizarre periods when junk bond and other monies can be raised in blind pools for deals that are still unnamed. Forgetting the lesson that chickens sit on the table, not at it, investors are hoping to dine with Turner, the Belzbergs, and Perelman, just as sixty years ago they tried to sup with Insull.

It is worth our while to take a look at one of these companies, Allied Stores Corporation, which in 1987 issued $1.15 billion of junk bonds and preferred stock.[47] Campeau Corporation, a Canadian company, successfully completed in 1986 a hostile tender offer for all of the outstanding stock of the original Allied Stores ("Old Allied") for about $4 billion. Old Allied was a rather good company. It had about $700 million of debt and $1,300 million of equity, representing a debt:equity ratio of roughly 1:2, about normal for the industry. Coverage of fixed charges was adequate, ranging from about 2.4 times in poor years to 3.8 in good ones. Old Allied's principal business, department stores, is capital intensive, and its earnings of about $160 million after taxes represented a return on equity of about $12\frac{1}{2}$ percent, which was good for that industry.

The new Allied Stores Corporation was essentially the same company but with a hollowed-out capital structure. The buyer had not only paid twenty-five times Old Allied's earnings in its last fiscal year but had borrowed almost all of the purchase price from banks and an affiliate of First Boston Corporation, its investment adviser. Campeau's own cash contribution did not cover even the financing fees and merger expenses. Allied's total debt jumped to $3.8 billion, and its annual interest charges (on a pro forma basis, to reflect the new capital structure) soared to $465 million, far in excess of its earnings. Instead of pretax profits of $290 million, the company now had a pro forma loss of $143 million. Cash flow became negative. Its loan agreements required that Allied raise $1.1 billion by selling a number of divisions that collectively were unprofitable, but even so, pro forma earnings of the remaining businesses would not equal interest charges. The company had no tangible net worth.

Allied Stores was not the worst of these junk bond issues, but it did have some unusually gamey aspects. The sole underwriter of this issue, First Boston, was the same investment banking firm that had provided Campeau a bridge loan of about $850 million for the takeover, and almost all the proceeds were used to repay that loan. Who was to make the usual due diligence inquiries? The worse Allied's prospects, the greater the incentive to complete the offering. In particular, the $200 million of new Senior Notes were not truly senior. Near the front of the prospectus there was a single paragraph that lumped together a number of "risks" in one dense statement, but it looked like pure boilerplate, with none of the detail or numbers that would have helped to alert an investor. Only by turning back further, and reading the last few lines of a paragraph that carried over to the next page, would an investor have learned that the new notes, while *senior* to $700 million of new debentures, were effectively *junior* to $1.3 billion of existing debt by reason of the company's holding company structure.

An SEC report in 1986 concluded that the risks in junk bonds are "fully obvious to the investors participating in the market for these financial instruments.''[48] Investors are rational and will not knowingly buy, at least not for long, a bad deal. Ordinarily, it is true, the market has its own self-correcting mechanisms. To a large extent, however, the institutional buyers of these junk bonds may not be the ones ultimately left holding the bag. Instead it may be the Federal Savings and Loan Insurance Corporation, which insures the numerous savings and loan associations that, already being insolvent and having nothing further to lose (of their own), have been willing to shoot craps with junk bonds and other high-risk securities. (There's the moral hazard at work again.) Or it may be the pensioners who have assumed, quite unbeknownst to them, the risks of annuities purchased at low cost by their employers from insurance companies that invested heavily—as much as 65 percent of their assets—in high-yield junk bonds. (The benefits of the low cost belong to the employers; the risks belong to the employees.) New York and some other states have begun to limit the junk bond holdings of insurance companies, but in many cases the exposure is far too large. Or it may be the pensioners and elderly who, having come to depend on the 12 percent interest being paid just a few years ago by money market funds, have been vulnerable to the sales pitch for the new high-yield mutual funds being marketed. The prospectus for one of those funds was accompanied by pictures of senior citizens playing a vigorous game of tennis, but in fact their eyes were not on the (right) ball. The portfolio listed some fine old companies, but the investor simply had no way to know that while the history of these companies was solid, the capital structures were a mess. The literature contained nothing specific enough to enable the investor to realize that he had assumed the risk of a major loss of principal.[49] Here was a simple disclosure issue. The SEC should have looked at these various questions, but it didn't, relying instead on uncritical assumptions about free markets.

By some measures, the growth in corporate debt has not been excessive. For example, the market value of all debt of nonfinancial corporations is a smaller percentage of the market value of corporate equities than it was in the mid-1970s. Several factors, however, are particularly disturbing. The soundness of a bond depends primarily upon the ability of the issuer to meet its obligations out of current income rather than asset values, and the coverage of net interest charges shows substantial and consistent deterioration. In one year's time the dollar value of junk bonds increased by 37 percent, and they currently account for about 20 percent of all marketable corporate bonds. Short-term debt has also risen dramatically, even during a period of economic expansion. By borrowing heavily, and borrowing short-term, corporations have lost much of their flexibility to deal with an economic downturn or a rise in interest rates.

5. It may be the bidders, as much as or more than the targets, who are the dummies

When First Interstate Bancorp. was bidding for BankAmerica in 1986, an associate of Joseph Pinola, First Interstate's chief executive officer, said of him:

> Joe sees this as a once-in-a-lifetime opportunity. To him, this is like the price of a wedding ring. When you find the right lady, do you really care how much you have to pay?[50]

One should ask not only for whom the marriage bells ring, but who is paying for the honeymoon. The pruning deadwood thesis assumes that it is the targets that are not maximizing shareholder returns. Enter the princesses and their premium offers, and the targets become princes. On reflection, however, if there is managerial dishonesty, indifference, or incompetence, it is quite as likely to appear on one side of the transaction as the other. Is it enhanced skill or enhanced ego—or a combination of these and other factors—that has led so many bidders to pay almost $2 for what had been selling in the market for $1?

Appraising the motives of the bidders in $180 billion a year of transactions is an invitation to overgeneralize. Congressmen like to revile "raiders" who dismantle factories and create unemployment. But the bidders should not be nice guys. They are supposed to do the dirty work that others may have been too timid to tackle. Malcolm Salter and Wolf Weinhold, however, concluded that while some easy-to-achieve tax, leverage, and other purely financial benefits can be expected to flow from takeovers, that may be all that takeovers do well.[51] The process is much less congenial for the more complex, but more sustainable and useful, tasks of combining the production and design facilities and coordinating the marketing and distribution systems of two formerly distinct organizations. Hostile bids may overcome the resistance of a feeble but entrenched management, as in the case of Pullman in 1980. But it is equally plausible, and consistent with the Salter and Weinhold study, that bids will often be made by those who have not succeeded at their own business and, like U. S. Steel bidding for Marathon in 1981, are simply seeking to find better—and better-run—businesses elsewhere.

Every merger boom brings out a rash of people long on financial skills but with few credentials for the more drawn out, laborious, intricate process of running a business day to day. Real gains depend on long-term commitments of resources, and commitments by people and to people.[52] A few years ago it was noticed that a growing proportion of companies were headed by people whose backgrounds were in law, accounting, and finance—almost everywhere but in product design, manufacturing, or marketing. The same has happened with takeovers. A high proportion of the hostile bidders are people whose skills are solely those of Wall Street. The Bass brothers, Bilzerian, Jacobs, Icahn, Belzbergs, Edelman. Some brag that they can buy the people needed to run a business, thereby underscoring their ignorance.

BUYING GOOD COMPANIES AT BAD PRICES

This list of factors that help produce takeovers is by no means complete. With premiums as high as 100 percent, there is, for example, an enormous temptation for financial ruffians to buy just enough stock either to put the target into play or, even quicker, to force the target to repurchase their shares at a hefty premium. The Belzberg brothers "greenmailed" Ashland Oil and three other companies within a period of four weeks.[53] Donald Trump bought 9.9 percent of the shares of Bally Manufacturing (just below the 10 percent threshold at which he would, under federal law, have been locked in for six months) and sold them to the company three months later at a $30 million profit. Shortly before that, he bought enough shares of Holiday Corporation, and made enough threats and attracted enough attention to sell the shares in the open market at a $35 million profit.[54] Such operations have much the same smell as the old market pools of the 1920s, but if a buyer stretches out the operation for two months instead of two weeks and makes the right noises about wanting to buy the company, it is difficult to prove a violation of the laws against manipulation. Why work for a living?

The most striking aspect of takeovers has been not so much this cause or that but the recurring willingness—familiar for at least sixty years—to buy good companies at bad prices. The herd instincts of Wall Street sometimes fail to be satisfied until what may once have been a good idea becomes overextended. The silly season sets in.

Only fifteen years ago we saw professional investors, the money managers, exaggerate the value of growth stocks to the point where they paid as much as seventy to eighty times earnings for the so-called nifty-fifty—Xerox, Kodak, Avon, Polaroid, and others—which were such good companies that price was thought to be unimportant. (Losses of as much as 80 percent in these ''one-decision'' stocks made price once again seem important.) More recently we have seen pricing bubbles in the gambling stocks, oil-drilling stocks—yes, even the now depressed oil-drilling stocks—and high technology stocks.

The speculation that is so visible in the market for stocks also infects from time to time the market for mergers. In the 1960s there emerged the idea that by bringing several companies under a single roof, good management techniques and low cost financing could be brought to businesses that had theretofore operated with mom-and-pop structures. Economists built elaborate theories to explain the efficiencies of the conglomerate form.[55] But Harold Geneen acquired at ITT not six or eight companies but over 270. Litton, Commonwealth United, Whittaker, Gulf & Western, and others did much the same. Some of them had management skills, but some were conglomerates in form with no substance. The stock market loved them all—at least for a while. The market wanted steady earnings increases, and Geneen and the others created accounting techniques and other gimmicks to meet the demand. Ultimately, of course, the lesson was learned that it is difficult enough to wear two or three hats. ITT and the others sold off businesses by the dozen. When the dust had settled, there was little to show for all the effort. Earnings had grown at first, but then the heavy debt and the difficulty of managing hundreds of diverse businesses took their toll. Stock prices rose for a while, too, but eventually the glamour faded and the prices collapsed. Mueller has concluded that the typical company acquired in a conglomerate merger has disappeared entirely.[56]

Now the pattern was repeated with tender offers. Target company shareholders did well, of course, but the bidders' did not. By the summer of 1987, with stocks at an all-time high, the bidders should have been priced out of business. How could they pay a premium over market when the Standard & Poor's 400 Industrials were already priced at twenty times the underlying earnings, when the acquired business could earn on the purchase price only about 7 percent before taxes, and when the lenders wanted to be paid 12 percent interest? Zero-coupon bonds were the answer for a while. No need to worry today about interest that doesn't have to be paid until a thousand tomorrows.

For a while, too, some of the dicey deals that are already out there may survive. Carl Icahn may indeed have put TWA on a profitable footing. Scovill has fended off its creditors, but at the cost of selling the only really good business that it owned. (Scovill illustrates the old wisdom that in a liquidity squeeze, the most promising business gets sold first.) Metromedia got out from under its mountain of debt by finding an even more enthusiastic buyer, Rupert Murdoch, willing to assume an even larger mountain. Turner may be lucky, too, although the odds are long. But the business cycle has a disturbing tendency to keep coming around, and instead of using buoyant markets to strengthen their finances, too many companies, such as Uniroyal, Blue Bell, and FMC Corp., have sold out or restructured themselves on terms that leave little or no room for the other half of the cycle.

Tender offers, which began as a quite useful disciplinary tool for underperforming or even slothful managers, expanded fifteenfold and were increasingly bent into the sadly familiar shape of the public utility holding companies of the 1920s, the conglomerates of the 1960s, and other financial excesses. The discipline was gone, but the game and the financial gains continued. Greenmail profits of $25 million and $50 million were commonplace. The transaction costs were sinful. In the Beatrice buyout, the bankers and lawyers received $250 million for a few months' work. (The celebration dinner was held at the New York Historical Society, a suitably ironic place to record the event.) In the Revlon transaction, the total cost of various fees and separation agreements was over $200 million, more than 10 percent of the transaction. At an average of roughly 4 percent of transaction values, the fees have been aggregating about $6–7 billion a year. The bankers' access to the huge financing required on short notice for billion-dollar takeovers leaves unanswered some questions as to who has been calling the tune. As the current criminal investigations unfold, we may yet see that it has often been the bankers, not their nominal clients, who have created and then orchestrated the bidding opportunities.

THE PROPER USE OF TAKEOVERS

If the purpose is to discipline wayward operations managers, the tender offer should be a remedy of last resort. It is a very inflexible device. A bidder's financing is good for a very brief period. If he does not proceed with his bid, he loses credibility all around, and commitment fees to boot. There is almost no way to modulate his demands, to increase pressure, then relax it. Occasionally a bidder seeks to buy only a portion of the outstanding shares, not as a first step toward a takeover but because his intention is to own no more than that. But that is the rare case. In today's markets, a bidder's financing usually depends on buying the whole company, because only then will he have the assured access to the target's cash flow that he needs to meet his own interest charges. Under more normal circumstances an investor might have preferred simply to join the board of directors, elect new officers, or do none of these and simply begin discussions between management and some of the major shareholders, discussions that just might need more than the twenty business days allowed for the completion of a tender offer. After all, even assuming that a company has gone astray, it is not necessarily best that it be sold off. But tender offers do not allow such choices. The language of takeovers is quite correctly the metaphors of warfare: raiders, sharks, poison pills, parachutes, and scorched earth. There is little room for dialogue.

In almost casual fashion, we circumvent the board of directors and management of the company, the only ones who have been in continuing touch with its employees, suppliers, customers, and products. The market gives a signal, but the board has no further opportunity to take corrective steps or to shape its response to fit the case. Putting a company into play resembles in this respect a run on a bank. The logic of collective action, to use Olson's phrase, is that each shareholder/depositor will rationally tender his shares—withdraw his money, if there is a run on the bank—even though if collective action had been possible, all might have agreed not to close down the venture or shut the bank. While the market may have given a signal that something is amiss, the signal is already too strong, too final, to permit management to take remedial action. White knight or black knight, the company will almost always be sold to someone.[57]

The tender offer is also drastic in the sense that for many targets it is an almost continuously open season, with no recess. Even proxy contests typically can be waged only once a year, but for many companies takeovers are a month-to-month possibility. Rumors that your company is on someone's "hit list" are no small distraction for a CEO; and while frequently the rumors are but the work of speculators trying to turn rumor into fact, there is no way to know, and no way to put the rumor to rest. Phillips Petroleum reached an understanding with Pickens, and then had to do it again with Icahn. In no other institution is the continuity of the venture up for discussion so continually.

Instead of a remedy of last resort, we have made of it a financial device of first resort, with hundreds of bankers turning over every computer leaf, looking for companies whose price in the trading market may not match merger values, which are themselves increasingly the result of speculative breakup values rather than more fundamental operating income values. At a conference at Columbia University, Martin Shubik asked the right questions about this new ability to arbitrage between two markets:

> What responsibility does management have to close the gap between the stock market and a control redeployment of assets? Given that a hostile tender offer can give the small shareholder a premium . . . , is this arbitrage [across markets] a social good or is a different correction mechanism called for? . . . [A]sset conversion is at the core of good finance. Yet it is important to recognize the difference between good finance and good industrial policy.[58]

TAKEOVERS AND THE POPULISTS

Pickens and the other populists are saying that management is responsible for the market price, not only within one market but across markets. The shareholders own the company, and that's that. But however appealing at first blush, it is a view that makes little social sense. Shareholders aren't the purpose of the market game, industry is. The stock market is a mechanism to marshal savings for private enterprise and to allocate them to those who can use capital most profitably. These opportunities to arbitrage across markets are telling us that what may be efficient pricing for one purpose and one market (day-to-day trading) may not be efficient for another (the negotiated, whole-company market). They are also telling us that the stock market is simply not all that efficient, else such large price discrepancies would not exist. The stock market has never been more than a voting or betting machine, and votes and bets sometimes show great insight and sometimes not. Pickens is arguing, in effect, that we should sell the companies to make right the bets (votes), forgetting that financial markets exist to serve industry, not the other way around. It is interesting that a recent Harris poll shows that by a four-to-one majority, the public rejects Pickens's views and believes that the impact on the economy is more important than the shareholders' right to sell their stock at a big gain.[59]

Are we confident that the decision to liquidate the company should be granted so freely to outsiders—Pickens, Steinberg, or whoever else initiates the bid? Ultimately, better answers will emerge if we think in terms of institutions and structure rather than Pickens's rhetoric of property rights. Shareholders do need to participate, because there is a role—no, several roles—for them that if properly shaped, only they can fill. As it stands, however, the tender offer has serious defects.

Some investors will always make more money than others, and fortunately for society the disciples of Graham and Dodd are far more consistent winners. Regardless of how the pie is split, however, for the group as a whole there are no gains over time except those that reflect the earnings of the underlying operations. A share of stock is nothing more than a share in a business, the equity capital that has been committed to the venture more or less permanently. The shareholders have liquidity so that any of them, but not all of them collectively, might sell off their shares in the stock market. Collectively their capital has been turned into bricks and mortar. A collective way out will sometimes be needed, some way around a smug management that might *never* think it advantageous to liquidate. A persistently depressed market price may signal that there is smugness within the company, and the longer it persists the clearer the signal. But a market price that sinks below breakup values may also signal only some routine failure of the market mechanism having nothing to do with the enterprise. Think of it this way: When shares of the *Washington Post* sold in the 1970s at an 80 percent discount, the answer for shareholders was to buy stock, to correct the price, not to sell the company.

SHAREHOLDERS AND MANAGEMENT:
BACK TO BASICS

Sharpest blade or dull tool, we have come back to the starting point. There is a need for shareholders to take more of an interest, to keep management vigorous. Delaware and the other states have frustrated those efforts, which in any event would be difficult to pursue. Tender offers, that surgical blade, will sometimes be useful, and the fact that the tender offer has been bent out of shape does not mean that the underlying dilemma is not still with us. A long-standing problem, a potentially bright new solution, but then serious distortions set in. One of the great risks in this conflict is that corporate managers will seek to capitalize on the abuses to eliminate voting rights and tender offers both, keeping the capital of shareholders but not the bother. The data suggest that what is needed is to refocus the blade and channel it back into useful service. In the meantime, we are reminded once again how little recourse the shareholders have.

Business managers like to argue that Wall Street's short-term focus is having a contagious effect on their own investment horizons. Accepting the conclusion that both Wall Street and Main Street are much too concerned about next quarter's earnings release, it is questionable whether Wall Street is the primary culprit. The extent and causes of the decline in America's competitive position are issues that outrun a book on the role of the shareholder. But while there is a good deal of criticism to be leveled at money managers and security analysts, after all it was the corporate vice presidents who put their feet to the fire, holding them accountable for quarter-to-quarter results. Wall Street reinvented the concept of excessive debt, making it all but impossible to approve projects having more than a twelve-month payback, but industry embraced it. We should be careful about blaming Wall Street for more than its own errors.

THE INACTION IN CONGRESS

The sharp and divisive debate about tender offers has created an environment in which Congress finds it exceedingly difficult to reach a consensus. The Williams Act, adopted in 1968, remains essentially unchanged. The SEC's rule-making powers have been used very sparingly, e.g., to extend the minimum offer for all bids from ten days to twenty business days (about twenty-six calendar days), to discourage partial bids ever so slightly, and not much more. In the meantime, the tactics of both bidders and targets have changed dramatically. Hearings yes, bills yes—over sixty bills in the second session of the ninety-ninth Congress—but nothing more.

Some of this congressional passivity may reflect a certain awe of finance, as well as the accepted principle that it is the marketplace that should decide these contests. Government should remain neutral. No doubt correct, at least in the sense that the SEC should not pass on the merits of individual tender offers, should not pick winners and losers, any more than it puts a stamp of approval on new stock issues. Whatever the law, it should be administered case by case in a neutral fashion. There is, however, no greater need here than elsewhere for policy judgments also to be neutral, and some restraints on both targets and bidders would be helpful.

The tactics of takeovers will be examined in chapter 6. The substantial failure of the pruning deadwood thesis does not mean that target managers should be free to adopt the weighted voting schemes and scorched earth defenses that too often leave the shareholders worse off than before the bidding began. Some not-too-complicated modifications of the rules affecting both targets and bidders will then be suggested in the final chapter.

An appropriate framework for those modifications should now be fairly clear. To see the tender offer as having failed is very tempting. After all, it is a loss, not a gain, to encourage hostile bids for successful companies. Nor should we have allowed the so-called market for corporate control to become the plaything of financial speculators, so that the only ones who profit consistently are the greenmail ruffians and arbitrageurs, not those who would buy businesses in order to operate them. But neither should we forget the acute shortage of other monitoring mechanisms, the history of managerial indifference, and the insensitivity of the states to shareholder interests, all of which argue for the retention of hostile bids in some form. Unfortunately, the debate has generally been conducted in absolutist terms, with Chicago School folk having no doubt about the desirability of tender offers and others contrarily insisting on the managers' right (and ability) to operate free of all shareholder control. The middle ground has been a lonely place.

If tender offers were working well in the mid-1970s, perhaps we should chill the currently overheated climate, reserving takeovers for the relatively few cases where the benefits are more likely to exist. At the same time, there should be restrictions on the targets' ability to defend the castle by throwing (shareholders') money at the raiders or by other tactics that the shareholders themselves, if given the opportunity, would reject. It is unlikely, however, that we can fashion any rational scheme for tender offers in a market of speculative excesses, an island of calm in a sea of turbulence. The congressional hearings have tended to focus on tender offers as a thing apart from the general frenzy on Wall Street, but speculation is not that easily quarantined.

If we can break the hold that the states have on internal corporate affairs, it should be possible to create in public corporations some of the more routine control mechanisms that exist in private companies and thus relieve this excessive reliance on the tender offer. The tender offer was so thoroughly welcome, because the more obvious processes by which shareholders might have exerted pressure lay thoroughly dormant. Even the much criticized Wall Street Rule of love 'em or leave 'em is partly a function of the lack of suitable alternatives. The tender offer needs to be weighed, therefore, as but one of a number of potentially useful corrective measures.

Appendix

Table 5-2

Return on common equity (ROE), targets,
bidders, and target-controls
(one to five years before the bid)
(weighted basis)[60]

	B-5	B-4	B-3	B-2	B-1
targets	13.1%	11.5%	13.5%	17.2%	16.4%
bidders	10.7	10.0	14.2	13.5	14.1
target-controls	12.9	12.9	15.8	18.3	16.8

Table 5-3

Mean debt: equity ratio of targets,
bidders, and target-controls
(one to five years before the bid)
(weighted basis)

	B-5	B-4	B-3	B-2	B-1
targets	76%	79%	78%	77%	82%
bidders	62	63	59	54	52
target-controls	84	84	83	82	85

Table 5-4
Return on equity (ROE), targets,
bidders, and target-controls
(one to five years before the bid)
(weighted basis)

	B-5	B-4	B-3	B-2	B-1
	(1975–1978 bids)				
targets	8.7%	6.0%	7.8%	10.0%	11.5%
bidders	9.4	9.7	11.4	12.0	13.9
target-controls	10.0	10.1	11.0	13.0	15.4
	(1981–1983 bids)				
targets	14.5	13.1	15.3	19.0	17.4
bidders	11.0	9.5	15.6	14.1	14.1
target-controls	13.1	13.2	16.8	19.6	17.2

Table 5-5
Return on equity (ROE), targets,
bidders, and bidder-controls
(three years before the bid
to five years after takeover[61])
(weighted basis for targets and bidders)

	B-3	B-2	B-1	T+1	T+2	T+3	T+4	T+5
	(1975–1978 bids)							
targets	7.8	10.0	11.5	—	—	—	—	—
bidders	11.4	12.0	13.9	14.8	15.3	16.6	17.6	17.2
bidder-controls	13.2	13.3	13.6	14.6	15.2	14.9	14.3	13.0
	(1981–1983 bids)							
targets	15.3	19.0	17.4	—	—	—	—	—
bidders	15.6	14.1	14.1	4.5	8.5	8.9	n.a.	n.a.
bidder-controls	15.1	15.6	14.8	12.4	12.9	13.2	n.a.	n.a.

⌣ 6 ⌢   Takeover Tactics: The Hole in the Regulatory Scheme

The institutional and regulatory framework should not be any more disjointed than the economy of the nation it is intended to serve.

T W O   C H A P T E R S of this book deal with tender offers because issues exist at two quite different levels. There are, first, the larger, social questions of the extent to which takeovers are good or bad for economic efficiency, and when indeed constructive, the extent to which they have a unique role to play or should be thought of as but one of a number of available devices and processes. These were dealt with in chapter 5.

Unfortunately, the hot debate about the overall value of takeovers has tended to overwhelm the more specific questions of tactics. As a result, an array of wholly unnecessary abuses has crept into the process. Takeover proponents have long argued for unrestricted tender offers, and that is essentially what we have. Bidders have developed a variety of quite unfair tactics: two-tier bids, greenmail, bids without committed financing, tipping of the bidding plans to a favored inside group . . . almost anything goes. The central problem is that fairness is not something that inheres in tender offers. By circumventing the target company board of directors, the bidder seeks to deal directly with a dispersed, disorganized group of shareholders. The process is vulnerable in a number of respects to practices that are neither economically efficient nor fair.

All of these and more have been matched by the almost equally unrestricted tactics of targets, such as poison pills, crown jewel lockups and dual class voting stocks, most of which would have been unthinkable just a few years earlier. Excess bred excess.

A balance between bidders and targets could have been maintained without these abuses. The core problem is that a proper legal framework for tender offers is missing. A very slender statute, the Williams Act, was passed more than twenty years ago and remains essentially unchanged despite the dramatic developments that have occurred.

In 1968, when Congress adopted the Williams Act, the emphasis was on maintaining neutrality between bidders and targets. Those "neutral" rules were set at a time when takeovers were still being played at a sandlot level and few rules were needed. Require a bit of disclosure from the bidder so that the target shareholders could choose intelligently between the Christians and lions. Provide for shareholders enough time to consider the offer and to give individual shareholders, and not just the professionals—there was no army of arbitrageurs then—a chance to participate. Congress was loathe to tie bidders' hands beyond that, and in the context of the times that was a reasonable judgment.

THE TACTICS ESCALATE

Within a few years, however, the bidders became much more aggressive. The bankers—and the arbitrageurs, too—assembled huge pools of cheap capital that could put into play billion-dollar companies and essentially seal their fate as independent entities. Because the disclosure rules remained very loose, bidders were often able to acquire 10–15 percent of a target's shares, arrange complex financing, and alert arbitrageurs and others to the possibility of a bid, all without giving the targets anything more specific on which to act than an earful of rumors. Some acquiring companies went still further, assembling in the open market large blocks of stock, enough to acquire outright control. So long as they did not make a formal tender offer or anything that too closely resembled one, such "creeping tender offers" were not covered by the Williams Act. In time, tender offers were made "subject to financing" in amounts of a billion dollars or more, permitting a growing array of speculative operators to stimulate the market and reap huge greenmail and arbitrage profits, without a firm obligation to buy so much as a single share.

The bidders came to enjoy an enormous competitive advantage. Until 1979,[1] the rules under the Williams Act required that bidders keep open their offers for a minimum of only seven to ten days. Time worked for the bidders. The message to the target company shareholders was very simple: what had been a $40 stock could be sold for $60 or $70, payable in cash. There was not much for the shareholders to ponder, except the possibility of competing bids (don't tender your shares until the bid is about to expire) or of proration if the bid was for less than all the shares. Whether the bidder was a good guy or bad guy was irrelevant, if a shareholder could turn $30,000 into $50,000 in a few days' time.

TARGETS UNDER PRESSURE

The target companies were operating within much more difficult constraints. A tender offer is made at a time of the bidder's choosing, almost by definition a poor time for the target. For example, Giddings & Lewis, a machine tool company, had for some time rejected the overtures of AMCA International. AMCA's interest was understandable. Giddings & Lewis was in many respects a picture-book company, very profitable and still investing heavily in research and development. In 1981, however, a number of other machine tool companies—not Giddings & Lewis—reported sharply lower earnings, and although the Giddings & Lewis backlog remained exceptionally high, its stock fell along with the others. That was when AMCA turned from a friendly to a hostile suitor.

Regardless of when an offer materializes, the target company is at a big disadvantage. It can tell its shareholders that the bidder is a very unsavory fellow, but that would be counterproductive. The more *unappealing* the bidder, the more eager the shareholders will be to take the money and move on. In some cases the targets are left to shadowbox with acquiring companies that never do make a formal tender offer, such as would have invoked the timing and other restrictions of the Williams Act. In the takeover of TWA, for example, Carl Icahn simply accumulated 20 percent, then 30 percent, and eventually a controlling or "blocking" position in open market transactions.

LITIGATION AS A FIRST DEFENSE

For a time the targets relied heavily on litigation as a defense, claiming violations of the disclosure rules,[2] the antitrust laws,[3] or the definition of what constitutes a tender offer.[4] Almost any excuse for a lawsuit would do, and the necessary papers lay ready and waiting in the word-processing machines. In response the bidders heaped mostly useless disclosures on top of one another, to the point where the offering materials became dense and unintelligible and required two whole pages, rather than one, in the *Wall Street Journal*. Soon even two pages were not enough. Eventually the courts rejected many of these pasteboard defenses for what they were, saying that takeovers should be resolved in the market, or as one judge put it, ''a pox on both your houses.''[5] Eventually, too, the SEC extended the minimum period that a tender offer must remain open to twenty business days. The Commission had initially proposed a thirty-business-day period, but then settled on twenty.[6] That is enough for shareholders to evaluate a bidder's offer, but it still leaves the defense to play a high-stakes, catch-up game on very short notice. The twenty business days, equivalent to about twenty-six calendar days, may have seemed sufficient for a thoughtful, considered response/defense, but in practice it is pitifully brief. The target company management by definition has no experience in the obscure world of two-tier, front-end loaded bids and the like. Yet if it does not quickly demonstrate its willingness to resist, the arbitrageurs will own so much of its stock that the only question will be the identity of the ultimate buyer. What is a target to do?

A GROWING ARRAY OF FINANCIAL DEFENSES

What happened is that target companies threw up a series of extraordinarily creative, if often destructive, defenses. Unlike the earlier litigation responses, which patently were little more than diversionary tactics, targets now began to challenge the bidders' tender offers more directly. Target managements began, in effect, to fight money with money—not their own, of course, but shareholders'. For example, they began to repurchase target company shares, at prices far above where they had been selling only a few weeks earlier, often far above where they had ever sold. Sometimes the purchases were in the open market or by a bid to all shareholders, but often they were on a highly discriminatory basis. The target might buy back only the bidder's shares in return for an agreement, sometimes explicit and sometimes not, that the bidder would not soon again stalk this particular company. Texaco did that in the case of the Bass brothers, Gillette with Perelman, and Disney with Steinberg. Unocal offered to buy back everyone's shares *except* the hostile bidder's. Even the open market purchases, made at inflated prices and in anticipation of defeating the bid, left individual shareholders holding stock in a poorer company, often with little room for a bad tomorrow.

These defensive tactics became a new art form, one with its own jargon. Early on, there were the ''scorched earth'' defenses, meaning that targets purchased otherwise unwanted businesses in a crude, last-minute attempt to create an antitrust defense or otherwise render themselves unattractive. Later there appeared the ''crown jewel lockups'' and still later the ''poison pills.'' A lockup involves a sale of the target's best business, usually the object of the bidder's desires, hoping thus to deflect the bid but in any event leaving the target a very different company. A poison pill entails the issuance of a new and otherwise worthless security that entitles the target company shareholders to buy the *bidder's* stock on the cheap. A cynic might have observed that targets seemed to be selling the good and buying the bad, but that of course was precisely what was happening. These new, essentially financial rather than legal defenses occasionally drove off the bidder altogether. Mostly, however, they succeeded only in buying time and providing the opportunity to improve on the price and/or the congeniality of the eventual merger partner.

In time still more ''complete'' defenses were developed. Target managers allied themselves with a banking group and became bidders for their own companies, sometimes in competition with a hostile bidder but sometimes without an outside offer having surfaced. In effect, the managers were saying that if the shareholders were happy to take a substantial premium over market from anyone, why not from us? More recently still, with the consent of the New York Stock Exchange, there has emerged the ''perfect'' defense of splitting a company's common shares into two classes, with the insiders keeping a class of stock with such superior voting rights as to render the company all but immune from takeover for all time.

THE COURTS' RELUCTANCE TO INTERVENE:
THE BUSINESS JUDGMENT RULE

It is easy to blame target companies for some of the more blatantly destructive defenses, but the rules were astonishingly lax. One of the more notorious cases was that of Marshall Field and Company, a lagging but still valuable department store chain that attracted over time an impressive number of suitors. To ward them off, to create an instant, do-it-yourself antitrust defense, the incumbent management systematically negotiated to buy stores in precisely the area, sometimes the very shopping center, where the suitor of the moment was doing business. Sometimes the negotiations were dropped when the threat waned, but Marshall Field ultimately bought many of those stores, including several that were concededly ''dogs.'' The Field shareholders were left poorer than if no one had sought their company. Despite Field's well-documented willingness to shoot itself in the foot in order to remain independent, the court did not even allow the case to go to the jury.[7]

In the face of a hostile bid, a target company board can place a large, preemptive block of shares in the friendly hands of a so-called white squire[8] or agree to sell off its "crown jewel" business for whatever price a fast auction will bring.[9] And the courts are likely to treat the case as if it were a matter of business judgment—in which great deference is routinely paid to the directors' decision. This reliance on the business judgment rule is key. The alternative would have been to apply the much stricter and arguably more appropriate duty of loyalty rules applicable to conflict of interest cases. Under those rules, these transactions would have been judged by whether the terms were scrupulously fair, and on that basis many of them would have failed.

Applying state law, the courts in *Marshall Field* and other cases adopted a policy of minimal restraint, refusing to overrule the judgments of target company boards, except in those (obviously rare) situations in which the desire to defeat the bid was the sole or primary purpose. In general, unless the target was caught red-handed with a single, naked motive, a smoking gun, it was free to defend itself howsoever it chose. A "primary purpose" test is essentially a good-faith test, highly subjective in character. Given the carefully orchestrated board meetings, only in exotic cases were the target managers unable to satisfy that test. To make matters worse, despite the subjective nature of the inquiry, courts sometimes imposed on the plaintiffs, of all people, the burden of proof of the defendant directors' malevolent intent. The effect, as one dissenting judge said, is to "clothe directors, battling blindly to fend off a threat to their control, with an almost irrebuttable presumption of sound business judgment."[10]

There is some recent evidence of the emergence of a new, stricter business judgment rule under which these defensive tactics would be subject to greater scrutiny. But the evidence is spotty, and some of the praise for these new, "tighter" rules is quite self-serving. Sometimes a target simply cannot find a white squire willing to buy the stock it is trying to put into friendly hands so as to dilute the bidder's position. If the target company management then tries to issue the additional shares to itself, or to an employee benefit plan that it controls, the courts will probably intervene.[11] While they still extend the customary deference to the board if it tries to tilt the bidding against the black knight,[12] or in favor of a particular white knight,[13] they are more reluctant to do so if the white knight is a sham, one created by management and its banking cohorts simply to mount a bid.[14] This sort of palpable self-dealing has become increasingly suspect, even if, as in the *Revlon* case, a majority of the directors are nominally independent.[15]

Perhaps these cases represent a new direction in the law, but if so, it seems more like a minor tack than a dramatic heeling about. Some of the brave new talk about restricting target company defensive tactics has come in cases where the defensive tactics were upheld,[16] not rejected, so that the talk was not very brave at all. Or it has come in cases where the self-dealing was so explicit and intrusive as to leave the courts little choice.[17] In the more usual situation, where the target managers' conflict does not extend beyond the "mere" desire to defeat the bid, where there is no money or stock passing to or from them personally—except perhaps for golden parachutes, which seem not to matter—the old and easy rules are probably still in effect.

With close to a trillion dollars in mergers and acquisitions in the last few years, with litigation for years an almost reflex response to any "unsolicited" offer, the numerous and varied court decisions do not, of course, all square with one another. But some patterns do emerge. Even when striking down palpably objectionable defensive tactics, the judges have taken care not to cast too wide a net. They tend to rely as much as possible on the business judgment rule rather than invoking the duty of loyalty,[18] thus maintaining for targets and courts alike a high degree of flexibility and discretion. Or they rely on factual distinctions so narrow as to have the same effect of preserving their freedom in deciding future cases.

POISON PILLS:
A STUDY IN ROUGH JUSTICE

In *Moran v. Household International, Inc.*,[19] the Delaware Supreme Court sustained in principle that recent invention, the poison pill. Since then over four hundred companies have adopted one version of it or another. In its most common form, the poison pill entails the distribution to the target company shareholders of a right to purchase one share for each share held at a price far above current market and therefore of no present financial significance. The pill continues to be of no consequence, unless during the ten-year life of the rights the target is acquired, *and* the acquiring company (or someone else) has previously purchased some designated percentage, e.g., 20 percent, or more of the target company's common shares. In that event, the rights "flip over," entitling the once-upon-a-time target company shareholders to purchase shares of the *acquiring* company at a 50 percent discount from market value. (To permit friendly mergers, the rights do not trade independently, and the target board has the power to redeem them at a nominal price, until the 20 percent trigger is activated.)

The SEC argued in the *Moran* case that the pill would preclude not only some but all hostile bids. The pill does not prevent a bidder from purchasing shares, but it does of course discourage the second-step merger without which a bidder cannot achieve the complete ownership of the target's assets and income stream that it (or its lenders) normally require. After it had lost in the Delaware courts, the Commission asked for comments on "the appropriateness of federal intervention."[20] Proponents of the pill responded that the intent of the poison pill is only to strengthen the hand of the target board in obtaining for shareholders the full merger-value of their shares. Martin Lipton, who invented the pill, noted that of thirty companies that had adopted the pill and were the object of a hostile bid, sixteen had in fact been acquired, in almost all cases at a price higher than the initial bid.[21] In effect, Lipton contended, the pill's value is as a bargaining chip and, as the Delaware Supreme Court had suggested in *Moran*, the board's ability to retain a pill in the face of an actual offer is subject to a rule of reason.

On the face of them, poison pills are a radical defensive tactic: target company shareholders are offered a 50 percent discount on the *bidder's* stock. When they first appeared, all the wise men (this author included) said that pills were patently illegal. Yet the courts have accepted many pills. They have rejected others. But they have decided the cases on the basis of such ephemeral distinctions as to make it plain that they are less concerned with fashioning a rule of law to deal with this innovative tactical development—and to provide for litigants some prospective guidance—than with resolving the immediate dispute and doing rough justice in the particular case. A law office memorandum on the legality of the poison pill would have to note that the result may depend on whether the pill had been created well before a bidder emerged or only in the heat of battle,[22] whether the battle entailed a proxy fight or a tender offer,[23] whether the pill "flipped" into enhanced rights in all respects or only voting rights,[24] whether the pill flipped immediately upon the bidder's acquisition of the partial interest in the target or only in the event of a second-step merger,[25] whether the target feared a "bust-up" junk bond bid or one that was more soundly financed,[26] and whether the court found that the pill in question "deterred coercive takeover attempts without [however] entrenching incumbent management."[27] Surely this is an unworkable body of law. Since the law of poison pills has only begun to develop, other permutations are no doubt in prospect, but these will do.

In the overall scheme of things, the pill is not notably more objectionable than other defensive tactics, and in some respects it is much less so. The SEC notwithstanding, all defensive tactics are designed to block a bid, sometimes at great cost. Greenmail payments of the kind sustained in Delaware usually induce the putative bidder to go away.[28] The scorched earth tactics by Marshall Field, sustained under Delaware law, also caused the suitor to go away. The Seventh Circuit allowed Brunswick Corporation to sell to a white knight its most valuable subsidiary, even though it obviously spelled an end to the bid by Whittaker Corporation.[29] The notorious Pac-Man defense—"I'll eat you before you eat me"[30]—makes no sense financially. The quarry turns into hunter and mounts a counter-tender offer for the bidder: as in the Bendix-Martin Marietta contest, each of the two owns a majority of the other's stock and indirectly of itself. But the bidder did go away.

"The business judgment rule," then Commissioner Bevis Longstreth said, "was not meant to bear the weight of the conflicts that emerge from change of ownership and control situations. While it works well for ordinary business transactions, it does not appear to work at all when the potential conflict between duty to self and duty to shareholders becomes acute."[31] The courts have accepted Pac-Man and these other bizarre inventions, in opinions that are no more systematic or enlightening than those on poison pills. Except in California, even something as discriminatory as greenmail seems to be acceptable.[32] The validity of lockup options often turns on whether they are designed to terminate an auction or only to stimulate the bidding, as if a privately negotiated sale did not also terminate the auction.[33]

THE FAULT IS WITH CONGRESS.

This defensive maneuvering seems at first blush to constitute outrageous behavior on the part of target boards—and for that matter, not much of a credit to the courts. But much of it represents a sometimes more, sometimes less, but generally rational response on both their parts to a dilemma not of their making. It is the direct and almost inevitable result of a federal statutory scheme, the Williams Act, that was adopted at a time when tender offers were first developing but which has neither kept pace with the dramatic changes in the market nor granted to the SEC sufficient authority to do so.

The Williams Act was casually conceived as a compromise, after a much stricter, antitakeover bill had failed. Floated off with the reassurance that it was intended to be neutral and to allow shareholders to make the decision, the statute imposed only minimal restraints on bidders. The Act left bidders free to escalate their tactics and to adopt greenmail, two-tier tender offers, creeping offers, and so on, as they acquired the necessary capital, respectability, and experience. As little as it did with respect to offensive tactics, however, Congress did almost nothing at all with respect to defensive responses. The implicit assumption was that the internal affairs of a corporation are a matter of state law.

The necessary forum where a fair and efficient balance between bidders and targets could be struck never came into being. The void in the statutory scheme was eventually filled, of course, as all voids are, but it was filled badly. With some intermediate steps, the spectacle emerged that we are now witnessing, a conflict in which a federal agency, the SEC, ostensibly regulates but increasingly champions the rights of bidders; and the states, with no authority to regulate the bidders' side of the process, are drawn into the conflict on behalf of targets. Congress never created the mechanism by which one side could be restrained if the other were. The tactics have inevitably escalated or, more accurately, degenerated so that the balance between bidders and targets has been achieved at ever lower levels.

Takeover bids had been used by the British for some time, but until the early 1960s they were virtually unknown in the United States. Until then, the preferred method for one American company seeking to acquire another without its consent was by a proxy contest. But proxy fights didn't work well. They sometimes dragged on interminably, and they had become dreadfully expensive. If the dissidents lost, they had nothing to show for their money except some paper ballots. In a tender offer, the bidder invests in shares, not votes, and by conditioning his offer appropriately, the bidder does not have to buy any unless he gets a majority. Moreover, while the proxy contest had been subject to intensive federal regulation since 1934, the tender offer—at least the cash offer—was not.

The Williams Act was first conceived as an antitakeover measure. One of its sponsors, Senator Harrison Williams, railed against "white-collar pirates":

> In recent years we have seen proud old companies reduced to corporate shells after white-collar pirates have seized control with funds from sources which are unknown in many cases, then sold or traded away the best assets, later to split up most of the loot among themselves.[34]

Having failed to win support for a promanagement bill, the sponsors, Senators Williams and Kuchel, who reportedly had been trying to protect Columbia Pictures, adopted an alternative proposal that originated with the SEC. The Commission was unwilling to support a bill that would alter its traditionally neutral role in control contests but was also eager not to offend Senator Williams, the chairman of the powerful Subcommittee on Securities of the Senate Committee on Banking and Currency. It was decided, according to George P. Michaely, Jr., the then chief counsel of the SEC's Division of Corporation Finance, that:

> the SEC [should] tell Williams that it could support a bill fashioned along the lines of the SEC proxy rules (tender offers were, after all, *somewhat* akin to proxy contests) and oriented mainly toward disclosure to stockholders. This was perceived as an excellent idea, because the SEC was quite experienced at administering disclosure statutes and could assume a neutral stance while doing so. Furthermore, it was believed that Senator Williams would be happy if he had a bill the SEC would support.
>
> [In] due course a new bill, ultimately introduced in the 90th Congress as S.510 with Williams and Kuchel as co-sponsors, was drafted for [them]. . . .
> The drafting of S.510 did not end the SEC's involvement. Senator Williams intended to schedule hearings and [Chairman] Cohen was "invited" to be a principal supporting witness. He had to support the bill and had to have some reason to do so. Accordingly, the famous "gap" in disclosure was discovered and in due course roundly condemned, although it had not been perceived as a problem. . . . Great care was taken to inject the idea of neutrality . . . in order to deflect possible attacks on the bill, thereby making the SEC's job of supporting the bill, which it did not relish, a little easier.[35]

Adopting this proposal wholeheartedly, Senator Williams made it plain that he was now taking "extreme care to avoid tipping the scales.

. . . S. 510 is designed solely to require full and fair disclosure.''[36] Earlier proposals that would, for example, have required bidders to submit tender offers to the SEC for comments before publication were cut way back. Apart from disclosure, the Act covered only a few substantive matters, such as those permitting shareholders to withdraw previously tendered shares and requiring that bidders accept shares pro rata in the event of overacceptance. There was, however, as another SEC official later said, no intention "to regulate tender offers as an economic phenomenon."[37]

It is astonishing that the Williams Act, casually conceived, written in a spirit of compromise and minimalism, thereafter updated in only minor respects, remains the entire legislative framework for the regulation of takeovers. Disclosure was not a great issue at the time, nor is it today, but by providing some disclosure and little else, the Act largely satisfied the then widespread concern that tender offers, still a newly developing phenomenon, might be killed off. Perhaps that was a satisfactory solution at the time, but the list of eventual problems that it failed to solve is now longer than those that it did. Just on the bidders' side, the Act fails to deal with

(a) the increasing prevalence and ease of greenmail, in one form or another;

(b) the ability to make bids without financing commitments, and therefore without any obligation to buy shares, a condition conducive to a variety of abuses;

(c) the ten-day "window" that allows bidders to accumulate large additional blocks of stock during the ten days between the time they first acquire 5 percent of the outstanding shares and the deadline for filing the requisite report with the SEC;

(d) the two-tier bid that allows bidders to pressure target shareholders to accept the front-end offer, even while facing what may be a low second-step offer, payable in cheap paper, or indeed no second-step at all;

(e) the absence of a definition of the term "tender offer," which fostered early on the so-called "creeping tender offer" and discriminatory purchase prices. More recently it has permitted Hanson Trust and others to cancel a bid and then a few minutes or hours later to "sweep the street," buying from arbitrageurs, and them alone, large blocks accumulated during the pendency of the offer. More recently still, while one bidder was waiting to complete a formal tender offer for shares of Newmont, another simply bought 16 million shares in the open market, sufficient to achieve absolute control; and

(*f*) the wholly unnecessary insider trading abuses growing out of a pattern by which putative bidders could "secretly" raise billions of dollars in financing, involving directly or indirectly talks with dozens of potential lenders, and escape responsibility for the inevitable consequences simply by labeling the information "confidential."

There are also serious unresolved problems on the targets' side, too, but with relatively minor exceptions Congress had never intended to address them. The most serious failure, however, was not the failure to correct this or that abuse by bidders on the one hand or targets on the other, but the simple, inevitably ruinous failure to deal with them both in some comprehensive fashion, either directly or through the creation of an administrative mechanism that could respond promptly and flexibly to the inevitable changes.

There is no smoke-filled or other room where the necessary bargains can be struck. Consider, for example, the issue of how long to require that a bidder keep its offer open. From the bidder's point of view, the shorter the better. It is true that for the shareholders to consider the bid, and the bid alone, not much time is needed. But if the target is to offer the shareholders choices, such as a merger with a white knight, a restructuring of its capital, or the like, then the target will need time to seek out and negotiate alternatives. After all that is done, *the target may still need substantial additional time to obtain financing, prepare proxy material, submit it to the SEC for review, solicit proxies, and hold a meeting.* If the target is trying to open the bidding, and not just to defeat the bidding, then it seems clear (except to some financial economists who favor initial bidders to the exclusion of others) that the shareholders stand to gain. The more bidders, the higher the price.

It is sometimes said that bidders are entitled to have their offers become effective and then close promptly, and that it is inconsistent with the purpose of the Williams Act to permit delay. The Supreme Court struck down an Illinois antitakeover statute on essentially the single ground that delay would unjustifiably burden takeovers.[38] But while delay almost certainly works against the initial bidder, it need not work against the target shareholders or the social welfare. If a company is to be sold, then let it be sold to the bidder for whom it has the highest valued use, i.e., the one willing to pay top dollar. And that takes time, often more time than is allowed under the present rules.

The sale of a Sherwood medical division by a beleaguered Brunswick or the lockup of a great oil field by Marathon ought not to be done in less time than it takes to buy and register a used car. Marathon, it is said, had one day in which to accept or reject the offer by U. S. Steel, including a lockup of the immensely valuable Yates oil field. Even assuming that Marathon was a not-so-reluctant victim of U. S. Steel's pressure, there was no time for it to negotiate in the way one would expect of a company with a $2.8 billion property at stake.

Management buyouts frequently produce top-dollar bids, but they tend to be complicated, time-consuming transactions. In one study of management buyouts, the premium of the winning bid over the market price thirty days before the first significant announcement jumped from 48 percent to 76 percent when there were three or more bidders.[39] These buyouts do not compete easily with tender offers unless the bankers have previously assembled a ready pool of capital, their own or someone else's, so that they, too, can proceed by an immediate tender offer and not wait for a shareholders' meeting.

The federal and state regulatory schemes are inconsistent, and no one, least of all Congress, has attempted to rationalize the two. Not surprisingly, bidders began to argue that the targets' defensive tactics were defeating the free bidding process that they claim to be the implicit mandate of the Williams Act. The SEC made essentially the same argument in a recent release, suggesting that if pills discourage bidders then there should be no room for pills under federal law, even if they pass muster under Delaware law. One federal court went so far as to hold that it was a fraud under the Williams Act for a target to lock up a crown jewel business, thereby frustrating a hostile bid. Quite obviously, however, that was an unwarranted reading of a statute that had been conceived as a disclosure statute and little else, and eventually the Supreme Court put it to rest.[40]

That still left the Constitution, of all things, as the one basis on which this federal/state conflict could be resolved. The Supreme Court addressed the issue in 1982 and again in 1987.[41] The court's jurisdiction, however, was confined to what in this context are relatively narrow issues, whether state antitakeover statutes have been preempted by the federal statute, and therefore violate the Supremacy Clause, and whether in any event they unconstitutionally burden interstate commerce in securities. The need for the court to decide two such cases within a few years tells us more about the shallowness of a federal regulatory scheme that fails to address fundamental issues than about the desirability of state statutes designed to rescue local targets. Takeover proponents argue that these statutes are designed to interfere with tender offers and with normal market activity. But as the Supreme Court concluded, many state law provisions, including some that have been on the books for years, have that same effect; and as a constitutional matter, it would be very difficult to distinguish one from the other.

The court's 1987 decision—sustaining the Indiana antitakeover statute—was unquestionably correct as a matter of constitutional law. With all the attention it has given to takeovers, Congress has had plenty of opportunities to take control of the process, and quite obviously it has yet to do so. But constitutional law aside, the result is to leave the states with large, if ambiguous, powers to deal with takeovers, and that could hardly be worse. The state legislatures have shown no disposition whatever to take an overarching, balanced view of the conflict.

Not a single state has considered whether to do something about the increasing trend toward dual class voting rights that entrench managers once and forever, or about scorched earth tactics, or the like. Many, if not most, of the antitakeover statutes were rushed to enactment in response to the urgent appeal of a then beleaguered target—Minnesota (Dayton Hudson), New York (CBS), North Carolina (Burlington Industries), and so on. Many of the statutes were drafted by corporate counsel and enacted a few hours later.

This fragmented scheme, regulating corporations here and financial markets there, is once again haunting us. We indulge the fantasy that there is a meaningful distinction between the federal regulation of stock purchases made to acquire corporate control on the one hand and the state regulation of internal corporate affairs on the other. The eventual balancing has been left to the Supreme Court, where the issues are to be decided not as a matter of financial or economic policy or institutional structure but on the remarkably narrow and unsatisfactory basis of constitutional law. Until Congress acts, until it takes a broadly encompassing view of the dilemma, there exists no other mechanism.

It would be difficult to conceive of a less satisfactory framework. A hostile bidder's initial offer may be 30 percent above market, but still well below the company's estimated auction value. It is not enough, however, that the target advise the shareholders that the price is low. Advice will not defeat a bid; only a counteroffer will do that. Some affirmative response is needed, and by and large only management can provide it.

But instead of rules for both sides, we have an unbalanced, crazy-quilt picture. On matters within its jurisdiction, the SEC writes quite detailed rules as to how bidders shall behave, while on the targets' side there are almost none. The law for targets is being made primarily in a common law process by judges who have time and again expressed their reluctance. The judges plainly do not want to write rules that might impose heavy civil liabilities on individual directors whose judgment may have been poor but who nonetheless acted in good faith. Nor do they want to make the larger public policy decisions—sensibly, too, because these are financial and economic issues that turn in the first instance on business values and ultimately on the impact on the economy as a whole. All that judges can do under such circumstances is to achieve a kind of pragmatic justice, in which, as P. S. Atiyah has written, "a decision [is] designed to achieve justice in the particular circumstances of the case, irrespective of the possible impact of the decision in the future."[42]

A congressional report concluded that these court decisions "wax and wane between holding defensive tactics inviolate, or giving greater scrutiny to management's actions."[43] Decisions depend on "flexible" interpretations of the business judgment rule that vary from state to state and case to case and offer virtually no guidance. Except in the *Norlin*, *Revlon*, *SCM*, and a few other cases of arrant self-dealing, the courts are not so much neutral as passive. And why not? The decision to restrict golden parachutes was made by Congress, not the courts, and the resolution of similar problems with respect to greenmail and scorched earth and two-tier bids must eventually come from Congress, too.

If management buyouts are to compete on equal terms with tender offers, but if the insiders are not to have unfair access to inside information, . . . and if it is greenmail that motivates bidders more and more often, and if . . . , and if . . . , then most of the answers will have to be found in principled rule-making and statutes, not in judicial decisions about the fiduciary duties of corporate directors. It is not just a question of whether greenmail, for example, is desirable or not. The appropriate remedies are simply not available to judges writing common law opinions. They have no power to levy taxes on golden parachutes, or to create short-swing trading penalties for hit-and-run greenmailers, or to insist that crown jewel lockups be submitted for shareholder approval.

Many of these defensive tactics are designed principally to create leverage for a board aware that hostile bids are rarely defeated except by a higher bid. But the process by which some defenses are approved and others rejected proceeds in a fashion that is at best disorderly and at worst opaque. The process ignores the deterrent and educational effects of law and the importance of planning in large, complex transactions. The recent practice, as Atiyah wrote, "appears to represent the abandonment of rule altogether . . . as the search for individualized justice has proceeded."[44]

THE BRITISH EXPERIENCE

There is a better model, for the British have solved quite well many of these very same issues. Yet not much is said about it, as if somehow to examine a more successful model would remind us of the failures of our own.

There is always difficulty in trying to transfer the experience of one country and culture to another, and it is true that significant differences exist between the British and American financial markets and their legal institutions. All of the British takeover business is conducted in the City, the London financial community, so that it is a good deal easier to think in terms of a flexible pattern of self-regulation, as they have done. Institutions own over 60 percent of the shares, and since they are in frequent touch one with the other, some defensive tactics, e.g., shark repellents, that work here simply would not get the necessary votes there. Nor is it likely that the London Stock Exchange would list some of the disjointed securities that are now appearing here, and since the Exchange is not as yet subject to serious competition from the over-the-counter market, that would be that.

But despite those differences, there are major similarities in market structure and liquidity. Indeed, it was the British who invented takeovers, and only they and the Americans among the major Western industrialized societies have allowed them to flourish. The British response is particularly interesting because they experienced early on some of the same problems that we encountered. Peter Frazer, a deputy director of the Panel on Take-overs and Mergers, speaking at Columbia University in terms that will sound painfully familiar to Americans, described a variety of abuses that had once been part of the British scene:

[T]he new system wiped out a whole series of abuses that used regularly to be part of the take-over scene. Big premiums to controlling groups, creation of minorities with no chance to get out, cash to insiders and exotic Chinese paper to widows and orphans, special deals for large institutions, . . . and various defensive tactics such as the issuance of new shares to friends etc were all virtually ended by the first Code in 1968. Many of the tactical ploys that would be unthinkable now were every day occurrences in the 50's and 60's.[45]

The terminology is different, but Frazer might as well have been describing partial bids, greenmail, front-end loaded bids, creeping tender offers, and "sweep the street" purchases of control by bidders on the one hand, and poison pills, scorched earth tactics, and white knight lockups by targets on the other. The particular mechanism adopted by the British was a nonlegislative, self-regulatory panel composed of representatives of the merchant banks, institutional investors, and others concerned with takeovers. While such a mechanism might not "travel" well to the United States, the comprehensive and balanced approach taken by the City Code on Take-overs and Mergers has much to recommend it. Objectionable defensive tactics largely dried up, primarily because the rules prohibit any significant transactions in shares or assets by targets faced with a hostile bid or the threat of one, unless the transaction is first approved by shareholders, which in most cases would be their death knell. Disputes as to the scope or meaning of the rules are resolved by the Panel on Take-overs and Mergers, and there is little of the continuing uncertainty that plagues target companies, as well as bidders, in the United States. Since the rules are process-oriented rather than duty-oriented, since in this case they are expressed in terms of a requirement of shareholder approval rather than the business judgment rule, target company directors have little fear that they may be called upon to defend their personal pocketbooks. The shareholders either approve those defensive tactics or they do not, and most likely that is the end of the matter.

While British targets do not have poison pills and other exotic "bargaining chips," there is less need for them. Bids remain open longer, usually more than fifty and often as many as seventy-five days after the first announcement, long enough to permit targets to produce reasonable, workable alternatives on which shareholders can then vote. (In addition, the process of soliciting proxies is much less time-consuming in Britain, because there is no need to clear proxy materials with a federal agency and because most of the shares are held by a few, easily reached institutions.) Coercive two-tier, front-end loaded bids are not permitted. Instead of years of litigation about Congress's intent two decades ago, when it used the term "tender offer" but did not define it—under circumstances that have long since changed—the British have precise trigger points that tell bidders and targets alike when an offer must be for all the shares, and not just part, when the bidder must include a cash alternative, and so on.

And despite this well-articulated, comprehensive regulatory scheme, takeovers are alive and well, steadily growing in volume, in Britain. The model is not different from that in the United States, namely, to enable shareholders to exercise a free, undistorted choice. The difference is that the British have been able to distinguish the larger economic issues from the more immediate questions of tactics and fairness. The process as a whole remains quite open and competitive even while the rules by which the game is played are continually adjusted.

SHAREHOLDER RIGHTS AND REMEDIES

The role of the shareholder in these takeover contests has always been somewhat ambiguous. The bidder's shareholders, of course, are rarely consulted at all, except if the bid involves the issuance of so large a block of stock that the New York Stock Exchange rules require shareholder approval. But the shareholders of the target are also little more than passive participants in the unfolding drama. The active participants, the bidders and target company managers, profess a great deal of affection and concern for the target company shareholders, but the line between affection and manipulation wears thin. Bidders insist that they are simply representing the long-suffering target shareholders and that under no circumstances will they accept greenmail payments to go away—but they often do so. Pickens has gone so far as to form an organization for the protection of shareholders. While he has made many a hostile bid, however, he has never completed one, settling time and again for greenmail. (Not much camaraderie there.) Target managements regularly claim that the bidder's price is inadequate, even though it may represent a premium of 50 percent or more over market; but then they often seem more eager to defeat all bids than to find a better one.

A SOLUTION TO SCORCHED EARTH AND
A NUMBER OF OTHER TARGET COMPANY ABUSES

Burning the village is not the proper way to save it. But a remedy is not hard to conceive. For a broad range of defensive maneuvers, such as lockups, the issuance of stock to favored white squires, scorched earth tactics, and greenmail, all that may be needed is an adaptation to the American context of the British City Code Rule 21. That rule requires shareholder approval of what the British, with a flair for understatement, call "frustrating actions." Such a provision, adapted to the American frame of reference, might read in substance as follows:

> No company which is the target of a takeover bid shall during the course of the offer, or even before the date of the offer if the board of the offeree company has reason to believe that a *bona fide* offer might be imminent, enter into any transaction or take any action which constitutes a structural change as to the target company, unless the change shall be pursuant to a contract entered into earlier, or unless the change shall have been approved in accordance with applicable state law but in any event by the holders of not less than a majority of outstanding shares entitled to vote generally in the election of directors, at a meeting called for the purpose and on such minimum notice as the Commission may prescribe.
>
> For these purposes, a "structural change" means
> (a) any acquisition or disposition of any significant amount of assets [e.g., 5 percent of total assets] otherwise than in the ordinary course of business, any issuance or repurchase of 5 percent or more of any class of equity securities, or any agreement or arrangement for any of the foregoing, and
> (b) any other transaction or action whether or not comprehended by clause (a) which, under such rules as the Commission shall prescribe, shall be deemed likely to affect significantly any of the following: (i) the business or assets of the company, (ii) the financial condition or capital structure of the company, or (iii) the voting rights of any class of securities of the company;
>
> provided, however, that the Commission may exempt any transaction or action, unconditionally or on specified terms, as not constituting a structural change.

This proposal for shareholder ratification raises a number of collateral questions, e.g., whether there is adequate time for a shareholder meeting and whether shareholders can be expected to vote with more interest than is ordinarily the case. These concerns, as well as countervailing restrictions on bidders, will be addressed in chapter 7. For the moment what is important is to see that if such a rule had been in effect, the shareholders of Marshall Field almost certainly would not have approved the purchase of those poorly performing stores to fend off a bid by Carter Hawley Hale. The same is presumably true of the greenmail payments by Gillette and a host of others. On the other hand, the lockups granted by Marathon to U. S. Steel would probably have been approved by the shareholders of Marathon, because they brought in a new, much higher bid.

Management Buyouts

For some defenses, however, a different response may be necessary. Two in particular are management buyouts and the use of classified voting stock. They require individual attention.

Substantial numbers of management buyouts (MBOs) first appeared in the mid-1970s. There were several contributing factors, but the most immediate was a major bear market. After rising to 1,036 in 1972, the Dow Jones Industrial Average dropped almost in half to 578 in 1974. A substantial number of small companies that had gone public in the new issue market of the 1960s found their stocks selling at particularly depressed prices.

Having only recently gone public, the top executives of many of these companies still owned controlling or even majority interests. Many, finding public waters no longer congenial, decided to return to the quiet shores of private life. By one device or another, their companies bought back the public shares.

These transactions were widely condemned. Public shareholders had been frozen out before, for example, when a parent operating company eliminated the minority shareholders of a publicly owned subsidiary. The market tolerated these parent-subsidiary mergers because they sometimes eliminated conflicts of interest in intercorporate transactions or helped achieve operating or tax efficiencies. By contrast, the MBO seemed like a purely internal or financial rearrangement. Management used the company's resources, its credit, and when necessary, its proxy machinery to eliminate all public ownership—an ownership that the management had offered only recently to the public at much higher prices.

While these early MBOs violated an old and useful taboo, they had only trivial economic consequences. The companies were remarkably small. According to one study, the mean market value of all the publicly held shares of forty-five companies that made going-private proposals and that were also listed on the American or New York Stock Exchange was less than $3 million.[46] In the mid-1970s no one would have guessed where the MBO would go.

The $1 billion management buyout of the mid-1980s has replaced the $3 million buyout of the mid-1970s. According to W. T. Grimm and Company, the total annual dollar volume rose from less than $1 billion in 1980 to $7 billion in 1983 and $9.5 billion in 1986.

Not all buyouts are suspect. To focus on those transactions where there is a significant conflict of interest, the term "management buyout," or MBO, is best used to mean the purchase for cash (or nonconvertible senior securities) of substantially all the equity interest in a public corporation in a transaction in which members of that corporation's management acquire a significant equity interest in the purchaser, and the purchaser is closely held and has not theretofore been an operating company or a subsidiary of one. Usually the purchaser's financing consists largely of borrowed money, hence the term "leveraged buyout," or LBO. That term, however, is also used to cover buyouts of mere subsidiaries or divisions of a company. These divisional divestitures are of little concern here, because the managers of the parent company are not on both sides of the table.

In a study of twenty-eight management buyout proposals, made from 1979 to 1984 and ranging in value from the $101 million bid for the Bekins Company to the $2.5 billion transaction for Esmark, the mean value of the companies, measured by the winning bids, was about $500 million. Because the firms are so much larger, the managers can no longer hope to own a controlling block of stock. Competitive bidding becomes possible. Unlike Mary Wells of Wells, Rich, Greene, Inc., whose famous proposal to take her advertising agency private so angered then SEC Commissioner A. A. Sommer, Jr., in 1974, it is not founders but professional managers who now make the bids. The CEO of Esmark owned less than 1 percent of that company's shares when he made his buyout proposal.

MBOs have in effect merged with the recent market for hostile takeovers in two respects. First, the larger the company, the more likely an MBO proposal will trigger an uninvited third-party offer and set off a reasonably good auction. Allowing for an occasional exception where the insiders still own a controlling interest, it is difficult to preempt the bidding. Second, MBOs have become a primary response to a hostile tender offer. It is the MBO proposal that frequently wins the bidding, offering top dollar to the target company shareholders even while enabling the management to stay on the job and receive cash or cheap stock for their stock interests in the old, public company and a much larger equity interest in the new, private one.

The new privately owned company (the ''newco'') that emerges from a management buyout has a number of advantages in the bidding. The insiders and their bankers who sponsored the MBO have access to information that is not available to a hostile bidder. The newco is often able to make more aggressive use of debt and various tax sheltering devices than could a public corporation; and while the debt:equity ratios of some of these companies may seem excessive, that is of no concern to target company shareholders who have sold out for cash. Private companies are freer than public ones to focus on cash flow rather than short-term reported earnings. More important still may be the substantial and positive incentives of the managers' once-in-a-lifetime opportunity to become seriously rich. A substantial equity stake for those managers is a part of every MBO, because the investment bankers and their clients need to win the managers' favor if there is to be a deal at all, and because the heavy leverage makes it only prudent to create special incentives.

While there are sometimes advantages, much of the praise heaped on MBOs is self-serving or a product of the enthusiasm that often greets each new development in corporate finance. Heavy debt-service requirements can sorely limit a company's flexibility. Research and development and capital expenditures are postponed, the theory being that in the near term the delay won't hurt. The newco has lost access to the public capital markets at the very time that it has weakened its financial condition. The most serious financial criticism, however, is that even if an MBO rejuvenates an aging management, the benefits will be short-lived. The pattern of these buyouts is that the participants expect a six-year payout. The financial plan typically calls for elimination of the excess debt in five to six years at most. By that point, the company will have reduced interest costs and can reschedule the remaining principal payments. The management group's employment agreements also expire at the same time, giving them the right to sell their shares in the new company, shares that will often have become remarkably valuable. And like most seasoned teams, they will expect to enjoy the good life and other fruits of their success, perhaps with a resale to the public.

The institutional investors who financed the buyout are under similar pressures. Usually they have two choices: (1) take the newly private company public again, leaving it to the allegedly perverse influence of the marketplace, or (2) sell the business as a whole, which will have much the same result, particularly if the buyer is publicly owned. No matter how the company is sold, however, the much-praised period of private entrepreneurship is likely to have been decidedly brief.

The problem is simply that when the advantages of private ownership are largely based on, or at least coupled with, a heavily leveraged capital structure, extremely generous but short-term compensation arrangements, tax-sheltering devices of equally short duration and an investor group that in all likelihood will not be content for long with merely paper profits, the arrangement is inherently unstable and will soon metamorphose into something quite different.

While the management buyout has changed a good deal in recent years, the basic conflict of interest remains. The owners of the business, the shareholders, are confronted—on a day not of their choosing—by a salaried manager who announces that he is not working for them anymore. By itself that's not too distressing, but when the manager goes on to say that he is taking the keys with him and that, using the company's credit and proxy machinery, he will shortly buy the business at a price that seems fair to *him* and the company's advisers, the conflict begins to build.

Management wants to buy as cheap as possible and still get the deal done. That conflict is not dealt with as easily as are greenmail and crown jewel lockups, by allowing shareholders to vote on the proposed buyout. It's like a dating game. Any one fellow looks good, and a girl will always go with him, unless she knows what the competition looks like. In the Stokely-Van Camp MBO proposal, for example, the principal shareholder-officer (who owned about 14 percent of the outstanding shares) offered a price of $50 per share compared with $38 before the announcement. Under the threat of a competing offer from Esmark, however, he raised the price to $55. Pillsbury then bid $62, and Quaker Oats ultimately won the bidding contest with its offer of $77 per share—fully 40 percent more than the top price bid by management.

Had there not been an auction, the shareholders would probably have accepted management's first offer, which was 32 percent over market, and surely would have rejoiced over the second offer, which represented a premium of 45 percent. Shareholders have no way of knowing the best price that an auction might bring unless there is an auction. Nor do the courts, which are notoriously (and understandably) reluctant to resolve issues of value. In that same study of twenty-eight management buyout proposals, the median premium of the winning bid over market price thirty days before the first significant announcement rose from 48 percent to 76 percent if there were three or more bids. Even if the shareholders suspect that someone is out there who, if given the chance, would outbid management, they are rarely in a position to do much about it.

MANDATED AUCTIONS

Unless there is an auction, the risks to shareholders are limited in substantial measure only by the imagination of the management group and its lack of scruples. It is easy to depress stock prices artificially so that the public can be offered a "premium" price—at a discount. The insiders can cut the dividend or increase it less than expected. The officers of a power company, Alamito, declined to meet with security analysts, thus withholding the type of access on which analysts and investment advisers depend.[47] On a more manipulative level, it is not difficult to accelerate investments in long-term projects or maintenance expenditures, both of which will reduce reported earnings in ways that do not diminish the company's intrinsic value. Since accountants are concerned primarily with the possibility that earnings may be overstated, it is easy enough to calculate reserves, inventories, and expenses on a "conservative" basis. Even if the stock market were as smart as financial economists would have us believe, it would still mark down the company's stock to reflect the increasingly obvious possibility of a corrupt intent.

The shareholders have currently been enjoying an auction—sometimes a vigorous auction, sometimes not. Because the market has been so active recently, the managers have been unable to monopolize the bidding. The shareholders often have, in practice if not in law, adequate protection.

While the courts have now made it clear that once a bidding contest begins, once a decision to sell the company has been made, the board of directors may not favor management's bid over someone else's,[48] the courts have not gone so far as to require that an MBO proposal trigger competitive bidding. Auctions are not assured. They began to appear only recently, and could as easily dry up. Managements preempt the bidding as best they can. In the proposed buyout of Scott & Fetzer and of Axia, Inc., the management groups each received a lockup stock option for about 18 percent of the outstanding shares. In the Northwest Energy MBO, the board of directors granted Allen & Company, an investment banking firm working with the management bidders, an option to purchase the company's most valuable asset, a pipeline, at book value.

The ultimately successful third-party bidder paid Allen more than $26 million to disconnect the pipeline option—money that presumably would otherwise have gone to the shareholders. More recently Revlon and SCM employed similar crown-jewel lockups to favor a management buyout proposal, and while the courts rejected both, the decisions left substantial room for such tactics in the future.

MBOs can be used to provide competitive bidding, but they can also be structured to forestall it. Depending on the nature of the business, outsiders may be unable to compete on reasonably equal terms with inside managers because of the information needed to bid intelligently. Or, as in the Malone & Hyde buyout, the bidding may be skewed in the direction of better benefits for management rather than a better price for shareholders.

Until the closing, most buyouts are vulnerable to a third-party bid, particularly one that begins by a tender offer. But by using a cash tender themselves, the MBO sponsors can greatly reduce the four to six months in which others have an opportunity to bid. For the first time, in the 1984 Malone & Hyde MBO, investment bankers made a management-backed tender offer for the public shares of the company—even while satisfying the margin requirements that had tripped up other MBOs. The plan exposed the management proposal to competitive bidding for less than one month, instead of several. Since then others, such as Amerace and American Sterilizer, have used the same technique.

Competitive bidding should be mandatory, but that is not to say that companies should be sold like pork bellies. So long as others have an opportunity to bid, there is no need to strip the board of its discretion in the selection of the buyer. A rule of open bidding simply separates the decision to sell from the selection of the buyer and enjoins managers against such shabby practices as moving to buy the company on their own terms and then, as has happened, deciding that the company is not for sale when someone else offers a better price. Such a rule would presumably require that the decision to sell be irrevocable—subject only to an upset price, terms of payment and other terms equally and fairly applicable to all bidders. And of course the information required to bid, and the time needed to do so, would also have to be available.

A rule of open bidding is difficult to challenge, either as a matter of law or economics. The rule restores some meaning to the traditional precept of undivided loyalty in a situation where the risks are high. It is much fairer than the law in many of the states, which relegates shareholders who object to a buyout to their appraisal rights. Appraisal is a proceeding that allows a dissatisfied shareholder to sue for the "fair value" of his shares, but only after the deal has closed. Eager to exclude other judicial remedies, New York and other states have tried to make the appraisal remedy more adequate, but there are major flaws in any remedy that requires individual shareholders to abandon their usually passive role and go to the courthouse. Very few will do it, it being, as one arbitrageur has said, a hard way to make a living. Acutely aware of this, managers have less incentive to offer a fair price, if by fair is meant the price that an auction would have yielded.

That is not to say that the rules would be easy to write, and one of the lessons is the need to give the SEC adequate rule-making power. Management buyouts are difficult to distinguish at the margin from parent-subsidiary mergers—in which the parent company freezes out the minority shareholders of a publicly owned subsidiary. It may be more difficult still to deal with the recapitalization transactions that have become so popular. Some companies, including Owens-Corning Fiberglass, CBS, Colt Industries, and Multimedia, have responded to takeover threats, or the possibility of one, not by a leveraged buyout but rather by buying back at a premium price a very large portion of the publicly owned shares, financed by massive borrowings. The effect is to leave varying amounts of stock in public hands but often to increase dramatically, by one device or another, the percentage of the balance held by management. In Owens-Corning, for example, the percentage of the voting shares controlled by management rose from 5 percent to 30 percent. The test for a mandated auction would presumably depend on the extent of the conflict of interest, that is, how aggressively the managers use the recapitalization transaction to enhance their own position. The precise line-drawing should be left to the SEC.

Classified Common Stock

Some responses to a hostile tender offer are so clearly appropriate as to raise no serious issue. Looking for a white knight who will pay a higher price is the obvious example. But in other cases the propriety is not so clear. With respect to selective stock repurchases—known as greenmail—lockups, and a number of other essentially financial defensive tactics, the suggestion made earlier in this chapter was simply to make shareholder approval a prerequisite. In the context of a takeover bid, with large stakes and with the shareholders very much on the alert, such a vote should operate not only as a useful but as a sufficient check. The shareholder vote is likely to be something more than the usual rubber stamp, because management's proposals will have an immediate effect on a pending third-party bid and, therefore, on present market value. With respect to management buyouts, however, something more was thought to be required, because without giving third parties an opportunity to bid, there is no way to know the proper price. Management is on both sides of the bargain, acting on behalf of shareholders to determine whether a sale is in their interest and to seek the best possible price, all the while acting in their own proprietary interest as purchasers.

About two hundred public corporations have recently taken, or proposed to take, a major additional step in the defense against takeovers. Dow Jones, Hershey Foods, General Cinema, and some other well-known companies have split their common stock into two separate classes, one of which has vastly superior voting rights. In one fashion or another the public shareholders wind up with Class A shares, the insiders get Class B shares, and each Class B share has as much as ten times as many votes as a Class A. Sometimes the public receives in return slightly higher dividends, sometimes not. The result is that a class with less than 10 percent of the equity might have as much as 50 percent of the votes.

Assume, for example, that management owns 91,000 of the one million shares outstanding and that management's shares constitute all of the Class B shares, which have ten votes per share. The public owns 909,000 shares of Class A stock, each of which has one vote. Management has 910,000 votes, and even assuming that all the public shares are voted, the Class A stock has only 909,000 votes. Absent cumulative voting, management elects the entire board of directors and has all the decision-making power. In reality, management may not own all the Class B shares, but by giving the Class A shares an extra 10 cents per share in dividends, it will persuade most investors—each of whom will rightly have concluded that others will opt for the Class A—to do the same.

These weighted voting proposals come in several different versions, but regardless of the distinctions they are not like other defensive tactics. Faced with a management buyout or crown jewel lockup, a bidder who is willing to increase his offer can probably still win the day. Even a poison pill can be defeated by an all-cash offer for all of the shares. But there seems to be no way to take over a company if the shares you buy don't have the votes. The corporation statutes permit these classified voting arrangements, and the courts have accepted the legislative writ. For corporate managers desperate for protection in a white-hot takeover environment, eager to preserve what they see as the interests of the corporation and those who work there, these nonvoting or limited voting stocks have enormous appeal, particularly now that "everyone" seems to be doing it.

Many of these classified voting arrangements have been put into place by a dividend, exchange offer, or other procedure in which the board of directors acted alone and without shareholder ratification. Assuming, however, that these classified stock proposals take effect only upon shareholder approval—as suggested by the New York Stock Exchange in 1986—why should there be any objection? Why should the shareholders not be free to relinquish their voting rights, so long as the decision is an informed one, with all the implications fully explored in the proxy material? It is, after all, only a slight twist on the Pickens notion—namely, the shareholders own the company and they can sell it, if they want to—to say, as has SEC Commissioner Charles C. Cox, that if "shareholders want to give up their voting rights, they should be able to."[49] ("The market is equipped to determine the value of voting rights," he added, meaning that if stock prices reflect the split in voting power, those who buy the Class A shares haven't lost anything.) And getting the necessary approval has been remarkably easy. The shareholders of United Artists, Wrigley, Church & Dwight, and others have approved unequal voting rights by very large majorities.

Phrased as an issue of shareholders' rights, the Cox laissez-faire position might seem appealing, but expressing the argument in terms of rights is misleading. One might as well argue, as some have done, that citizens have a right not to be taxed without their individual consent. Taxes to pay for police or fire departments are most certainly an infringement on a citizen's "rights," but that is not a useful formulation of the issue. Rather it is whether we need more or less police or fire protection, just as the issue now before us is whether we need shareholder voting as a constraint on management, or whether management will do its job well enough or even better if left on its own.

The proper questions are twofold: are nonvoting stocks too great a disservice to public shareholders, unless they agree or even if they do? And second, going beyond the rights of shareholders, does classified voting ultimately undermine the legitimacy of the corporate enterprise on the one hand and its efficiency on the other?

In corporate finance there is little that is new, or as that sage of base-ball, Yogi Berra, said, "It's déjà vu all over again." At the turn of the century the pattern of one vote per common share was the norm, and even preferred stocks were generally voting stocks. But thereafter bank-ers began to use a variety of techniques to achieve or retain control. Nonvoting preferred stocks were issued, and voting trusts were created, as were holding companies in which a pyramidal, highly leveraged struc-ture made it possible to retain at small cost the control of a far-flung utility network. Then, in the mid-1920s, there appeared for the first time in modern history the dual class common stock, one of the two typically being nonvoting.

Professor William Z. Ripley, who two years later wrote *Main Street and Wall Street*, the book that anticipated so many of the problems that later brought Wall Street to its knees, was the one who first sounded the alarm, in October 1925, at the Academy of Political Science in New York. He seized on the recent offerings of two well-known companies, Dodge Brothers, Inc., the automobile company, and Industrial Rayon Corporation, an "artificial-silk" company. Dillon, Read, the under-writer of the Dodge offering, sold to the public $130 million of senior securities and nonvoting Class A shares, keeping for itself all of the vot-ing Class B common stock for only $2.25 million. (Could it be that someone thinks the public can be fooled? The unwritten rule still seems to be that the public gets the A shares, but the B shares get the votes.) The Class A shares were listed on the New York Stock Exchange. The offering of Industrial Rayon consisted of 598,000 nonvoting Class A shares, with the remaining 2,000 Class B shares retaining exclusive vot-ing rights. Lashing out at investment bankers, Ripley said:

> All kinds of private businesses are being bought up by banking houses, and new corporations are being substituted for the old, in order that the purchase price (and more) may be recovered by sale of shares to the general public. But the significant change is that the new stock, thus sold, is entirely bereft of any voting power . . . and new preferred stocks are sold up to the hilt of the value of the assets, if not beyond. . . .[50]

Newspapers and magazines echoed Ripley's attacks, and a few months later President Coolidge, hardly an enemy of free markets, invited Ripley to the White House and let it be known that the Department of Justice was looking into the matter—although on what theory it is difficult to

imagine. It was jawboning, 1920s style, and it worked. Utility and railroad commissions began to reject nonvoting stocks.[51] Early in 1926, on
the eve of the meeting between the president and Ripley, the New York
Stock Exchange decided that it would no longer list nonvoting stocks.[52]

And that for all purposes ended the matter for almost sixty years. A
few companies took advantage of the more lenient standards of the New
York Curb (later the American Stock) Exchange, but the Big Board, it
turned out, had set a policy that was not only clear but widely accepted,
even by companies not listed there. The rule was informal and nongov-
ernmental, but it was generally adhered to until a few years ago, when
companies increasingly became willing to see their shares delisted. "Better over-the-counter than dead," one might say, but in fact the National
Association of Securities Dealers' over-the-counter trading system was
by now offering liquid, competitive markets and, to boot, many fewer
restrictions on internal corporate matters and, best of all, none whatever
on voting rights. The pressure for change, therefore, came from the Big
Board, which feared a loss of listings by companies that in turn feared
takeovers.

It was suggested that the SEC had sufficient power under the Securities
Exchange Act of 1934 to set minimum standards for the listing or trading
of stocks in the major markets. If not, there was always Congress. But
there was also a remarkable amount of debate about the very desirability
of a one share, one vote requirement or whether, as Commissioner Cox
believes, it is a matter that can safely be left to market forces.

So much of the debate in the 1980s echoes the discussion in 1925 as
to leave one in awe of Yogi's insight. In its recent proposal regarding
nonvoting shares, the New York Stock Exchange suggested that shareholder approval be required, the implication being that voting rights
were theirs to give away. Like his colleague Cox, Commissioner Joseph
Grundfest argued that since a new issue of nonvoting shares would be
priced to reflect the lack of voting rights, the buyers would not be de-
prived of anything.[53] "No one is [being] coerced," agreed Chairman
John S. R. Shad.[54] *But it is déjà vu all over again.* The concern in 1925
was not that the nonvoting Dodge Brothers shares could not be sold but
that they could be, and at a hefty price. If the market had rejected nonvoting stocks, then the market judgment would be final, but it didn't. A
more thoughtful response would have been to inquire as to why there
can be, as happened in 1925 and again sixty years later, both market
acceptance and public outcry.

It has also been argued, even by thoughtful people such as former Commissioner Sommer, that "adequate safeguards against abuse are provided to shareholders by independent directors sitting on a corporation's board and the NYSE requirement for . . . an independent audit committee."[55] *But it is déjà vu all over again.* In the more structured society of 1925, voting shares were said to be unimportant because of the high sense of ethics that prevailed among the reputable banking houses. It was sufficient, they said, to leave the matter as an issue of private conscience.[56]

And it is being argued, too, that voting rights are unimportant, a mere makeweight, because the shareholders almost never exercise the franchise—which is surely true. There are very few proxy contests, and it is hard to recall any management proposals that have been defeated. *But it is déjà vu all over again.* Ripley had to deal with the same argument that " '[a]ll the stockholders act like a flock of sheep.' . . . It will be objected that no real change is involved in these recent tendencies: that the stockholders never did, and never will, exercise their voting rights.' "[57]

There is no small amount of cynicism in the claim of bankers and business managers that they are willing to let the shareholders decide the voting rights issue. Would they be so deferential if they were dealing with 20 institutional shareholders, instead of 20,000 public ones? Hardly. Call it sheeplike behavior, call it a problem in collective action, but the issue is not whether shareholders will or will not accept nonvoting stocks. Shareholder ratification on an issue of this kind more nearly resembles a sword for managers than a shield for shareholders.

Commissioners Cox, Grundfest, and Shad seemed to be saying that shareholders own their voting rights in the same sense that they own their automobiles. Not so. They have rights to vote, not to be routinely traded away, in private transactions, but because of a deep and abiding fear of power without accountability. Arguably—and it is a very good argument—voting rights need to be strengthened, not weakened. Again it was Ripley, with great foresight, who suggested that the investment trusts, the institutional investors of the day, might be the solution:

> If suitably developed under proper safeguards, these concentrated investments, handled by competent persons who devote their entire time and attention to the matter, might well participate in corporate government in an intelligent and entirely helpful way.[58]

But the issue in any case is one of institutional structure, not private property. We are trying, and probably always will be, to sort out the checks and balances in the control of $3 trillion worth of corporate equities. Directors cannot sell their votes, and indeed there is case law that the shareholders cannot sell theirs, at least not individually.[59] One might as well speak of buying and selling votes in political elections. As Tobin said, any good second-year graduate student in economics could prove that voluntary sales of votes would increase the welfare of the sellers as well as the buyers. There is, in fact, a fundamental question as to whether prices that clear the market can be created for voting mechanisms. Recent results in game theory imply that they cannot be.[60] But Tobin was correct in saying that "the legitimacy of the political process rests on the prohibition of such transactions."[61] So too does the legitimacy of the private enterprise process.

Some weighted voting schemes are more reasonable than others. The one that limits the number of votes to be cast by any one shareholder, for example, does have a nice egalitarian touch. The difficulty is that there are no such populist principles motivating the corporate managers who, far from seeking to distribute power widely, adopt the particular package that best suits their own purposes. Arguably, too, a weighted voting system could be constructed in which the institutional investors would acquire greatly increased voting power, thereby motivating them to take a more active role. Professor Gunnar Hedlund and other Swedish economists have suggested that some such arrangement exists in Sweden, "where long-term holdings and very active voice on [the] part of owners are common."[62] But that ideal of countervailing power is not what is being suggested by the New York Stock Exchange. Corporate managers are seeking to become their own monitors, with no institutional checks other than that of a board of directors which in the new era would be entirely under their thumbs.

To deal with dual class voting stocks, some Chicagoans have jumped through hoops so as to save takeover bids. If investors choose to buy nonvoting shares, they have said, it should be of no concern to us. In the world of efficient markets they assume, the price will accurately reflect all aspects of the bargain. But, of course, if that process were carried too far, hostile tender offers would be in jeopardy. Some economists have, therefore, come to the interesting conclusion that new investors should be allowed to accept nonvoting shares, but existing ones should not.

Dual class voting stocks have implications and effects that do not stop with takeovers. They allow corporate control to be seized or retained by corporate officers or insiders—and perhaps even their grandchildren—not just to ward off raiders, but for all purposes. The executives are ultimately in a position to sell that control for a premium, leaving the ordinary shareholders to receive something less, or nothing at all. Where does it stop? Power without accountability will eventually be abused—just as it was abused by the investment companies and utility holding companies of the 1920s.

Time and again, in the Bankruptcy Act, the Investment Company Act, and the Public Utility Holding Company Act, Congress has taken steps to reinforce voting rights, and it may have to do so again. In the 1920s, it was the popular outcry and fear of congressional action that ended the debate and led the New York Stock Exchange to change its rules. The same is happening now. Senators and congressmen who are unsure about takeovers have few doubts about this sort of power grab. In 1987 the SEC, to ward off otherwise almost inevitable federal legislation, announced that it would hold hearings on a requirement of equal voting rights for all shares traded in the major markets, but with exceptions for shares—such as those of Dodge Brothers!—newly issued in a public offering or by merger. The solution in the 1920s was better, and it may yet be better here, too.

⌇7⌇ Beating the Wall Street Rule with a Stick and a Carrot, and Other Conclusions

We cannot, therefore, settle on abstract grounds, but must handle on its merits in detail, what Burke termed "one of the finest problems in legislation, namely, to determine what the State ought to take upon itself to direct by the public wisdom, and what it ought to leave, with as little interference as possible, to individual exertion." (John Maynard Keynes, "The End of Laissez-faire," contained in *Essays in Persuasion* [New York: Harcourt Brace, 1932], 312–313.)

Financial Markets and Business Managers

EARLIER CHAPTERS have described the profound changes that have taken place in the ways investors select and trade stocks. Reduced commissions, stock-index futures, and a variety of other new financial "products" have produced a virtual explosion in transactions that bear little, if any, relationship to fundamentals. The same astonishing growth has affected hostile takeovers and other mergers. Instead of occasional transactions, a highly liquid market in whole businesses has come to exist alongside the traditional market for shares of those businesses. Whole businesses have, in effect, become one of its more important "new products," as Wall Street learned to merchandise leveraged buyouts and corporate restructurings.

What happens in the marketplace inevitably spills over and affects the companies whose stocks are traded there. Chicagoans like to ignore the dysfunction of high stock turnovers, but it is silly to pretend that in-and-out investors have much to contribute to the market or to the companies whose shares they so briefly hold. There are no Chinese Walls between markets and corporations. The adverse effects are all about. Hostile takeovers were greeted as a device for disciplining managers, but the end product of excessive takeovers and greenmail has been to hasten the abandonment of the rule of one share, one vote, without which the more routine, continuing supervision of managers by shareholders cannot operate. It is only in the mythology of a fragmented regulatory scheme that we continue to believe, as we saw in chapter 6, that there is a functional separation between Main Street and Wall Street.

These and other issues that have emerged in the course of this book are part of a single fabric spun out of the threads of investors, markets, and corporations. Generally it is the discrete threads that are studied, one by one. Except in times of crisis, there is no important political constituency arguing for systemic changes that, whatever the collective benefits, inevitably antagonize important constituencies. (Lobbyists are rarely hired for public benefits.) Most of us would rather muddle along than go down an uncharted road on which there is for each of us the risk of more private loss than of compensating collective gain. With respect to the tax system, we knew for a long time that nothing less than a major overhaul would do. There is only now an emerging sense that something is amiss with respect to corporate control, takeovers, and financial markets. It may take a broad-based calamity—more painful than the one of October 1987—to develop anytime soon the necessary sense of public urgency.

The obstacles to an integrated approach to this triangular web of investors, financial markets, and corporations are daunting. An integrated approach means a federal approach, and not for fifty years has there been even a modest willingness in Congress to speak of corporate governance and financial markets in the same breath. The internal affairs of a corporation are in principle reserved for state regulation, the financial markets for federal, a distinction that for a long time was at least recognizable, even if not altogether viable. When the two merged, as they did in takeovers, whose very purpose is to use marketplace tactics to affect the internal workings of the target company, the distinction lost any semblance of virtue. Still it persists. Even groups as thoughtful as the draftsmen at work at the American Law Institute seem unwilling to rearrange the tactics of both bidders and targets in a single document, lest they breach the party wall separating what belongs to Washington from what is Delaware's.

We try to muddle through. Over sixty bills on takeovers and related issues were introduced in a single session of Congress, but none of them moved. Congress professes not to want to tilt the balance between bidder and target, but it sits passively by while such states as New York and North Carolina enact aggressive antitakeover statutes.

This willingness, if not desire, to drift along rather than to rationalize the structure of the system stems in large measure from an inability to agree on goals. The explosion in the day-to-day, routine trading of stocks and "derived instruments," such as stock-index futures, troubles only a few observers. Even at the SEC, the burst of trading in options and futures is not worrisome, except in the trivial respect that it affects closing prices once each calendar quarter or in times of market chaos. And so there is no agreement, nor yet even debate, as to whether such trading has serious implications for market efficiency, or for corporate control and governance. We continue to think in discrete boxes—the shareholder rights box, the junk bond box, the trading box, and so on.

HOW BEST TO KEEP MANAGEMENT'S FEET TO THE FIRE

If there is little, if any, consensus in Congress, it reflects the raging conflict among lawyers, economists, and academics. There is agreement in some minor respects. There is, for example, agreement that managements sometimes have a personal agenda that conflicts with that of the shareholders. Lawyers use such terms as "shirking" and the "corporate opportunity doctrine," and economists "agency costs," but underlying them all is the biblical lesson that none of us is beyond temptation, least of all when entrusted with other people's money. It is a waste of good computers and empirical research time that so many young scholars earn their doctoral wings trying to prove (or disprove) that proposition.

There is also agreement that shareholders have a role to play as monitors of management, keeping them as honest, competent, and diligent as possible. The "as possible" is an important qualification, however. Economists have wisely warned against what they call the "Nirvana fallacy," meaning that while some managers and some companies will surely fail, it does not mean that the corporate institution has failed.

How the shareholders do their monitoring—that is the question. Financial economists generally believe that it is sufficient if shareholders express their approval or disapproval by transactions in the marketplace. And, of course, investors have been behaving in ways that only those economists could approve—buy, buy . . . sell, sell, all at a furious pace. Just how little else they do was demonstrated recently by the College Retirement Equities Fund (CREF), one of the nation's largest investors—over $28 billion in a single fund—with few constraints on its freedom to speak out. CREF submitted a proposal at the 1987 shareholder meeting of International Paper Company opposing the company's poison pill, which like the similar plans adopted by four hundred or so other corporations, discourages some takeover bids. In its thirty-five-year history, CREF had not offered a resolution at odds with any management on an internal governance issue, but according to one of its officials, "[s]o many companies have [poison pills] that *we can't register our disapproval by selling our stock and investing elsewhere.*"[1] Despite an extraordinarily diversified portfolio, it took a fund as conscientious as CREF thirty-five years to take a public stand, and even then it did so on the cheap, relying primarily on its right under the federal securities laws to put a statement in management's proxy material rather than soliciting proxies independently.

For those economists with a neoclassical bent, however, the failure of the proxy machinery to generate much interest or enthusiasm is not serious. Managers' feet are kept to the fire, they believe, by a series of market-based pressures—not just the stock market, but also the markets for the goods and services their companies sell, markets for their own services as managers, and even markets for directors' services. The development of hostile takeovers in the 1960s was a particularly welcome development, one that seemed to round out the scheme. In economists' jargon, takeovers were quickly converted into a "market for corporate control," thus conferring on them the ultimate legitimacy.

What distinguishes these neoclassical, Chicago School economists is their conviction that markets alone will suffice to keep managers acting responsibly and, second, their deep and abiding sense that interference in this process can only make matters worse. They sit approvingly, or at least silently, by while the daily volume on the New York Stock Exchange soars from 3 million to 100 million and then to 160 million shares. They do not object or even raise questions, fearing, it seems, that if they peered under the stones of this trading frenzy, they might find slugs and worms. Sell, sell . . . buy, buy.

When these intellectual foxes were still scattered in the academic brush, there was less to worry about, but some of them are now in the chicken house. The federal securities laws were intended to put a floor under the race for the bottom by which the states had failed to provide even minimally adequate protections for shareholders. (The state corporation laws, it will be recalled, do not so much as require that the proxy card provide a place to vote "no" as well as "yes.") But with its new members and shorter memory, the SEC has the temerity to suggest that state law might be copied by the federal. State corporation laws enable shareholders to waive a long list of protective provisions. Seeing by some strained logic this aspect of state law as a potential model, the SEC suggested in 1986 that perhaps shareholders should be permitted to waive now, with respect to some *unknown,* future transaction, their right under the Williams Act to have a tender offer made to all holders, and not just to a select few.[2] What is so striking is that the Commission might better have been thinking about extending the so-called all-holders requirement rather than curtailing it. As more companies adopt dual class voting stocks, there is a growing risk that bidders will in time simply buy the supervoting shares—as happened recently with Resorts International—with the public left out in the cold.

AN EXIT-VOICE ANALYSIS

Modern finance and economic theory did not create the gypsies on Wall Street and other problems confronting us, but like any one-lens mechanism, it lacks depth perception. Einstein said that we should make things as simple as possible, but no more so. As a starting point for tying together various problems affecting investors, corporations, and financial markets, the exit-voice analysis suggested by Professor Albert O. Hirschman for social and economic problems in his provocative book *Exit, Voice, and Loyalty,* may be somewhat more complex, but it provides a much more dynamic framework.

The terms "exit" and "voice" have become part of the vocabulary of economic and political theory. The term "exit" refers to the classic market mechanism of exit-and-entry by which, for example, consumers switch products, voters change parties, workers refuse bad jobs and accept good ones. The second, voice mode of response refers to the more political process by which a dissatisfied worker, instead of quitting, asks for a higher salary or better working conditions. In the political process, from which Hirschman adapted the concept, voice refers not just to voting but to the letter writing, the clubhouse politics, and the bargaining by which a democratic society functions.

Exit is the sort of neat, impersonal mechanism on which economists thrive when they speak of the invisible hand of the marketplace. In a model market, with perfect competition and perfect information among anonymous buyers and sellers, there is not much room for haggling, complaining, letter writing, and the rest of the give-and-take of voice.

It is not surprising, therefore, that it was an economist, Milton Friedman, who suggested that schooling would benefit from a voucher system that entitled parents to switch (exit) to the school of their choice, subject only to acceptance. The implication was that a voucher system would improve the schooling of all children in the long run, although in the first instance it is a mechanism of escape from deterioration, not one of recuperation. Indeed, by draining off many of those who care most about education, exit diminishes the likelihood that those who remain will have sufficiently long bootstraps to lift themselves out of the rut. In neoclassical theory that loss tends not to matter much, because there is no particular virtue to restoring a school or other institution to good working order. It is assumed—although not always true—that a school that does not work well will be promptly replaced by those that do.

Voice mechanisms are not nearly so neat or private as exit. If the diner in a restaurant dislikes the canned fruit salad, he can decide not to return, i.e., exit, but his only other choice is to speak up, expressing himself on the tinny taste of the oranges more or less forcefully, more or less directly. He has to decide whether to send the offending fruit back to the kitchen or to articulate his displeasure more directly by speaking up, either to the waiter or, even one notch higher, to the maître d'. But while voice is messy, it can also communicate in much more subtle, richer, and better-modulated fashion than a simple stay-or-leave decision. Not surprisingly, each has its place. That diner probably discovered as much, depending on the availability of other restaurants, the seriousness of the defects in this one, and the loyalty with which he has patronized it. If he is not a known customer, if he has exited too often, his voice may not count for much. He may then have no choice but to exit again.

Exit-voice analysis makes a marvelous contribution to thinking about investors, the stock market, and corporations. Unfortunately, not much attention has been paid to it in corporate finance. Hirschman, quoting Graham and Dodd, saw immediately the relevance of his analysis to the modern corporation,[3] but he has said that he did not feel sufficiently comfortable in dealing with financial markets to take the matter further. Some vigorous work has been done in Sweden, reflecting in part the long experience there of "active" investors, the perception of a growing threat to that structure and culture, and the willingness of Professor Gunnar Hedlund and others to think in terms of control mechanisms beyond the market.

Soups and stocks are different.

A decision not to buy the common stock of Campbell Soup affects that company much less directly than a decision not to buy its soup. The company suffers no loss of revenue or profits, because its shares, unlike the soup, are almost invariably purchased from other investors, not the company. The supply of shares is largely static, the only open question being the identity of the particular holders. Beyond that, the factors influencing the buy/don't-buy decision with respect to the shares are not nearly so much under the company's control as in the case of the soup. Campbell's has the ability to determine largely the price as well as the quality of its soup. The company can try to manage the "quality" of its stock, but having done so, it can influence the price only indirectly and only over longer periods of time. Some macroeconomic factors affecting stock prices, such as interest rates, are wholly outside its control.

Just how much the company, even if it could do so, ought to concern itself with the day-to-day price of its shares is not all that clear. Its function is to deliver the goods, and beyond that to treat shareholders fairly. Certainly it has no obligation to boost the price without regard to value, for if so the result would be self-defeating. To be sure, some companies do act as perennial boosters, applying to stocks the same marketing instincts they learned with soup. But to what end? The true value will eventually win out. A company may succeed for a time in putting a high price on its shares, but in the process it will by definition have lost those shareholders who bought on fundamentals and be left with those who, however they may think of themselves, are speculators at heart and will behave as such when the cycle turns. And if the purpose is not to boost the stock price, but only to help it stay close to "true value," it is even less clear that Campbell's has available to it many effective choices.

THE WALL STREET RULE

Even at the far lower turnover rates that once prevailed, there was concern that the Wall Street Rule—love 'em or leave 'em—was perpetuating bad management and bad policies.[4] With so many alternative investments available, it was unthinkable for all but the most committed investors to resort to voice. Voice requires a sense of commitment, some stake in the outcome, and therefore some continuity of interest. If it is too cheap and easy to go elsewhere, the incentive is lacking. No-fault divorce laws, for example, may undermine voice—and marriage:

[R]ather than being an action of last resort (like strikes, which are always costly), divorce can become the automatic response to marital difficulty with less and less effort made at communication and reconciliation.[5]

In corporate life, not only voice has been allowed to atrophy. Whatever message was implicit in the trading itself has been diluted and submerged in the near-frenzy of trading currently engulfing the securities markets. What should a corporate CEO learn from or about his shareholders, as he watches the tumultuous trading in his company's shares? Let us assume that he is the president of Median Corporation, a manufacturing company that bears a striking resemblance to the average large, publicly owned American corporation. Median Corporation enjoys a return on equity of about 12 percent, and its earnings do not fluctuate a great deal. But while the business is stable over the longer term, investors come and go with dazzling frequency. Some are shareholders from January to May, others from March to November, and so on, each trying to take a larger share of the average annual gains by hoping that the immediately good news will happen during his watch.

Our CEO's first and most enduring reaction will probably be that the owners of his business are fools and do not appreciate how hard it is to make a dollar. Why else would they take the earnings that required such skill and sweat and dissipate such a large proportion of them by switching in and out of different stocks, feeding the brokers instead of themselves? If he has read Keynes, he might generalize a bit and add that his shareholders come and go at a rate that makes a "fetish of liquidity," competing with others in a trading game that diminishes the collective result.

Given the frenetic trading, it follows that the CEO of Median Corporation receives from his shareholders very few questions or messages about the company's business, except perhaps as they relate to the earnings for the ensuing six months or other events during their brief stay (or in the case of security analysts, the equally brief stay of clients who might now buy the shares). None of the mushrooming interest in stocks and the stock market has been translated into increased interest in the voting of stocks, shareholder meetings, or any of the other "voices" that might improve the overall results. Nor will it. It is useless to expect those trading in options for IBM stock, where the volume exceeds that in the stock itself, to take much of an interest when their "investment horizon" is 90 or 120 days. They are making bets, not investments, with winning and losing defined by market perceptions, rumors, and whether IBM's next new product is introduced in 43 rather than 83 days.

Exit is a powerful tool. As the recent events at General Motors attest, when customers quit and market share drops, management receives strong signals. New products, better service . . . something has to change. But while the signals may be strong, they are often, as Hirschman suggested,[6] quite unrefined and inarticulate. General Motors supplements its sales data with extensive interviews and surveys of consumer preferences, to see how to proceed.

However fuzzy the message may be when a customer stops buying an Oldsmobile, it is a good deal more ambiguous when the customer who quits is not someone who closely identified with the product in the first place. Consider the business traveler at the airport car rental agency who picks an Oldsmobile for a one-week trip. Like as not, the real choice he made was only that he wanted a mid-size car, or whatever, and he drove away in an Oldsmobile because it was the brand offered to him by the clerk. The initial selection did not represent a considered choice, and so the decision on his next trip to rent a different car—to exit from Oldsmobile—may not signal much, if anything at all. The average institutional investor today is very much like that traveler, except that he is "renting" a stock rather than a car. Hedlund points out that the market in stocks is likely to be even less responsive, voice-motivated than for Oldsmobiles:

> [The] loyal GM customer does not suffer that much more trying one final time to convince the company to improve, rather than selling his car today. In financial markets, it is *precisely* by selling before anybody even knows that you are dissatisfied that you make money.[7]

Too easy and frequent exit may have a depressing effect not only on the utility of voice mechanisms but on the value of marketplace discipline as well. General Motors asks why customers stopped buying Oldsmobiles, but it is safe to assume that it wastes little time finding out why this or that pension fund has sold its stock.

TAKING A STICK TO THE WALL STREET RULE
The fifty-year-old suggestion by Keynes that we discourage stock trading in some fashion or other now seems compelling. That is not to say that

even if share turnover were 10 percent annually, instead of ten times that figure, the shareholders of our large public corporations would behave much like the twenty shareholders of a family business. They did not in the 1950s, when turnover was far less. The Wall Street Rule is not a new insight. Until we stop this hyperactive trading, however, there is no possibility of a solution to the longer-term concerns of how best to encourage shareholders to act like those owners of a local factory rather than holders of a parimutuel ticket.

Several factors may influence the shape of the solution:

- *Tax-exempt investors.* The rules should apply to tax-exempt as well as fully taxable investors.
- *A universal rule or a selective one.* One possibility, of course, is to deal just with institutional investors, who are not only among the most serious offenders but the ones whose behavior patterns are most easily changed. If money managers are churning, we could simply make the fund managers, rather than those whose money is *being* managed, bear the "excess" transaction costs. Perhaps that would suffice, and it would be consistent with the Investment Company Act under which Congress imposed on money managers unusually strict fiduciary duties. The question is whether if the institutional junkies go off to the trading-abuse center, would other addicts voluntarily take the cure? Unfortunately, there is nothing much in the history of Wall Street to suggest an optimistic answer.
- *Sticks, not carrots.* We are talking primarily about sticks, not carrots, to create the necessary incentives. One positive incentive that has been adopted, although for very different reasons, is the weighted voting scheme of companies such as J. M. Smucker, which offer more votes to those who hold their shares for at least three years or so. For the modern, gypsy investor, however, votes are not much of a carrot.
- *Better and worse sticks.* As for sticks, they almost inevitably rely on the tax system. One is a graduated tax of the kind suggested by Felix Rohatyn, with the tax decreasing in proportion to the length of the holding period. Depending on the rates, such a tax would help, but it is dangerously vulnerable to lobbying efforts that would whittle away at the holding periods and at the rates both. Only a few years ago, after trading had already reached

epidemic proportions, the securities industry persuaded Congress to cut the holding period for long-term capital gains treatment from one year to six months. The same problem exists with the recent proposal of House Speaker Jim Wright, that a flat 0.5 percent tax be levied on all stock transactions. Because both proposals have a genuine potential to raise revenues—Wright's purpose was to do just that—there is no clearly correct holding period or tax rate. The Congressional Research Service indicated that Wright's proposal would cause stock prices to decline by about 10 percent, and while that estimate seems far too high, it is the sort of argument that is likely to be made again and again. There would be enormous pressure to cut back the holding period and the tax rate both, once the initial appetite for reform has been satisfied.

- *A "nontax" tax.* There is a more attractive model in the short-swing trading rules under Section 16 of the Exchange Act. Section 16(b) provides that all gains by insiders from the purchase and sale (or sale, then purchase) of company shares completed within a six-month period shall be paid over to the company itself. What makes Section 16(b) so relevant is that it was not the purpose of the short-swing trading rules to increase corporate revenues. Who got the money was less important than who lost it, and who lost it was less important than sending a clear "no-fraud" signal to the players at the nineteenth hole. Hopefully, no one would lose, although the experience, of course, is that some few do inadvertently fall into the trap.

Applying this analysis, Buffett's proposed 100 percent tax on all gains, including those of otherwise tax-exempt investors, from the sale of stocks or derivative securities held for less than one year is very attractive. In substance it is a nontax tax. While it sounds confiscatory, it is not. Unlike most taxes, this one is designed not to collect money but to change behavior. (The tax system is involved at all only because it provides the necessary reporting mechanism.) More important, it seems well designed to change radically investors' perception of the role and function of Wall Street. The investor could get his money back at any time, if he sold above cost, but "there would be no profit to [him] from [his] capital allocation decisions unless they had a time horizon of at least one year."[8] In short, the emphasis is on the buy-side of the transaction, the purpose being not to impose a penalty on those who, for whatever reason, decide to sell but to announce that stocks are not the proper vehicle for short-term holdings.

Options and index futures, which are the exactas and daily doubles of the Wall Street racetrack, would disappear. Greenmail might not entirely disappear, but the ante would go up for those who now put companies into play at no cost to themselves. Fewer of our graduates would find their careers producing the synthetic futures and other "new products" on which Wall Street now feeds. It is hoped that more of them would find careers making new products on which the country as a whole could grow. Except for the brokers, and those few who commit inadvertent and innocent errors—recidivism is unlikely—there would be only winners and no losers.

This proposal is easy to understand and relatively easy to implement. A number of exemptions would be required. For example, only voluntary sales in the market should trigger the tax, not mergers or other "forced," sale-of-the-company transactions. (There would thus remain a role for the more useful forms of arbitrage.) An exemption would be needed for stock exchange specialists and other market-makers, and also for new issues of stock. But these are not very substantial matters. If a major purpose of financial markets is to direct real investment in physical and human capital to its socially more productive uses, and if short-term speculation drives a wedge between personal and social gains, then why not, as Buffett proposes, eliminate the rewards of such behavior?

Is Buffett's proposal realistic? True, the nontax turnover tax is not likely to be adopted any time soon, and surely not while stocks are roaring ahead, as they were until recently. But to be realistic one should think not just of what can be pushed through in the short term, but what if adopted, would work well in the long term. The proposal meets that test admirably. Once in place, the nontax tax would give off clear, workable signals, and if the short-swing trading rules are an example, it would be relatively safe from political tinkering.

USING A CARROT AS WELL AS A STICK:
SHAREHOLDER NOMINATED DIRECTORS
Useful as it is, the nontax tax is not a panacea. It will not rid us of the Wall Street Rule or the tendency to think of stocks as trading instruments divorced from the ownership of a business. It is true that there has always been the potentiality for leadership among institutional inves-

tors, but for sixty years or more these hopes have remained unfulfilled. The initiatives taken by some of the major public and private pension funds and by the Investor Responsibility Research Center suggest that this may be a time to think more ambitiously. But it is too much to expect investors to take the initiative, to exercise leadership, without some special inducements. In addition to the stick, some carrot is needed.

There have been proposals recently that major shareholders, those owning, for example, at least $500,000 worth of a company's shares, be granted access to the proxy materials in order to solicit votes in competition with management; or that the outcome of the voting be publicized, in order to put pressure on otherwise passive money managers; or conversely, that there be instituted a secret ballot, to free those same managers from the pressures of CEOs who ask the managers of their pension funds to vote "correctly."

These suggestions are well intentioned, but they miss a very important point. The problem is that in many respects, shareholders resemble other large, dispersed groups, such as factory workers, taxpayers, and farmers. There is a common interest that argues for higher wages, a cleaner environment, or higher farm prices, as the case may be. But if the resolution depends on individual action and exhortation, nothing happens. Each farmer, for example, keeps planting as large a crop as possible, even though the common interest lies in reducing output. Like former President Ford's WIN buttons—"whip inflation now"—soft talk doesn't work. The benefits of curtailing farm production—what economists call a "collective good," in this case the higher crop prices—are available to all, including those who do not cut back their acreage. (Indeed, those who cheat may be twice blessed, having more to sell at higher prices.) Nor are prices affected by the decision of any given farmer. Each of them continues to plant the maximum, therefore, all the while hoping for laws that would require him to plant the minimum.

What is true of farmers is also true of the shareholders of a large public corporation when it comes to the messy, time-consuming, sometimes expensive chore of getting out the vote or otherwise taking an active role as watchdog. Money managers get new moneys by what they earn on the old, not by their willingness to be good corporate citizens at General Motors and General Electric. Even the relatively simple task of reading proxy statements and voting one's own shares is neglected. Banks assign the task to low-level employees who, as one bank officer wryly noted, still have time left for their regular duties as cashiers. Either coercion or some selective inducement is required.[9]

Coercion is probably what works best for farmers, and through the union or closed shop it provides the necessary discipline for unions, too. No one approves of coercion as such, and there has been a vigorous debate about right-to-work laws and the freedom of workers to choose for themselves whether to join a union. There are reasonable arguments against unions, but if one concludes that collective bargaining is useful and a lively labor movement desirable, then it is not a good argument that workers should be free to choose individually whether or not to belong. The issue, as Olson said, is more properly phrased as to whether "the results of the unions' activities justify the power that society has given them."[10] One cannot have both stable unions and "free choice," and the arguments for right-to-work laws tend merely to mask an underlying hostility to organized labor.

Buffett's proposed nontax tax is obviously coercive. Like the workers unwilling to pay their union dues voluntarily, money managers are unable to step out of the crowd, to make portfolio commitments that last even a year, without some assurance that others will be equally constrained. But there the similarity ends. The workers at a tire plant in Ohio are already a group.

Not so the shareholders, who without the Buffett tax are not yet a group that can be defined with any continuity. Six months from now, many of today's shareholders of, say, GM or GE will have changed places with each other. Some of what they learned at the first company will be useful at the next, but most of it will not. Different industries, different managements, different capital structures and accounting procedures. Much of what they learned is company-specific, and indeed knowing that they will soon move on, and knowing that they already own shares in three hundred other companies, it is difficult to invest very much in learning about any of them. It is as if the rubber workers in Ohio might tomorrow become auto workers in Michigan, and sometime not long after that, steel workers in Alabama. The contribution of the Buffett tax, therefore, is that it encourages more stable and enduring relationships between shareholders and companies. The weakness of it, taken alone, is that the economically rational bank will still be inclined to leave the proxy voting to a cashier.

The Buffett stick helps to create the group and give it continuity of interest, but only a carrot, some special incentive, will induce members to step forward and provide the necessary leadership for the rest. The Investor Responsibility Research Center, and individual funds, such as CREF, have tried to mobilize shareholder opinion, but in a large, latent group social pressures are not a sufficient catalyst.[11] It is true now, and it was equally true when shareholders traded at a more leisurely pace. For fifty years or more, scholars have argued eloquently against the tendency of investors who, having exercised great care when buying stocks and again when selling, unhappily suspend those critical judgments between times. The advice was sensible, but of course nothing came of it.

This supine attitude, this willingness to approve whatever proposals management submits, is of course the contradiction that lies at the root of some free-market economists' argument that shareholders are free to abandon even their most fundamental rights, if only they have the opportunity to vote on it. Rather than asking how such votes can yield uniformly affirmative results, they take these Iron Curtain plebiscites as if there had been paid proxy solicitors and cohesive action on both sides of the issues and not just on one, as if the issues had been framed and presented on a level playing field and not on a tilted one.

Mr. Georges' arrogance

One major hurdle is that the shareholders have never had access to the nominating procedures for directors or the proxy machinery, except by a we-they confrontation that fund managers are understandably reluctant to undertake. CREF's previously discussed proposal with respect to the International Paper poison pill was hardly a radical one, asking only that the shareholders be given the opportunity at some later date to vote on an antitakeover device that is of dubious value, except as a bargaining chip. But it provoked an arrogant, hostile response from John A. Georges, the CEO of the company, who seemed to resent CREF's efforts to force a shareholder vote "on a matter [which] the board has decided." He wrote to the CEOs of over three hundred other companies to ask that they "instruct" their pension fund managers to vote with him on the issue. Whatever their nominal or legal independence, pension fund managers are hard put to fend off such tactics. It is reported that pressure was also put on individual members of CREF's own board to withdraw the proposal, and a proxy soliciting firm that was interviewed was willing, but reluctant to act on CREF's behalf.

International Paper's hostility was really quite bizarre. Some governmental pension funds, it might be said, are managed with an eye to the press and for political advantage. But CREF, with a large portfolio, and a picture-perfect board, is not that. Relying on distinguished counsel, eschewing the use of proxy solicitors even in the face of Mr. Georges' hostility, CREF is about as respectably tweedy as it could be.

The episode at International Paper was not unique. Numbers of bank trust departments and insurance companies report having encountered similar threats. Even without overt pressure, there is a strong temptation for financial institutions not to tempt the fates.[12] In the case of Rockwell International, however, there was a particularly odd twist. The CEO requested that his counterparts at other companies instruct their pension managers to vote their shares of Rockwell International at the 1987 annual meeting in favor of a dual class voting structure, one that would thereafter restrict voting rights. If approved, the new structure would make any such further requests unnecessary.

The grievance procedures that unions long ago won for their members do not yet exist in anything like adequate form for shareholders. Shareholders, relying on the Wall Street Rule, have chosen to quit instead of speak out. Relying on exit, they have used voice mechanisms so rarely that the necessary dialogue has yet to develop. The place and process for it do not exist. On the few occasions they they do speak up, shareholders somehow pick on ephemeral issues, such as a poison pill, rather than on more fundamental aspects of corporate structure, such as the right of shareholders to approve substantial business acquisitions or new stock issues. They seem to care only about issues that affect current market values.

Even the most responsible, least demagogic of shareholders, such as CREF, are greeted by a heavy-handed response, as if they have no right to ask for a shareholder review of that which the directors have once addressed. Mr. Georges' insistence on the finality of directors' decisions is consistent with a nominating procedure that is an almost entirely closed affair. He probably had forgotten that it was the shareholders who had elected those directors, but given the election practices that have evolved over the years, the oversight was understandable.

Shareholder nominated directors:

the proposal

Against that background, the proposal is that there be given to shareholders the exclusive right to nominate, separately from the nomination of directors generally, a significant but still minority number of additional directors, e.g., 20–25 percent of the board. Specifically, in addition to management's slate of candidates for the usual number of directors, shareholders should be allowed to elect a minimum of two directors out of a short but separate list of candidates, appearing in the same proxy statement. *This second group of candidates, however, is to be nominated not in the customary fashion, not by the incumbent board of directors, but by shareholders directly.* The list of candidates would consist of those with the most nominating votes and would contain perhaps two times as many candidates as the number of seats to be filled. Shareholder nominated directors would have the same duties and rights as the rest. The process mimics in a sense the long-standing New York Stock Exchange requirement that the board include independent directors, but it takes the concept of independence one step further back in the process. Independence of management would mean something more than not being either on the company payroll, its New York lawyer or the like. Since nomination has until now been tantamount to election, it is intended, with respect to a minority of directors, that directors be selected by the shareholders in substance as well as form, and that they owe their positions to persons and organizations whose stock ownership is substantial. (This new class of directors might be thought of as being "very independent" directors.)

A somewhat similar proposal for shareholder nominated directors was made thirty-five years ago,[13] but it was much less feasible then. Now, with institutional investors owning 50 percent and more of many companies, it should be fairly easy to open up the nomination process, without fear that it will somehow be trivialized by corporate gadflies and others whose interests may be primarily personal, social, or political—or anything other than the inherent profitability of the venture. Thus the proposal is not intended to give representation to labor or to so-called public interest groups. The process is frankly designed to encourage the election of candidates nominated by major institutions. CREF, for example, owned more than $70 million, about 1.5 percent, of International Paper common stock. Whatever might be said about perennial gadflies, CREF and others like it are not that.

Why not encourage institutional investors to participate in corporate governance before the event rather than voting with their feet after? In a sense the prevailing criticism by shareholders and management of each other is correct in both directions. Shareholders have gotten little respect, but they haven't deserved much. Executives talk of a responsibility to other interest groups—the workers, the community, and so on—to escape what they see as the short-term, stock price obsession of most investors. Provide a bridge between owners and managers, and it just might turn a we-they conflict into a continuing dialogue about how best to satisfy the interests of both. Not that the conflicts will disappear. In mature companies, for example, shareholders almost surely are seeking higher payouts than managers would prefer. But the boardroom is the appropriate place to work it out.

Structured dissent

The potential benefits would run to managers as well as shareholders. It may be that at General Motors, the personal chemistry between H. Ross Perot, the director who owned a huge amount of company stock, and the CEO was simply too corrosive, and one of them had to leave. But Perot, who resigned, was in some respects just the sort of investor-director for whom we are looking, one who walked into showrooms, kicked the tires, and asked tough questions. One of the weaknesses of the American public corporation is that we have never developed very well what sociologist James S. Coleman has called "structured dissent." Within the company, some CEOs encourage it, but others merely pay it lip service; and employees, never completely sure which camp their own CEO falls in, play it safe. Presidents and chairmen have such complete power to make and defeat the careers of their subordinates that dissent is muted. At the board level, some directors speak up, but many do not. Not enough time, not enough information, emotionally too identified to be critical, many boards tend to be much too permissive. The CEOs who most need a loyal thorn in their sides are least likely to have one.

The purpose of the present proposal is not to unseat corporate executives. They would still make the decisions, they would still frame the issues that go to the board, and they would still draw on the loyalties that develop over years of collaborative effort. But there is something to be learned from the consensus-building ethic of the Japanese, or the patterns of cross-ownership by which the *keiretsu,* an interlocking group of companies, provide for each other the institutionalized oversight and participation to which Coleman was referring. IBM for a time owned a substantial stake in Rolm, but then opted to buy the balance. Instances where otherwise independent firms own substantial minority stakes in one another for a significant period of time are remarkably rare in the United States. The present proposal, for directors who are selected as well as elected by shareholders, seeks to create some such continuing, unconfrontational channels by which the owners of the business communicate with the managers.

David A. Walker, an executive director of the Bank of England, put it well:

> The point is obvious enough that a major investor cannot take a mature view about the future of a company unless he has some first-hand knowledge of the quality of the board. . . . Equally, it is very unsatisfactory for a board to labour under the impression that major shareholders would not support long-term projects when the matter has not been discussed with them.[14]

The merchant bank analogy

Shareholder nominated directors would resemble in some respects the influence exercised over German corporations by the major banks of that country. Because West Germany does not have restrictions such as those in the Glass-Steagall Act, banks are able to combine their lending functions with the ownership of corporate shares. The banks sometimes control quite large blocks of stock and are able to put representatives on the boards of major corporations. Looking at the power exercised by American corporate managers, largely free of internal accountability, it is tempting to see something of value in a merchant banking system, where power is in such "responsible" hands. If the company slides too far down, if management is weak, if capital is being wasted, the banker, and the directors through whom he acts, are in a position to do something about it informally and at low cost. That was the positive side, after all, of the role of J. P. Morgan, George F. Baker of First National Bank and a few others who, working in close contact with one another, so largely shaped the structure of American industry in the late nineteenth and early twentieth centuries.

Merchant bankers have not been part of the American industrial and financial culture for many years, and they raise troublesome questions about concentration of power and other potential abuses. There was a negative side to the Money Trust that Morgan built. The closest thing we have seen to a Morgan in recent years is Kohlberg, Kravis & Roberts, the most important of the firms specializing in leveraged buyouts. The firm puts together large, complex companies, financing, and people in ways that Morgan would have admired, and it then fills a supervisory role—not managerial, but at times intervening a good deal more aggressively than the ordinary director—that Morgan would have recognized. The difference, however, is that most of these private companies are soon sold off or they go public, and in either case KKR's role is soon diluted.

Perhaps the pattern will change, but until now they have been more eager to get good prices than to amass power.

The role of the institutional investor

With the growth in professionally managed funds, it may now be feasible to have some of what Morgan contributed, without the loss of competition and other drawbacks of a Morgan. Being a minority on the corporate board, the shareholder nominated directors would not be able to replace corporate officers or exercise control as a merchant bank might do, but they would have the power to shape opinion on the board and to act as a catalyst. Over half the directors of large public corporations are outsiders. As anyone familiar with boards of directors can attest, these independent directors, each of whom owns the obligatory 100 shares of stock and sometimes a bit more, tend to listen carefully when the fellow who owns all those "tickets"—786,214 shares of International Paper common stock, in the case of CREF—does the speaking. The more the board listens, and the more influence a shareholder nominated director acquires, the less the temptation for an investor to sell the company's stock. The savings in trading costs alone would exceed by far the direct and indirect expenses of the additional balloting.

But more than any out-of-pocket savings, there is a decent possibility here of stimulating a change in culture and behavior. By their participation in corporate affairs, by increased voice and loyalty, institutions may begin to reshape their investment decisions in ways that in time would alter the attitude and conventions of investment management. Money managers, able to place their candidates on this or that board, may actually become interested in the companies they own. They may begin to act more as owners of a business, in part because they would be constrained by the nontax tax, and in part because they would begin to develop that better understanding of particular companies that comes only with time and commitment. (Intimacy sometimes breeds something better than contempt.) Better understanding means better knowledge of problems as well as strengths, but it is a curious commentary on the trader's mentality that he continually seeks out the risks and problems of the company that he does not yet know.

Ultimately we should be seeking something more than a police officer on the corner. The discourse on corporate governance in the United States tends to rely on such concepts as monitoring, supervision, and oversight, all of which are relatively shallow. The discussion of what role shareholders might play has not gone beyond that, because at least in the American context and culture, with its intense reliance on agency and market theory, there has been little chance of something better and richer. It is not true elsewhere. As Hudlund notes, Japan, Germany, and Sweden have developed "interpersonal networks" and solutions that are deeper than the level of a proxy statement. In Sweden, for example, "people often talk about 'owner responsibility' (ägaransvar), and this includes *much* more than overseeing managers."[15] There is a very reasonable argument, therefore, that the proposal made here is much too modest, and that investors should be looking for more than merely a 20–25 percent representation on the board. It is a reasonable suggestion, but it overlooks the cultural factors that eventually win out over bright new mechanisms. The fact is that in the American context there is no recent experience whatever in a useful exchange of views between owners and managers. A confrontational attitude is still the prototype, and changing it will take time.

SHAREHOLDER NOMINATED DIRECTORS: POTENTIAL PITFALLS

There are a number of significant issues raised by this proposal for shareholder nominated directors, but two are particularly important. The first is whether institutions would respond to the opportunity, whether the carrot is large enough to shake investors out of their apathy. CREF's holdings at International Paper were substantial enough that its designee would almost surely have been one of the nominees to appear in the proxy material, with a strong chance for election. The question is whether CREF—and others like it—would be interested enough to take the opportunity, now that it could gain a seat in the boardroom without a bruising fight. The singular aspect of what CREF did at the International Paper annual meeting in 1987 was to breach the Wall Street Rule, to speak to its fellow shareholders. But it spoke only with respect to the rights of shareholders to sell their shares with as little interference as possible, in short, only with respect to issues affecting current market prices. It is difficult to infer from that any great interest in sitting on boards and getting their hands onto more complicated issues. What is good for investors may not, after all, be good for money managers.

The shareholder nominated director proposal is frankly in the nature of an experiment for which there are no precedents. Pickens and others have been complaining about shareholder rights, but he studiously forgets that in the long run one cannot have power without responsibility.

Graham and Dodd understood it better. They closed the relevant portion of each of the last two editions of *Security Analysis* with a plea that investors begin to act like owners of a business:

> But if the stockholder is to regard himself as a continuing part-owner of the business in which he has placed his money, he must be ready at times to act like a true owner and to make the decisions associated with ownership. If he wants his interests fully protected he must be willing to do something on his own to protect them. This requires a modest amount of initiative and judgment. It is not beyond the competence of American investors. . . .[16]

The difficulty is that investors have no experience acting as the owners of a business, and any proposal along those lines is necessarily experimental. Will they respond at all, and if so, will they respond in collaborative fashion or will each of them go it alone? Might some few respond so vigorously that they would be able to place representatives on so many boards as to raise questions about conflicts of interest and competence? One suspects that groups with common ties would form to assure the nomination of candidates acceptable to the group, sometimes with such substantial support that nomination would be tantamount to election. If investors thus began to act like owners of a business, the managers might then begin to treat them as such, rather than as officious meddlers. For a variety of reasons, J. P. Morgan was treated with plenty of respect, but since his day we have not seen public shareholders who, even through surrogates such as Morgan, took an active interest. It's new ground. The guess is that for appropriate reasons of prestige, power, and peer group pressure, the institutions would slowly but surely take advantage of the opportunity to move from the outside to the inside. But it is only a guess.

Conflicts of interest and potential lawsuits

In the wake of the recent insider trading disclosures, there may be concern that if institutions were to nominate directors, they would be increasing their exposure to liability. If correct, or even if perceived as correct, the proposed election procedures would not achieve much. But while money managers do not see themselves as being paid to take risks, it should be said that the risks here are relatively modest, and the concern is partly a product of inexperience. There are for most directors only a few days a year, if any, that they are privy to material inside information of the kind that raises issues under the law. Thousands of directors live comfortably with those restrictions, partly because day to day there is no issue and partly because practices have developed to avoid even the suspicion of taint. (For example, the better practice is not to trade for forty-eight hours or so after the release of the quarterly earnings so as not to jump the gun.) Second, it ought to be at least as possible for investors to develop procedures like the Chinese Wall of investment bankers so that the information a director receives at board meetings does not become water fountain gossip back at the mutual fund offices. Third, it would always be available to investors to nominate business school deans, security analysts, industry specialists, and others who could represent shareholder interests effectively but whose knowledge would not be imputed to the investor.

In the present climate it may be too much to expect that we can persuade institutional investors to ignore the risks of litigation. The perception of risk has far outrun the reality, but it is the perception with which we would have to deal. And those lawsuits are troublesome even when they are baseless. Ultimately, some statutory or regulatory changes might be needed to assure investors that the knowledge of a designated director is not to be casually imputed to those who nominated him.

Maintaining the independence of these new directors

A second major concern is that some corporate managers might try to subvert the new process to assure the election of shareholder nominated directors who meet their definition of congeniality. It could be achieved in a variety of ways, such as by pressuring institutional investors to vote ''correctly,'' or one step better, by asking one or more of them to nominate ''congenial'' candidates in the first place. The issue is complex, but if it turns out that the ''very independent'' directors are no more independent than the rest, if management controls or even substantially influences the nomination of these directors, too, there is not much point to the proposal.

To preserve the independence of these newly minted directorships, it might be enough to require very complete disclosure in the proxy material of what management has done to promote its favored candidates. In theory, disclosure would put the shareholders generally on notice that some of the shareholder nominated directors are ''tainted''—or blessed, depending on the point of view—by association with management. They could then vote their choice, knowing that management had sponsored this or that nominee. The difficulty with disclosure as the primary solution, however, is that it supposes that the election process is not as tilted as it is, by management's control of the proxy machinery, by the rational apathy of shareholders, and by the willingness of at least some managers to manipulate the web of corporate relations and dealings.

In the final analysis, there seems to be no very good reason why, if management already controls the nomination, and in practice the election, of ten directors, it should be allowed to exert much influence on the election of the remaining two or three. If responsible institutional investors have to fight their way onto the board, nothing has been gained. The question, then, is whether, in the process by which those remaining two or three directors are chosen, it is permissible to gag management. In some broad sense of free speech, obviously it is not. Corporate officers are not disabled from speaking up. We sometimes forget, however, that "management's" proxy statement does not really belong to management, and that being a corporate resource, paid for with corporate funds, the rules can be changed. The federal proxy rules already invite a good deal of flexibility. If necessary, the rules might be changed so that management, to keep its privileged access to the corporate proxy machinery, would have to agree to maintain a decent neutrality with respect to the nomination and election of the shareholder nominated directors.

Managers might welcome this new class of independent directors. Whether the issue is a proposed business acquisition or the appointment of a special litigation committee to consider a threatened shareholder suit, the process gains legitimacy by having the formal approval or participation of a director who realistically owes his election to someone other than management. But they might not welcome it. It is fair to assume that executive compensation, on which there are now no effective restraints, would in time come under much closer scrutiny. The same is true of those once-in-a-lifetime opportunities to take a company private. There is legitimacy, it is true, in having on one's board these very independent directors, but not many of us go to bed at night thirsting for legitimacy. The tenure of some CEOs is painfully short, often a reward for years of loyal service; and dissent, no matter how "structured," might not seem the most agreeable way to spend it.

The two proposals—a nontax tax and shareholder nominated directors—are modest in their design, and yet it is not easy to feel confident that they will work. They are intended, first, to force investors to think more like part-owners of a business in the sense of buying only those stocks they are prepared to hold for a year, and second, to encourage at least some of them to become better informed and more directly involved in corporate affairs than they have ever been. Will they take the bait? The basis for optimism is that the bait has never been so good, nor have there been institutional investors of a kind and number so likely to take it. But even if investors mend their ways, the corporate managers will also have to take a longer view of what is good for the company and themselves. It is a breathtaking challenge, made only slightly less so by the absence of any good alternatives.

THE ROLE OF THE HOSTILE TENDER OFFER

We have tried to make takeover bids carry too much freight, too much of the job by which corporate managers are supervised, monitored, guided, and disciplined by shareholders. The real disservice of the Council of Economic Advisers and others like it is that by focusing our attention on this one remedy, they have deflected attention from all the others. Perhaps the temptation was understandable. After all, the issue of how best to create for shareholders an effective role in overseeing management had proven to be very stubborn, and any potentially workable solution was bound to be attractive. But when Marris and then Manne began to think about the disciplinary effects of takeovers, the number of such transactions was so small that what they were expessing was little more than a hope. We needed then as we do now to think more comprehensively, to understand that takeovers are by their nature expensive, drastic surgery, often conducted on patients who don't belong in surgery. The goal is how best to communicate with management and to influence its behavior. Takeovers do that, but it is not scripture that if the payout to shareholders is too low, if management is holding on to too much of the earnings and making bad acquisitions, the shareholders' only and best relief is to wait for a tender offer. If we can see that, rules for takeovers will be a good deal easier to work out. The issue is not whether takeovers are useful, but how useful they are and in what respects, and to what extent we ought to rely on takeovers to the exclusion of voting and other ongoing, internal mechanisms by which shareholders might participate.

There are some major difficulties with hostile tender offers as they now exist in American finance:

- *Tender offers don't work as well as advertised.* Some transactions are undoubtedly ''good'' for the economy, in that they displace some tired old managements or move assets to higher valued uses, but tender offers are just too complex a phenomenon for us to believe that there is a single key, such as improved efficiency. It defies common experience to think that the simple, happy explanations of the 1960s, when there was a mere trickle of takeovers, would still suffice when the faucet has been turned on full. Without reviewing again the data in chapter 5, it is worth recalling that there is no significant evidence that target companies *as a group* need this resuscitation. Common experience also tells us, and the data in chapter 5 again confirm, that we should not accept at face value the pretensions and motives of bidders who, without so much as a look at the targets' books, are willing to pay premiums of 80 percent over market. Complexities need to be explained, not explained away.

- *We have failed to distinguish the larger economic and social issues from questions of tactics and fairness.* As a result, a variety of unnecessary abuses have crept into the process. Takeover proponents have argued for unrestricted tender offers, and that is essentially what we have. Two-tier bids, greenmail, bids without committed financing . . . almost anything goes. And these are matched by essentially unrestricted tactics by targets, such as poison pills, crown jewel lockups, and dual class voting stocks, that would have been unthinkable just a few years ago. Happily, greenmail and bids without financing are not intrinsic to tender offers, and it goes almost without saying that something more than the creative skills of Martin Lipton, who invented the poison pill, ought to constrain defensive tactics. A balance between bidders and targets could be maintained, if so desired, without including greenmail, poison pills, and the like.

- *The regulatory framework for tender offers is a mess.* A wispy little statute, the Williams Act, was passed more than twenty years ago. It regulates bidders only a wisp, targets virtually not at all, leaving the escalating conflicts to be worked out by judges who are properly reluctant, seeing what few and inadequate tools they have been given. No forum has been created where the necessary balance can be struck. No adequate administrative mechanism has been created that would permit the rules of the takeover game to be adjusted without an act of Congress. As the conflict intensified, everything became fodder. Ultimately, even long-standing, unquestioned rules of the New York Stock Exchange—such as those requiring that the public receive only fully voting shares and that shareholders have the opportunity to vote on the issuance of large new blocks of stock—were threatened, as the delicate balance between bidders and targets fell into the cracks between what was properly within the federal purview and what belonged to the states. No attempt was made to rationalize the two.

- *We have thoroughly confused the function of the public shareholder.* This is the most serious difficulty with tender offers, the one that permeates all the public debate. Pickens argues that the shareholders own the company and if they want to accept a premium offer, that is their right. Can that be? Modern corporations depend on the commitment of capital to such long-lived investments as plant, equipment, and oil exploration. Shareholders are free to play a short-term game, to think of stocks as highly liquid assets. Nothing wrong with that, so long as they are simply selling their shares to others who similarly intend only to sell to still others of like mind. Indeed that is, as we have seen, the genius of the stock market. It enables investors to rely on the trading market for the liquidity they need, even while the managers invest and reinvest capital and earnings according to the quite different timetable of the business. The terrible dilemma of takeovers, at least at the abundant rate we have been witnessing, is that they give to shareholders—the equity investors whose dollars were thought to have been the most firmly committed at the business level—a license to disinvest *collectively* as well as *individually.* As Scherer noted, "long-term resource commitments—the sine qua non for achieving real economic gains—become less secure and less subject to the pursuit of confident, steady-handed policies."[17] Given the almost total absence of any machinery for collective decision-making by shareholders, there is a fundamental flaw in the notion that they are wholly free to sell off the company and not just their shares individually. The dilemma is how to have those "confident, steady-handed policies" and takeover bids both—how to retain takeover bids for the inevitable contingencies without undermining the necessary conditions for the more ongoing real operating gains.

A legislative framework

There are solutions to many of the difficulties with tender offers, but no optimal solution. Optimally, the solution is to encourage those takeovers that are most likely to be consonant with improved efficiency, discourage those that are a product of financial speculation, all the while permitting target managers to build moats around the castle only insofar as comports with the best interests of the shareholders. The optimal solution is obviously an impossible one, even if the tactics were static, which they are not. The Delaware Supreme Court was able to identify Pickens as a speculator, but ordinarily it is not possible to screen the bidders with such easy confidence. About all that can be done is to raise the threshold for bidding to discourage those faint of heart and light of purse, in the hope that the bidders who do in fact know how to squeeze out of a target additional productivity or better asset allocations will not be deterred. What also can be done, when bids do emerge, is to encourage more open, competitive auctions in the reasonable expectation, basic to economic theory, that those who are willing to pay the highest price for the target will generally put its resources to the best use. But there is no test that would allow only "good" bids to hatch.

While the optimal solution continues to evade us, a good many relatively easy changes would go a long way toward curing the awesome defects in the present arrangement. Assuming that a nontax tax of the kind described earlier has been adopted, the problem of how to discourage those willing to take greenmail will have been largely, although not completely, solved. So too will the destabilizing impact of large scale arbitrage operations designed merely to put companies into play. In addition, such a tax would make it unnecessary to consider the various proposals for confining voting rights to those who have held their shares for some minimum period, such as six months, because all shareholders either would have held their shares that long or would intend to do so, which is almost as good.

Beyond that, the major legislative objectives on the bidding side of the process are not very complex. One objective is to preserve hostile tender offers, but to put a heavy chill on the purely financial incentives. *It is a terrible thing to see a well-managed company put into play.* It is terrible not only for that particular company, but also for the message that it gives to all the rest. The second objective is to make the bidding process more fair by minimizing what would otherwise be unfair, or at least unequal, treatment of target company shareholders. Fairness is not something that inheres in tender offers. By circumventing the target company board of directors, the bidder seeks to deal directly with a dispersed, disorganized group of shareholders. Such a process is vulnerable in a number of respects to results that are neither economically efficient nor fair.

Extend the minimum period for tender offers

Within that framework, there are a number of useful proposals that have already been made at congressional hearings and elsewhere. It is particularly important to extend the minimum period that a tender offer must remain open. It would permit target company executives to respond in a more considered fashion, saving them, and indirectly their shareholders, from the bad judgment and fatigue that come from sleeping on couches and floors. A statutory merger may take three to four months, but it has never been explained why the rules permit a hostile tender offer, made without warning, to terminate in twenty business days, i.e., three to four weeks. Bidders don't like the added time, but then bidders don't like competition. More time would mean a better auction and better prices for shareholders. A minimum period of ninety days, for example, would also allow sufficient time for targets to make the necessary SEC filings and to solicit proxies, if, for example, the company intends to issue a large block of new shares, sell off a crown jewel or effect any of the other changes covered in the proposal described in Chapter 6. Extending the duration of tender offers would also render unnecessary many of the state antitakeover statutes, that being their primary purpose.

The British experience is instructive. While the rules do not require it, offers generally remain open for nearly sixty days from the first mailing of the documents to the closing off of the bidding. Frequently, too, the bidder must, because of leaks or the like, announce its intentions even before the formal commencement of the offer, thus adding two to three weeks more, or a total of as much as seventy-five days. And the British do not have to cope with the delays inherent in our regulatory structure if the target decides to submit to shareholders a counterproposal.

Eliminate the conspiratorial bidding
and other useless practices

Other desirable changes, which need not detain us long, include (a) a requirement that bidders have in hand committed financing for the entire offer, and (b) earlier and more complete disclosure of bidders' stock accumulations and the secret formal or informal arrangements by which they may, in one fashion or another, have conspired to bid together. It would also be helpful if target company shareholders could *individually* reject a bid without being excluded from it in the event that a majority of the shareholders do indeed accept it. A number of suggestions to deal with this last problem have been made, mostly entailing a shareholder vote on the tender offer. But so long as bidders are paying premiums of 50 percent and more over market, a vote is an empty formality. This is why the state statutes mandating a shareholder vote are simply a device for delaying the bidder. In any event, the British have come up with a simple solution, by requiring in effect that offers that are accepted by more than 50 percent in interest of the shareholders must then be left open for a further fourteen days. This also provides protection for the "widows and orphans" who might otherwise be left out.

Insider trading

A good many bidders act as if the law permits them directly or indirectly to let dozens of prospective lenders know of their intentions, even the identity of the putative target, without making public disclosure. By putting each of the tippees on notice that the information is "confidential," the bidder and his banker have escaped responsibility for the inevitable leaks. Under American law that works, assuming that the bidder and his financiers have not crossed over some ill-defined line and formed a conspiracy of sorts. In this case, the British do much, much better. Under the City Code, an announcement is required when there is "an untoward movement" in the price of the target's shares, when "rumour and speculation" are rife and there is reason to believe that the potential offer is the cause, or when "discussions are about to be extended to include more than a very restricted number of people." Recently the Code was amended to require disclosure by those who own 1 percent or more of the shares of a company once it is involved in a takeover. We could do better, too. If 100 people know about the bidder's intentions, we might as well let 100,000 know, and that would solve the problem of insider trading. The prohibition against insider trading is sometimes described as one of "abstain or disclose," and it is easy enough to require disclosure. True, the bidder's plans might have to be revealed earlier than he would like, but that would be of concern only to those eager to favor initial bidders.

Partial bids

Apart from a nontax tax and extending the minimum period for a tender offer, the most significant improvement would be a rule requiring that bidders who accumulate more than 15 percent of a target's shares shall promptly bid for all the rest at a single, no less favorable price. The exact figure would depend on the level at which one believes that the balance of control tips, but 15 percent seems about right. (There would be some exceptions to such a rule, of course—for example in the case of stock purchases approved by the target. There is no reason to forbid IBM from owning 25 percent of a Rolm, as part of a pattern of investment and technical exchange and cooperation.) Such a rule would solve many of the problems growing out of Congress's failure to define a tender offer, and it would also be conducive to bids that are fair and soundly financed. It would eliminate front-end loaded and other partial bids. If coupled with a requirement of a cash alternative, such as the British have, it would remove the otherwise great temptation to use the proposed ninety-day minimum offer period as an occasion to switch from cash tender offers to those payable with newly issued, speculative securities.

Speculative financing

Congress has not acted for almost twenty years, and there is little reason to believe that it can keep step with a market as dynamic as take-overs. A requirement of committed financing, for example, might promptly be overtaken by the growing practice by which investment bankers make "bridge loans" to their bidder-clients, the loans to be repaid, as in the Allied Stores case, out of a public offering shortly thereafter.

Junk bond financing is difficult to deal with in isolation. Attempts in the past by the Federal Reserve Board or Congress to limit speculative financing of mergers have failed and would probably fail again. The problem is partly a function of the ease with which any fixed restriction on the flow of funds can be circumvented. In one sense, the problem grows out of a corporate tax system that foolishly favors debt over equity financing, but that problem will not be solved any time soon. In any event, the problem is not on the issuers' side of the loans, where the regulation has been, but on the lenders'. Borrowers are always willing to take large amounts of money on inadequate security, and why not? What needs further examination is why the lenders have become so accommodating.

While takeover-related debt is a concern, it is only a part of the larger concern about a banking system that in recent years has stumbled on loans for less-developed countries, the oil industry, and real estate. Much of the explanation lies in a deregulated banking environment that has created enormous pressure to find earnings to offset a much higher and more volatile cost of funds. Having found higher yield, less creditworthy sources of income, the banks also discovered new "securitized" markets, which permit banks to convert loans into marketable securities that can then be repackaged and sold off. In effect, the banks, by securitizing their loan portfolios, are able to free up their capital and, just as importantly, they no longer have the same concern over the borrowers' longer-term creditworthiness or the value of their collateral. Like any other merchant, a banker's focus is simply on the spread between the current cost of his inventory—in this case, money from deposits or other sources—and the price at which he can "sell" the money as loans that will leave the store, just as any other merchant's inventory does. The old-fashioned, flinty-eyed banker is a relic of Jimmy Stewart movies. With consequences that we will not fully understand until the business cycle has come full circle, banks are no longer performing their traditional role as guardians of the nation's credit.

Another part of the explanation is that other financial intermediaries, such as insurance companies and mutual funds, have also found it profitable to adopt an extremely short-term horizon on the bonds and other "high yield" loans in their portfolios. The accounting earnings may be satisfactory, but they are suspect because often the borrowers are not obligated to make substantial payments until much later.

What is surprising is how little of these junk securities have been bought directly by individuals—as distinguished from savings institutions, mutual funds and insurance companies. A closer look than the SEC and other federal agencies have been willing to take might have disclosed some serious market imperfections and externalities, as economists say. Translation: some very heavy losses may fall not just on the dealers in junk, but on a largely unsuspecting public or, through federal bailouts, on all of us.

The rhetoric of free markets

These limitations on bidders may smack of disrespect for free markets. The short answer, perhaps, is that no one cares much for truly free markets. The markets we prefer we then designate as free. (Sometimes that is expressed as "believing is seeing.")[18] A model or free market would include, for example, large numbers of buyers and sellers. Yet when the Williams Act rules were modified to encourage competition, by extending the minimum waiting period to twenty business days, many takeover proponents objected. They want the initial bidders to be able to capture targets for less than fair market value. Truly free markets are as scarce as hen's teeth. One can talk of a "market for corporate control" in which managers compete on a level playing field, but the tax structure, the state corporation laws, the rational apathy of dispersed shareholders, speculative influences in the stock market, and other factors make it unlikely that takeovers operate in a state of nature.

Not only does a natural order not exist, but in transactions such as these it is unattainable, and if attainable, undesirable. Individual self-interest does not *necessarily* operate in the common or public interest, and indeed as we have seen just a few pages back, sometimes it does not necessarily operate even in the interest of the individual, if that is defined properly. The present task, then, is to see in what ways the legal and institutional framework can be structured so that competition and individual efforts can work effectively as an instrument of control. By all means, that task should be approached with humility. In the case of takeovers, for example, we surely do not want government to set prices. But that is a far cry from saying that society has no legitimate interest in the legal and market framework within which those transactions occur.

Defensive tactics

Turning to the target side of the ledger, some defensive tactics are a good deal easier to deal with than others. Loosely called financial defenses, these are the crown jewel lockups, poison pills, and other exotically labeled tactics by which the target company seeks to issue or buy its own shares or other securities, or to trade in corporate assets, its own or someone else's. There is no hard and fast rule about these transactions. Some of them may indeed be desirable, although under the circumstances management's motivations—and the likelihood of the company's selling too cheap or buying too dear—are worrisome. The solution suggested in chapter 6 was to require that any material transactions of this kind, in the face of a pending or threatened tender offer, be submitted to shareholders for approval. To judge by the British experience, such a solution would work well. Management would keep the all-important right to pick and choose its response to the tender offer. It would lose only the right to act unilaterally, and even then it would need to consult shareholders only in those cases where the defense might alter significantly the nature or value of the shareholders' investment.

There is, to be sure, a question of how diligently the shareholders would exercise this veto power. After all, shareholders have been approving a variety of shark repellents, even in the face of increased activism by some institutions. Why would the rational apathy, the ignorance and indifference, that infect so much of shareholder voting elsewhere not operate when a Marshall Field proposes to buy ''dog'' stores or a Gillette asks to buy back shares held by a raider?

In the first place, shareholders would have the benefit of much more timely and complete disclosure about these transactions, and that alone would help discipline managers. But beyond mere disclosure, there is every reason to believe that shareholders would be more vigorous in voting on shark repellents that might deprive them of a then *pending offer* to pay a premium on their shares of 50 percent or more. With so much money on the table, a tender offer commands attention, vitiating the ignorance that is the keystone of shareholder indifference.

There is disclosure even now, of course, in the proxy materials for the various antitakeover proposals made routinely at a time when *no offer* is pending. But it is disclosure of a very abstract, conjectural sort, without names and numbers. It is disclosure of the loss of a potential opportunity, at some unknown time—in short, a remote possibility of the kind that an economically "rational" investor might not even bother to read. Or if he did, he might discount it to a present value of little consequence to himself, particularly if, like the average investor, he does not expect to own the stock for very long.

CEOs, such as Mr. Georges, might still be able to use the old-boy network in the manipulative fashion observed earlier in this chapter so that numbers of institutional investors, whatever their inclinations, might not be free to vote on the merits. But if lots of money turns on the vote, and if the third-party bid is clearly superior, it is going to be a long, hard pull for Mr. Georges, much harder than the vote-in-a-vacuum that he won on a poison pill of no present significance.

FICTIONS AND MORE FICTIONS

Surely no one has failed to notice that in hostile tender offers, the exclusive concern of state legislatures has been to help build a moat around the castle. Indeed, it would be rather silly for Delaware to legislate away poison pills, unless New York did, and none of the states has indicated any interest in a commission that could act jointly. All proposals for restricting poison pills, greenmail, and other target company maneuvers, therefore, have been made at the national level. The particular tools vary. In the case of golden parachutes, it was the Internal Revenue Code. By limiting the tax deduction, Congress sought to set a ceiling on the payments. In the debate on dual class voting stock, it has been the rules of the New York Stock Exchange and other major trading markets. For greenmail and scorched earth tactics, it has been a series of proposed amendments to the Williams Act. But whatever the device, it has been recognized that if the goal is clear, if the time for experimentation has passed, then the solution should not depend on local options.

Because of pressures to maintain the traditional respect that Congress pays to states' rights, some fictions had to be developed. On the one share, one vote issue, for example, the fiction was maintained for a long time that the National Association of Securities Dealers and the stock exchanges might enter into a voluntary agreement, an agreement that would be blessed by the SEC but would not otherwise be "tainted" by federal action. Another, even less workable fiction is that Congress should prohibit objectionable defensive tactics if they are adopted during the pendency of an actual or threatened takeover, but not if adopted beforehand. Fearing to be seen as intruding on managerial decisions except in the context of an immediate takeover, bills have been introduced, such as H.R. 2172 in the 1st Session of the 100th Congress, which would forbid golden parachutes and poison pills only if first adopted by a target board *after* a hostile bid has emerged. Needless to say, the standard advice of takeover defense lawyers to their clients is that earlier is better, and the authors of the bill undoubtedly knew that these proposed provisions would have no effect. But they were impaled on the fiction.

Still another, and perhaps the most dubious, of these fictions is the assumption that takeovers are the only problem that Congress needs to address. Why does Congress stop at the water's edge? It is takeovers that raised the issue of one share, one vote. But the public's right to vote has profound implications for public corporations year in, year out, in a variety of ways having nothing to do with tender offers. The same is true of golden parachutes, those multimillion-dollar payments that ease the pain for executives confronted with a hostile bid. Some of the payments are a function of takeovers, but increasingly they have become just the tip of the iceberg of routine compensation packages that are equally inflated. (It was recently disclosed that the former chairman of E. F. Hutton, who left under pressure, received a one-time payment of $4 million on retirement. In addition, he was to receive consulting fees of $3.5 million, and his pension was increased from $185,000 annually to $650,000.[19] One can only guess what the payments might have been if there had been less criticism of his performance.) And the same is true of greenmail. The repurchase of blocks of stock from a single holder, without giving the public the opportunity either to participate or to approve, has always raised obviously troublesome conflict-of-interest questions. Wholly apart from takeovers, many countries largely or entirely forbid the practice.

Cary's Legacy

Under the pressure of takeovers, the pretense of a broadly workable federal-state distinction has largely broken down. The federal government cannot regulate only bidders' tactics, at least not without unfairly tipping the balance, and it cannot regulate targets' responses without intruding on matters traditionally reserved for the states. Nor is it feasible to differentiate that which takes place in the context of a tender offer from that which does not. Takeovers are the primary object of law reform at this time, but by probing deep into the structure of the modern American corporation, they force us to reexamine long-standing fictions and defects.

Bill Cary, who taught at Columbia Law School and was for several years chairman of the SEC, suggested that we retain the federal-state distinction but that we reshape it along the same lines as the rules of the major stock exchanges. The states and the exchanges should be free to compete for corporate business—for charters in one case, and for listings in the other—on whatever terms they see fit, subject only to certain minimum standards. As we saw in chapter 4, Cary's proposal provoked a howl of protest. The fear, of course, is that once its nose is in the state tent, the federal camel will choose to sleep there.

The "nose" of the federal proxy rules has been in the tent for some time. Nothing unseemly has happened, and much of what has been discussed here is little more than an extension of the proxy rules. What is the point of proxy rules designed to assure investors of a right to be informed of the issues and to mark their ballots "nay" as well as "yea," if their stock is nonvoting? What is the point of proxy rules if, under state law, management can issue bushels of new shares and effect fundamental changes in the character of the business without consulting shareholders?

It is enormously tempting to suggest that we pay off Delaware, which has held hostage our corporation laws for over half a century, and have done with it. The price would not be large. Delaware's total revenues from corporate franchise taxes were less than $120 million in fiscal 1986, or on average less than $3 million for each of the other forty-nine states.

Perhaps there is some value in keeping local values alive, but in this case the values are not local. Delaware is regulating businesses located in California, Illinois, and indirectly everywhere.

Except for the $3 million, Delaware has no interest in what happens to an Illinois-based company. Of course, for public companies, the issue is not so much where the factories or offices are located. Corporation laws don't regulate labor, environmental and other truly local concerns. In their important aspects, they deal principally with the rights and protections of shareholders who are the product of national (and international) securities markets and live almost everywhere but Delaware. And Delaware has no more substantive interest in the outcome of these matters than in whether an Illinois factory belches smoke.

Cary resisted the temptation to suggest a federal corporation law, and that is still good advice. His proposal was simply for a federal minimum standards act, applicable to all public corporations. (A copy of the relevant portion of his proposal is attached as an appendix to this chapter.) He anticipated marvelously many issues that were quite dormant in 1974 but have since come to the fore under the pressure of takeover tactics. He was concerned about setting fiduciary standards for insiders, nonvoting shares, and a requirement of more frequent shareholder approval of major corporate transactions. Cary described it as setting minimum standards for corporations, but perhaps it is better thought of as a bill of rights for shareholders that neither corporations nor states could eliminate. Cary obviously did not have to deal with such recent issues as management buyouts or the state antitakeover statutes, and one can question some aspects of his proposal. But he did not pretend, nor need we, that his suggestions offered a precise model.

Some such bill of rights is appropriate, and not just to solve the takeover riddle. Cary wasn't thinking about takeover reform. His proposal is an essential aspect of solving the riddle that transcends tender offers, the proper role of the public shareholder in the modern American corporation. Encourage shareholders to think of their stocks as part ownership of specific businesses by setting some modest restrictions on turnover to which they would easily adapt. Being a part-owner, behaving as much as possible like one of the twenty shareholders of a closely held corporation, would entail obligations and responsibilities—thus the obligation not to whip the trading of the stocks of American industry into a speculative froth that diverts talent and resources from the business of the nation. But since the money managers are driven largely by a fear of being out of step, the nontax tax that would enforce that obligation ought soon be seen as more of a benefit than a burden. Trading costs would dry up, and markets made up of investors rather than speculators ought to be much less subject to manic-depressive pricing.

The tax is only the first step, a necessary but not sufficient step. Shareholders should have the opportunity to communicate with and influence management in ways that would more nearly resemble those available to the twenty shareholders of a closely held business. Such opportunities can be created at the board level, without threatening managerial hegemony and efficiency. This can be done by creating for major shareholders the right to participate in board decisions, after management has formulated its plans but before they have been cast in concrete and announced to the world. As Cary suggested, these opportunities can also be created by enlarging the occasions on which the shareholders as a whole are consulted. There would still be a place in the scheme for takeovers, the market for corporate control, but as in most other organizations such all-or-nothing devices would be relegated to a lesser role, one of last resort after other remedies have failed. Such a revised structure would be consistent with a distinction to which Cary often referred, that between finance capitalism and industrial capitalism, between what enriches brokers and what enriches the nation.

Appendix

William L. Cary, "Federalism and Corporate Law: Reflections Upon Delaware," *Yale L. J.* 83 (1974): 663, 702 (footnotes omitted).

The proposal is to continue allowing companies to incorporate in the jurisdiction of their choosing but to remove much of the incentive to organize in Delaware or its rival states. Such companies, nevertheless, must be subject to the jurisdiction of the federal courts under certain general standards. To illustrate, some of the major provisions of such a federal statute might include (1) federal fiduciary standards with respect to directors and officers and controlling stockholders; (2) an "interested directors" provision prescribing fairness as a prerequisite to any transaction; (3) a requirement of certain uniform provisions to be incorporated in the certificate of incorporation: for example, authority to amend the by-laws, initiate corporate action, or draw up the agenda of shareholders' meetings shall not be vested exclusively in management; (4) a more frequent requirement of shareholder approval of corporate transactions, with limits placed upon the number of shares authorized at any one time; (5) abolition of nonvoting shares; (6) the scope of indemnification of directors specifically prescribed and made exclusive; (7) adoption of a long-arm provision comparable to Section 27 of the Securities Exchange Act to apply to all transactions within the corporate structure involving shareholders, directors, and officers.

Notes

CHAPTER 1: Investment Versus Speculation

1. Walter Werner, "Management, Stock Market and Corporate Reform: Berle and Means Reconsidered," *Colum. L. Rev.* 77 (1977): 388, 392.

2. Benjamin Graham and David L. Dodd, *Security Analysis* (New York: McGraw-Hill, 1st ed., 1934), 228, 305 306.

3. Edward S. Herman, *Corporate Control, Corporate Power* (New York: Cambridge Univ., 1981), 7.

4. Alfred D. Chandler, Jr., *The Visible Hand: The Managerial Revolution in American Business* (Cambridge: Belknap, 1977), 361.

5. Werner, "Management," 393.

6. Ibid., 392.

7. Andrew Sinclair, *Corsair* (Boston: Little, Brown, 1981), 164.

8. Graham and Dodd, *Security Analysis,* 4th ed., 213; Sinclair, *Corsair,* 126–130.

9. Arthur S. Dewing, *The Financial Policy of Corporations* (New York: Ronald, 1920), II–153.

10. Dewing, *Financial Policy,* 167.

11. Sereno S. Pratt, *The Work of Wall Street* (New York: Appleton, 1903), 42 (emphasis added).

12. Pratt, *Wall Street,* 45.

13. Edgar L. Smith, *Common Stocks as Long-term Investments* (New York: Macmillan, 1924).

14. Robert Sobel, *The Big Board: A History of the New York Stock Market* (New York: Free Press, 1965), 127.

15. Graham & Dodd, *Security Analysis,* 4th ed., 409–410.

16. Ibid., 410.

17. Ibid., 2d ed., 2–3.

18. Herman, *Corporate Control,* 119.

19. William Z. Ripley, *Main Street and Wall Street* (Boston: Little, Brown, 1927), 317.

20. Robert M. Blair-Smith and Leonard Helfenstein, "A Death Sentence or a New Lease on Life," *U. Pa. L. Rev.* 94 (1946): 148, 162 n.49.

21. Blair-Smith and Helfenstein, "A Death Sentence," n.15; Joel Seligman, *The Transformation of Wall Street: a history of the Securities and Exchange Commission and modern corporate finance* (Boston: Houghton Mifflin, 1982), 127.

22. Sobel, *The Big Board,* 142–43.

23. Sinclair, *Corsair,* 183.

24. Ibid., 155.

25. John M. Keynes, *Essays in Persuasion* (New York: Harcourt, Brace, 1932), 94.

26. Daniel Seligman, "Don't Fret About Program Trading," *Fortune* (Oct. 13, 1986): 87, 92.

27. SEC Advisory Committee on Tender Offers: *Report of Recommendations,* July 8, 1983 (separate statement of Easterbrook and Jarrell), 118 (multilith ed.).

28. John G. Cragg and Burton G. Malkiel, *Expectations and Share Prices* (Chicago: Univ. of Chicago Press, 1982).

29. Jack Hirshleifer, "The Private and Social Value of Information and the Reward to Inventive Activity," *Amer. Econ. Rev.* 61 (1971): 561.

30. Sobel, *The Big Board,* 244.

31. Graham and Dodd, *Security Analysis,* 2d ed., 2.

CHAPTER 2: Rule No. 2

1. Graham and Dodd, *Security Analysis,* 1st ed., 3.

2. Ibid., 12, 23.

3. Ibid., 4th ed., 41.

4. Ibid., 1st ed., 614.

5. Ibid., 370.

6. Graham and Dodd were not under any illusions on this point. They were aware that security analysis, as they defined it, was only for those with native ability, flair, and a "courageous, independent spirit"—an unlikely combination that would seem to bear out the 5 percent estimate in the text (Preface to *Security Analysis,* 3d ed., viii).

7. *The Collected Writings of John Maynard Keynes XII* (ed. Donald Moggridge) (New York: Macmillan, 1983), 103–104.

8. Ibid., 38–39.

9. Ibid., 58–59.

10. Ibid., 108.

11. Ibid., 56–57, 79–83. Even as to such details as second-grade bonds and new issues, Keynes and Graham and Dodd were like two (or three?) peas in a pod. Ibid., 58, 107; Graham and Dodd, *Security Analysis,* 1st ed., 50, 286.

12. Keynes, *Collected Writings,* 160–161.

13. Frank H. Knight, *Risk, Uncertainty and Profit* (Boston: Houghton Mifflin, 1921; rev. ed. 1971, Univ. of Chicago Press), 214, 226.

14. John M. Keynes, *The General Theory of Employment, Interest and Money* (1st ed. 1936; New York: Cambridge Univ. Press, 1973 ed.), 149.

15. Keynes, *General Theory,* 148.

16. John M. Keynes, *A Treatise on Probability* (Edinburgh: R. and R. Clark, 1921), 30.

17. Benjamin Graham, *The Intelligent Investor* (New York: Harper & Row, 4th rev. ed., 1973), 277, 283.

18. Dewing, *Financial Policy,* 167.

19. See, e.g., Jeffrey N. Gordon and Lewis A. Kornhauser, "Efficient Markets, Costly Information, and Securities Research," *N.Y.U. L. Rev.* 60 (1985): 761, 776–777.

20. Cragg and Malkiel, *Expectations,* 73–74.

21. Keynes, *General Theory,* 152.

22. Dennis C. Mueller, *Profits in the long run* (New York: Cambridge Univ. Press, 1986), 135–37.

23. Lawrence Lederman and Michael Goroff, "Recapitalization Transactions," *Rev. Sec. & Commod. Reg.* 19 (Nov. 19, 1986): 241, 245.

24. Graham and Dodd, *Security Analysis,* 1st ed., 493.

25. Ibid., 2d ed., 10–11.

26. Graham, *The Intelligent Investor,* 268 (prices not adjusted for stock splits).

27. Stephen Figlewski, "Market 'Efficiency' in a Market with Heterogenous Information," *J. Pol. Econ.* 86 (1978): 581.

28. Louis Lowenstein, "Pruning Deadwood in Hostile Takeovers: A Proposal for Legislation," *Colum. L. Rev.* 83 (1983): 249, 281, n.131.

29. Keynes, *General Theory,* 156.

30. Graham and Dodd, *Security Analysis,* 1st ed., 341.

31. Graham, *Intelligent Investor,* 1959 ed., 190–192.

32. Sanjoy Basu, "Investment Performance of Common Stocks in Relation to Their Price-Earnings Ratios: A Test of the Efficient Market Hypothesis," *J. Fin.* 32 (1977): 663; Sanjoy Basu, "The Relationship between Earnings Yield, Market Value and Return: Further Evidence," *J. of Fin. Econ.* 12 (1983): 129; David A. Goodman and John W. Peavy, "Industry Relative Price-Earnings Ratios as Indicators of Investment Returns," *Fin. An. J.,* July–Aug. 1983, 60.

33. Werner DeBondt and Richard Thaler, "Does the Stock Market Over-react?" *J. Fin.* 40 (1985): 793.

34. See, e.g., Burton G. Malkiel, *A Random Walk Down Wall Street* (New York: Norton, 2d college ed., 1981), 162–171; Robert J. Shiller, "Fashions, Fads and Bubbles in Financial Markets," in *Knights, Raiders and Targets: The Impact of the Hostile Takeover* (New York: Oxford Univ. Press, ed. John C. Coffee, Louis Lowenstein and Susan Rose-Ackerman, 1988) (forthcoming), ch. III; Graham, *Intelligent Investor,* 4th rev. ed., xvi.

35. *J. Fin.* 41 (1986): 529, 533 (emphasis added) (footnotes omitted).

CHAPTER 3: The Performance Game

1. SEC, *Staff Report on Corporate Accountability* (1980), 380–381.

2. Marshall E. Blume and Irwin Friend, *Recent and Prospective Trends in Institutional Ownership and Trading in Exchange and OTC Stocks* (Rodney White Center, Univ. of Pennsylvania, working paper, 1986) (Appendix) table 27.

3. "The Battle for Corporate Control," *Bus. Week* (May 18, 1987): 102, 104.

4. Ripley, *Main Street and Wall Street,* 107.

5. SEC, *5 Investment Trusts and Investment Companies* (1938), 371.

6. SEC, *Institutional Investor Study Report,* H.R. Doc. No. 64, 92d Cong., 1st Sess. (1971) 2530.

7. Ibid., 4.

8. *New York Stock Exchange Fact Book* (1986), 71.

9. Berkshire Hathaway Inc., *1981 Annual Report,* 51–53.

10. Source: CDA Investment Technologies, Inc.

11. Scott McMurray and Beatrice E. Garcia, "Regulators Brace for Wild Stock Swings," *Wall Street J.* Dec. 5, 1986, p. 6, col. 1.

12. Haim Levy, "The Capital Asset Pricing Model: Theory and Empiricism," *Econ. Journal* (Mar. 1983), 145.

13. *NYSE Fact Book* (1987), 17; CCH *Fed. Sec. L. Rep.* No. 1213 (Jan. 22, 1987), 12–13 (SEC Chairman J. Shad).

14. McMurray and Garcia, "Wild Stock Swings."

15. Goldman Sachs, *Anatomy of the World's Equity Markets* (Sept. 1986), table 1.8.

16. Source: Salomon Brothers, Inc., Jan. 1987.

17. Kenneth Gilpin, "Program Traders' Impact Seen Waning," *N. Y. Times,* Jan. 3, 1987, p. 30, col. 1.

18. *In the matter of Behel, Johnsen & Company,* 26 S.E.C. 163 (1947) (450 percent turnover in three years).

19. Max G. Ansbacher, *The New Stock Index Market* (New York: Walker, 1983), 24.

20. Goldman Sachs, *Creating synthetic futures with options* (Jan. 1985), 7.

21. "Great Wall St. Traders," *Hermes* (Colum. Bus. Schl., Spring 1986), VII (comments of Michael Steinhardt).

22. Letter to author from Mallory Factor Inc., Jan. 20, 1985.

23. John Pound and Robert J. Shiller, *Speculative Behavior of Institutional Investors* (manuscript, June 1986).

24. Ibid., 10.

25. Robert J. Shiller, "Do Stock Prices Move Too Much to be Justified by Subsequent Changes in Dividends?" *Am. Econ. Rev.* 71 (1981): 421. In a subsequent study, Shiller found standard deviations of about twice what they "should" be. See also Kenneth D. West, *Bubbles, Fads, and Stock Price Volatility Tests* (manuscript, Dec. 1987).

26. Warren Buffett, "The Superinvestors of Graham-and-Doddsville," *Hermes* (Colum. Bus. Schl., Fall 1984), 4.

27. Eugene Shahan, "Are Short-Term Performance and Value Investing Mutually Exclusive?" *Hermes* (Colum. Bus. Schl., Spring 1986), 26.

28. The returns average about 11.4 percent annually for the five-year periods, but for statistical reasons the average annual returns tend to exceed the compound annual returns.

29. James Tobin, "On the Efficiency of the Financial System," *Lloyds Bank Rev.* (July 1984): 1, 10.

30. Robert H. Jeffrey, "The Folly of Stock Market Timing," *Harv. Bus. Rev.* 64 (July–Aug. 1984): 102–103; Richard A. Ippolito and John A. Turner, *Turnover, Fees and Pension Plan Performance,* (manuscript, Feb. 1987), 7–8.

31. BNA, *Sec. Reg. L. Rep.* (Nov. 7, 1986), 1613 (Joseph Grundfest).

32. Tobin, "Financial System," 2.

33. Ibid., 14–15.

CHAPTER 4: Investors as Owners of a Business

1. F. M. Scherer, *The Ownership of U. S. Corporations* (manuscript, April 1987), 4.

2. William J. Baumol, *The Stock Market and Economic Efficiency* (New York: Fordham U. Press, 1965), 3–4 (quoting Fritz Machlup).

3. Cambridge: Harvard Univ. Press, 1965.

4. Adolf A. Berle and Gardiner C. Means, *The Modern Corporation and Private Property* (New York: Harcourt, Brace, rev. ed. 1967), 250.

5. See, e.g., Eugene F. Fama, "Agency Problems and the Theory of the Firm," *J. Pol. Econ.* 88 (1980): 288.

6. Daniel Fischel, "Organized Exchanges and the Regulation of Dual Class Common Stock," in *Knights, Raiders and Targets,* ch. XXXII.

7. Eugene F. Fama and Michael Jensen, "Separation of Ownership and Control," *J. L. & Econ.* 26 (1983): 294.

8. *Commentaries on Corporate Structure and Governance* (Phila.: Am. Law Inst.-Am., Bar Assn., ed. Donald Schwartz, 1979), 95 et seq.

9. Winthrop Knowlton and Ira M. Millstein, *Can the Board of Directors Help the American Corporation Earn the Immortality It Holds So Dear?* (manuscript, Apr. 1987), 42–43.

10. *Knights, Raiders and Targets,* ch. I (comments of Warren Buffett).

11. See, e.g., Henry G. Grabowski and Dennis C. Mueller, "Life-Cycle Effects on Corporate Returns on Retentions," *Rev. Econ. & Stat.* 57 (1975): 400; William J. Baumol, Peggy Heim, Burton Malkiel and Richard Quandt, "Earnings Retention, New Capital and the Growth of the Firm," *Rev. Econ. & Statistics* 52 (1970): 345; Baumol, Heim, Malkiel & Quandt, "Efficiency of Corporate Investment: Reply," *Rev. Econ. & Statistics* 55 (1973): 128; see generally John C. Coffee, "Shareholders versus Managers: The Strain in the Corporate Web," in *Knights, Raiders and Targets,* ch. VI.

12. Ripley, *Main Street and Wall Street,* 86.

13. Marshall E. Blume and Irwin Friend, *The Changing Role of the Individual Investor* (New York: Wiley, 1978), 207–208.

14. Ripley, *Main Street and Wall Street,* 203.

15. SEC Commissioner G. Purcell, Hearings, House Comm. on Interst. & For. Commerce, 77 Cong., 1st Sess., Pt. I (1941), 8.

16. Seligman, *Transformation of Wall Street,* 2.

17. John Brooks, *Once in Golconda* (New York: Harper & Row, 1969), 22–23.

18. Seligman, *Transformation of Wall Street,* 25.

19. Brooks, *Once in Golconda,* 67.

20. Seligman, *Transformation of Wall Street,* 25 (quoting Edmund Wilson).

21. Ibid., 24–31.

22. William Manchester, *The Glory and the Dream* (Boston: Little, Brown, 1973), 43–45.

23. Ibid., 17; Brooks, *Once in Golconda,* 66.

24. Seligman, *Transformation of Wall Street,* 71.

25. Irwin Friend, "Economic and Equity Aspects of Securities Regulation," in *Management Under Government Intervention: A View from Mount Scopus* (Greenwich: JAI Press, 1984) (Supp. 1), 31–58.

26. Manchester, *Glory and the Dream,* 72–78.

27. Seligman, *Transformation of Wall Street,* 76 n.11.

28. William O. Douglas, "Protecting the Investor," *Yale Review* 23 (1934): 521.

29. Seligman, *Transformation of Wall Street,* 87 n.61; Henry C. Simons, *Economic Policy for a Free Society* (Chicago: Univ. of Chicago Press, 1948), 58–60.

30. William L. Cary, "Federalism and Corporate Law: Reflections Upon Delaware," *Yale L. J.* 83 (1974): 663.

31. Ibid., 705.

32. Ibid., 701.

33. *Commentaries,* 319.

34. N.J. Stat. Ann. §14A, at x–xi (1969).

35. Seligman, *Transformation of Wall Street,* 536.

36. Note, "Law for Sale: A Study of the Delaware Corporation Law of 1967," *U. Pa. L. Rev.* 117 (1969): 861, 867.

37. Ibid., 888.

38. 488 A.2d 858 (Del. Supr. 1985).

39. "Bias in the Boardroom: Psychological Foundations and Legal Implications of Corporate Cohesion," *Law & Contemp. Prob.* 48 (1985): 83, 89.

40. BNA, *Sec. Reg. & L. Rep.* (Sept. 12, 1986), 1309 (comments of A. Gilchrist Sparks, III).

41. James J. Hanks, "State Legislative Responses to the Director Liability Crisis," *Rev. Sec. & Comm. Reg.* 20 (1987): 23.

42. Burroughs Corporation, proxy statement for Aug. 1986 meeting of shareholders.

43. Section 402 of the New York Business Corporation Law, as amended (1987).

44. Ralph K. Winter, "State Law, Shareholder Protection, and the Theory of the Corporation," *J. Legal Studies* 6 (1977): 251, 258.

45. Herbert A. Simon, *Administrative Behavior* (New York: Macmillan, 2d ed., 1957), 81.

46. Peter Dodd and Richard Leftwich, "The Market for Corporate Charters: 'Unhealthy Competition' versus Federal Regulation," *J. Bus.* 53 (1980): 259, 281.

47. See, e.g., Frank Easterbrook, "Managers' Discretion and Investors' Welfare: Theories and Evidence," *Del. J. Corp. L.* 9 (1984): 540, 550.

48. See *Medical Committee for Human Rights v. SEC,* 432 F. 2d 659, 676 (D. C. Cir. 1970), vacated as moot, 404 U. S. 403 (1971); Joel Seligman, "Stock Exchange Rules Affecting Takeovers and Control Transactions," in *Knights, Raiders and Targets,* ch. XXXI.

49. Mortimer M. Caplin, "Shareholder Nominations of Directors: A Program for Fair Corporate Suffrage," *Va. L. Rev.* 39 (1953): 141, 152; see also SEC, *Staff Report on Corporate Accountability,* 96th Cong. 2d Sess. (Sen. Comm. on Banking, Housing and Urban Affairs, 1980), A–36.

CHAPTER 5: Hostile Takeovers

1. Robin Marris, "A Model of the 'Managerial' Enterprise," *Quarterly J. of Econ.* 77 (May 1963): 185.

2. Henry G. Manne, "Mergers and the Market for Corporate Control," *J. Pol. Econ.* 73 (1965): 110, 112.

3. Henry J. Friendly, "Make Haste Slowly," in *Commentaries,* 525, 532.

4. Graham, *Intelligent Investor,* 4th rev. ed., 269.

5. Ibid., 269–270.

6. R. Duncan Luce and Howard Raiffa, *Games and Decisions* (New York: Wiley, 1958), 95.

7. Berle and Means, *Modern Corporation,* 251.

8. L. C. B. Gower, "Some Contrasts Between British and American Corporation Law," *Harv. L. Rev.* 69 (1956): 1369, 1396.

9. The Companies Act, 11 and 12 Geo. 6, §§209(1), 209(2) (1948).

10. See *Hanson Trust PLC v. ML SCM Acquisition Inc.,* 781 F.2d 264, 277 (2d Cir. 1986) (the "stockholders' fundamental right to make the 'decisions affecting [the] corporation's ultimate destiny.'''); *Norlin Corp. v. Rooney, Pace Inc.,* 744 F.2d 255, 258 (2d Cir. 1984).

11. *Council of Economic Advisers 1985 Annual Report,* 199; William J. Carney, "Fundamental Corporate Changes, Minority Shareholders and Business Purposes," *Am. Bar Found. Res. J.* (1980): 119–128; compare Frank Easterbrook and Daniel Fischel, "Corporate Control Transactions," *Yale L. J.* 91 (1982): 698, 708.

12. See e.g., Gregg A. Jarrell and Michael Bradley, "The Economic Effects of Federal and State Regulations of Cash Tender Offers," *J. L. & Econ.* 23 (1980): 381; Henry G. Manne, testimony before the Subcomm. on Telecomm. and Finance, Comm. on Energy and Commerce, U. S. House of Rep., Apr. 1, 1987.

13. Warren Law, "A corporation is more than its stock," *Harv. Bus. Rev.* 64 (May–June 1986): 80, 83.

14. Coffee, "Corporate Web."

15. Source: W. T. Grimm and Company.

16. Edward S. Herman and Louis Lowenstein, "The Efficiency Effects of Hostile Takeovers," in *Knights, Raiders and Targets,* ch. XIII.

17. Salomon Brothers Inc., *Prospects for Financial Markets in 1987* (1986), table 3c.

18. Source: Salomon Brothers Inc. (cited *Wall Street J.,* Jan. 2, 1987, p. 8b).

19. See Martin Neil Baily, "What Has Happened to Productivity Growth?" *Science* (Oct. 24, 1986): 441.

20. Herman and Lowenstein, "Hostile Takeovers"; see also Dennis C. Mueller, "Further Reflections on the Invisible-Hand Theorem," in *Economics in Disarray* (Oxford: Basil Blackwell, eds. Peter Wiles and Guy Routh, 1984), 159.

21. Touche Ross & Co., *The Effect of Mergers, Acquisitions, and Tender Offers on American Business: A Touche Ross Survey of Corporate Directors' Opinions* (1981), 12.

22. See Ellen B. Magenheim and Dennis C. Mueller, "On Measuring the Effect of Acquisitions on Acquiring Firm Shareholders, *or* Are Acquiring Firm Shareholders Better Off After an Acquisition Than They Were Before?" in *Knights, Raiders and Targets,* ch. XI.

23. Ibid.; see also Murray Weidenbaum and Stephen Vogt, "Takeovers and Stockholders: Winners and Losers," *Calif. Mgt. Rev.* 29 (1987): 157.

24. Richard S. Ruback, "Some Comments on the Sources of Takeover Gains," in *Knights, Raiders and Targets,* ch. XXI.

25. Michael Bradley and Gregg A. Jarrell, "Evidence on Gains from Mergers and Takeovers," in *Knights, Raiders and Targets,* ch. XV.

26. Ibid. See also Douglas H. Ginsburg and John F. Robinson, "The Case Against Federal Intervention in the Market for Corporate Control," *Brookings Rev.* (Winter/Spring 1986): 9.

27. Much of the data (and other data, too) are contained in Herman and Lowenstein, "Hostile Takeovers." Since writing that paper, the authors added data for an additional year, 1985, and for control groups and those new data are reflected in this book.

28. The 56 completed transactions grew out of hostile, unsolicited bids begun during the nine years 1975–1983, a period of rapidly growing activity. It did not matter that the winning bidder was a friendly, "white knight," so long as the initial bid was unsolicited and the target was acquired by some domestic company for which data were available in the COMPUSTAT data base maintained by Standard & Poor's. For purposes of comparability, foreign companies, as well as some others, such as banks and insurance and real estate companies, were excluded, but with these exceptions the H & L Study appears to have included all the major, hostile (as defined) takeovers begun in that nine-year period.

29. Herman and Lowenstein, "Hostile Takeovers"; see also Magenheim and Mueller, "Acquiring Firm Shareholders."

30. The data are shown on a weighted basis, meaning that the results are weighted by the total assets of each company in the group. (Ivac Corp. with total assets of $12 million thus counts less than another target, Conoco, with assets of $11 billion.) The effect is to tell less about individual companies but more about the overall economic impact of the process, which is, after all, what the debate has been about.

31. Michael C. Jensen, "How to Detect a Prime Takeover Target," *N.Y. Times,* Mar. 9, 1986, p. F3, col. 1.

32. Debt included the portion shown as current liabilities, which makes the ratios somewhat higher than those in other studies.

33. John Pound, *Are Takeover Targets Undervalued?* (Wash., D.C.: Investor Respons. Research Ctr., Jan. 1986).

34. "Life After Takeover," *J. Ind. Econ.* 36 (Sept. 1987) (forthcoming).

35. Pound, *Takeover Targets,* 30.

36. In 31 of the 56 takeovers (55 percent) the bidder had a better record than its particular target. The advantage was confined to the smaller targets, those of less economic importance.

37. Stephen A. Rhoades, *The Operating Performance of Acquired Firms in Banking before and after Acquisition* (Bd. Gov. Fed. Res. Sys., staff study 149, Apr. 1986).

38. Mueller, *Profits in the long run,* 220–221.

39. Comments at conference at Columbia University, Center for Law and Econ. Studies, Nov. 1985.

40. "Pruning Deadwood in Hostile Takeovers: A Proposal for Legislation," *Colum. L. Rev.* 83 (1983): 249, 306.

41. Graham and Dodd, *Security Analysis,* 3rd ed., 484–485 (footnote omitted).

42. Charles Steindel, "Tax Reform and the Merger and Acquisition Market: The Repeal of 'General Utilities,'" *Fed. Res. Bk. N. Y. Qtrly. Rev.* (Autumn 1986): 31, 32.

43. Ronald J. Gilson, Myron S. Scholes and Mark A. Wolfson, "Taxation and the Dynamics of Corporate Control: The Uncertain Case for Tax Motivated Acquisitions," in *Knights, Raiders and Targets,* ch. XVIII.

44. Until the law was further amended, tax lawyers were able to use a new loophole, known as mirror image liquidations, to avoid the impact of the repeal of *General Utilities.*

45. J. Elizabeth Callison, *An Analysis of Bid Premiums in Tender Offers for Forbes 500 Companies: 1979–1983* (manuscript, rev'd Nov. 1986): 16 (52 of 54 bids for cash).

46. Fed. Res. Sys., 12 C.F.R. Part 207 [Reg. G; Docket No. R-0562] Securities Credit by Persons Other Than Banks, Brokers, or Dealers; Purchase of Debt Securities to Finance Corporate Takeovers. Final interpretative rule.

47. Allied Stores Corporation, prospectus dated March 10, 1987.

48. SEC, Office of the Chief Economist, *Noninvestment Grade Debt as a Source of Tender Offer Financing* (June 20, 1986).

49. Prospectus, First Investors Fund for Income, Inc., Apr. 30, 1986, and accompanying literature; "What's under the rock?" *Forbes* (Feb. 23, 1987): 134 (insurance companies with 60–65 percent of assets in junk bonds and salesmen who claim not to know that).

50. Richard B. Schmitt and G. Christian Hill, "Bank American Directors' Decision on Bid May Create Dilemma for Adviser, Suitor," *Wall Street J.,* Nov. 3, 1986, p. 8, col. 1.

51. Malcolm S. Salter and Wolf A. Weinhold, "Corporate Takeovers: Financial Boom or Organizational Bust," in *Knights, Raiders and Targets,* ch. vii.

52. These concerns are the subject of a penetrating recent analysis by Andrei Shleifer and Lawrence H. Summers, "Breach of Trust in Hostile Take-overs," (Natl. Bur. Econ. Res., 1987).

53. Dan Dorfman, "The Intimidators," *New York* (Apr. 14, 1986): 29.

54. "Trump Ends His Struggle to Gain Control of Bally," *N.Y. Times,* Feb. 23, 1987, p. B2, col. 3; Laurie Cohen, "Bally to Buy Back Trump's Holding, Ending Bid Threat," *Wall Street J.,* Feb. 23, 1987, p. 2, col. 3.

55. Oliver E. Williamson, *Markets and Hierarchies* (New York: Free Press, 1975), 145–148.

56. Mueller, *Long Run,* 206.

57. Callison, *Analysis of Bid Premiums,* 17 (47 of 54 bids result in purchase by one or another of the bidders).

58. Martin Shubik, "Corporate Control, Efficient Markets, The Public Good, the Law and Economic Theory and Advice," in *Knights, Raiders and Targets,* ch. II.

59. Testimony of Louis Harris, House Commerce and Energy Committee, Subcommittee on Telecommunications and Finance, Apr. 1, 1987.

60. See note 30.

61. In the case of the 1980s transactions, adequate data for more than three years after the takeover are not yet available.

CHAPTER 6: Takeover Tactics

1. Exchange Act Release No. 16384, Nov. 29, 1979 [1979–1980 Transfer Binder] Fed. Sec. L. Rep. (CCH) ¶82,373.

2. *GAF Corp. v. Milstein,* 453 F.2d 709 (2d Cir. 1971), cert. denied, 406 U. S. 910 (1972).

3. *Gulf & Western Indus., Inc. v. Great Atlantic & Pacific Tea Co.,* 476 F.2d 687 (2d Cir. 1973).

4. *Wellman v. Dickinson,* 475 F. Supp. 783 (S.D.N.Y. 1979), aff'd 682 F.2d 355 (2d Cir. 1982), cert. denied, *Dickinson v. SEC,* 460 U. S. 1069 (1983).

5. "Marietta, Bendix 'Pac-Man' Tactics Cause Concern Among Merger Analysts," *Wall St. J.,* Sept. 24, 1982, p. 8, col. 1 (comment of Judge Young); see also *Hanson Trust PLC v. SCM Corp.,* 774 F.2d 47, 60 (2d Cir. 1985); *Northwest Indus., Inc. v. B. F. Goodrich Co.,* 301 F. Supp. 706, 713 (N.D. Ill. 1969).

6. Exchange Act Rel. No. 15548, Proposed Tender Offer Rules and Schedule, Feb. 5, 1979 [1979 Transfer Binder] Fed. Sec. L. Rep. (CCH) ¶81,935.

7. *Panter v. Marshall Field & Co.,* 486 F. Supp. 1168 (N.D. Ill. 1980), aff'd 646 F.2d 271 (7th Cir.), cert. denied, 454 U. S. 1092 (1981).

8. See, e.g., *Gearhart Indus., Inc. v. Smith Int'l, Inc.,* 741 F.2d 707 (5th Cir. 1984); *Treadway Cos. v. Care Corp.,* 638 F.2d 357 (2d Cir. 1980); *Carter Hawley Hale Stores, Inc. v. The Limited, Inc.,* 587 F. Supp. 246 (C.D. Cal. 1984).

9. See, e.g., *Whittaker Corp. v. Edgar,* 535 F. Supp. 933, 951 (N.D. Ill.), aff'd Nos. 82-13305, 82-1307 (7th Cir., Mar. 5, 1982).

10. *Panter,* 646 F.2d at 299 (Cudahy, J.).

11. See *Norlin Corp. v. Rooney, Pace Inc.,* 744 F.2d 255 (2d Cir. 1984); *Frantz Mfg. Co. v. EAC Indus.,* 501 A.2d 401 (Del. 1985).

12. *Unocal Corp. v. Mesa Petroleum Co.,* 493 A.2d 946 (Del. 1985).

13. See *Treadway Cos.,* 638 F.2d 357; *Carter Hawley Hale Stores, Inc.,* 587 F. Supp. 246.

14. See *Revlon, Inc. v. McAndrews & Forbes Holdings, Inc.,* 506 A.2d 173 (Del. 1986); *Hanson Trust PLC v. ML SCM Acquisition, Inc.,* 781 F.2d 264 (2d Cir. 1986).

15. *Revlon,* 506 A.2d 173.

16. See *Unocal Corp.,* 493 A.2d; *APL Corp. v. Johnson Controls, Inc.* No. 85-L-990 (E.D.N.Y. Mar. 25, 1985); see also Meredith M. Brown and Marc C. Cherno, ''The Business Judgment Rule,'' in *Ann. Inst. on Sec. Reg.* 17 (Prac. Law Inst. 1986).

17. See *Revlon,* 506 A.2d 173; *SCM,* 781 F.2d 264; *Norlin* 744 F.2d 255.

18. *Revlon,* 506 A.2d 173.

19. 500 A.2d 1346 (Del. 1985).

20. ''Concept Release on Takeovers and Contests for Corporate Control: Advance Notice of Possible Commission Actions,'' Exch. Act Rel. No. 23486, July 31, 1986, Fed. Sec. L. Rep. (CCH) ¶84,018.

21. Martin Lipton, *The SEC, the Poison Pill and Takeover Policy* (manuscript, Nov. 5, 1986), 4.

22. *Moran v. Household Int'l, Inc.,* 500 A.2d 1346.

23. *Dynamics Corp. of Am. v. CTS Corporation,* No. 86-C-1624 (N.D. Ill. April 17, 1986), aff'd 794 F.2d 250 (7th Cir. 1986), rev'd on other grds, 107 S. Ct. 1637 (1987).

24. *Unilever Acquisition Corp. v. Richardson-Vicks, Inc.,* 618 F. Supp. 407 (S.D.N.Y. 1985); *Asarco, Inc. v. M. R. H. Holmes A Court,* 611 F. Supp. 468 (D.N.J. 1985).

25. *Dynamics Corp.*, supra; *Amalgamated Sugar Co. v. NL Industries,* 644 F. Supp. 1229 (S.D.N.Y. 1986).

26. *Moran,* 500 A.2d 1346; *Revlon,* 506 A.2d 173.

27. *Edelman v. Phillips Petroleum Co.,* Del. Ch. C.A. No. 7899 (June 3, 1986), 16.

28. *Polk v. Good,* 507 A.2d 531 (Del. 1986).

29. *Whittaker Corp.,* 535 F. Supp. 933, 941; see also Robert Metz, "Brunswick's Bailout Plans," *N.Y. Times,* Mar. 6, 1982, p. D6, col. 3.

30. *Martin Marietta Corp. v. Bendix Corp.,* 549 F. Supp. 623, 625 (D. Md. 1982).

31. Testimony, Subcommittee on Telecommunications, Consumer Protection and Finance, House Comm. on Energy and Commerce, Hearings on Takeover Tactics and Pub. Policy, 98th Cong. 2d Sess., May 23, 1984 (Ser. No. 98-142), 345, 354.

32. Compare *Heckmann v. Ahmanson,* 214 Cal. Reptr. 177 (Cal. App. 2d Dist. 1985), with *Polk v. Good,* 507 A.2d 531. A recent decision suggests that Ohio as well as California may be an exception to the general rule. See *Samuel M. Feinberg Testamentary Trust v. Carter,* 652 F. Supp. 1066 (S.D.N.Y. 1987).

33. Compare *Whittaker,* 535 F. Supp. 933, with *Hanson Trust,* 781 F.2d 264.

34. 111 Cong. Rec. 28257 (1965).

35. Letter to the author from George P. Michaely, Jr., Sept. 15, 1983.

36. 113 Cong. Rec. 24664 (1967).

37. Testimony of Philip A. Loomis, Commissioner, SEC, Hearings on Regulation Under Federal Banking and Securities Laws of Persons Involved in Corporate Takeovers, Before the Senate Committee on Banking, Housing and Urban Affairs, 94th Cong., 2d Sess. (1976), quoted in SEC Rel. 16384, Fed. Sec. L. Rep. (CCH) 82,373 at n.31.

38. *Edgar v. MITE Corp.,* 102 S. Ct. 2629, 2640–2643 (1982).

39. Louis Lowenstein, "No More Cozy Management Buyouts," *Harv. Bus. Rev.* 64 (1986): 147, 149.

40. *Schreiber v. Burlington Northern, Inc.,* 472 U.S. 1 (1985).

41. *Edgar,* 457 U.S. 624; *CTS Corp.,* 107 S.Ct. 1637.

42. P. S. Atiyah, "From Principles to Pragmatism: Changes in the Function of the Judicial Process and the Law," *Iowa L. Rev.* 65 (1980): 1249, 1251.

43. *Corporate Takeovers: Public Policy Implications for the Economy and Corporate Governance,* Report of the Chairman of the Subcommittee on Telecommunications, Consumer Protection and Finance, House Committee on Energy & Commerce, 99th Cong. 2d Sess. (Comm. Print 99-QQ 1986), 48.

44. Atiyah, "From Principles to Pragmatism," 1257–1259.

45. Peter Frazer, "The Regulation of Take-Overs in Great Britain," in *Knights, Raiders and Targets,* ch. XXVII.

46. Harry DeAngelo, Linda DeAngelo and Edward M. Rice, "Going Private: Minority Freezeouts and Stockholder Wealth," *J. L. & Econ.* 27 (1984): 367.

47. Brenton Schlender, "Alamito Is Target of Four-Way Takeover Fight," *Wall St. J.,* Mar. 7, 1986, p. 6, col. 1.

48. *Revlon,* 506 A.2d 173; *Hanson Trust,* 781 F.2d 264; *Edelman v. Fruehauf Corp.,* 798 F.2d 882 (6th Cir. 1986).

49. *Sec. Reg. and Law Rep. (BNA) 18* (1986): 285.

50. 67 Cong. Rec. 7719-20 (Apr. 19, 1926).

51. Joel Seligman, "Stock Exchange Rules Affecting Takeovers and Control Transactions," in *Knights, Raiders and Targets,* ch. XXXI.

52. Ibid.

53. *Fed. Sec. L. Rep. (CCH) 18* (1986): 1356.

54. Ibid., 1805.

55. A. A. Sommer, *Two Classes of Common Stock and Other Corporate Governance Issues* (manuscript, 1985), 15.

56. Ripley, *Main Street and Wall Street,* 92–93.

57. Ibid., 96 (quoting Robert Herrick), 98.

58. Ibid., 107.

59. See, e.g., *Palmbaum v. Magulsky,* 217 Mass. 306, 104 N.E. 746 (1914).

60. Martin Shubik and Ludo van der Hayden, "Logrolling and Budget Allocation Games, *International J. Game Theory* 7 (1978): 151–162.

61. James Tobin, "On Limiting the Domain of Inequality," *J. Law & Econ.* 13 (1970): 263, 269.

62. Letter to the author from Gunnar Hedlund, June 24, 1987.

CHAPTER 7: Beating the Wall Street Rule

1. Barnaby Feder, "'Poison Pill' Challenge Loses," *N. Y. Times,* Apr. 15, 1987, p. D1, col. 3 (emphasis added).

2. SEC, *Concept Release on Takeovers and Contests for Corporate Control: Advance Notice of Possible Commission Actions,* Exch. Act Rel. 23486, Jul. 31, 1986, *Fed. Sec. L. Rep.* (CCH) ¶ 84,018.

3. Hirschman, *Exit, Voice and Loyalty,* (Cambridge, Mass.: Harvard University Press, 1970), 46.

4. Graham and Dodd, *Security Analysis,* 3rd ed., 616.

5. Albert O. Hirschman, *Rival Views of Market Society* (New York: Viking, 1986), 96.

6. Hirschman, *Rival Views,* 78.

7. Letter to the author, June 24, 1987.

8. *Washington Post,* Dec. 4, 1986.

9. Mancur Olson, *The Logic of Collective Action* (Cambridge, Mass.: Harv. Univ. Press, 1965), 44.

10. Olson, *Logic,* 88–89.

11. Mancur Olson, *The Rise and Decline of Nations* (New Haven: Yale Univ. Press, 1982), 24; see also Rexford E. Santerre and Stephen P. Neun, "Stock Dispersion and Executive Compensation," *Rev. Econ. & Stat.* 48 (1986): 685.

12. James E. Heard and Howard D. Sherman, *Conflicts of Interest in the Proxy Voting System* (Wash., D.C.: Institutional Investor Responsibility Center, 1987), 43–49.

13. Caplin, "Shareholder Nominations."

14. The Economist, Dec. 20, 1986, p. 126.

15. Letter to the author, dated June 24, 1987.

16. Graham and Dodd, *Security Analysis,* 4th ed., 674 (quoting 3rd ed.).

17. Scherer, *U.S. Corporations,* 18.

18. Harold Demsetz, "Two Systems of Belief About Monopoly," in H. J. Goldschmid et al., ed., *Industrial Concentration: The New Learning* (Boston: Little, Brown, 1974), 164.

19. Steve Swartz, "E. F. Hutton Plans Hefty Payments For Ex-Chairman," *Wall St. J.,* June 18, 1987, p. 7, col. 1.

⤳ Glossary ⤳

Arbitrageurs: Until recently, arbitrage was a low-risk operation. An arbitrageur would, for example, purchase a convertible bond at a price slightly less than the current value of the underlying common stock. He then would convert it into the stock and deliver the shares against a sale that he had already made, thus capturing a small but certain profit. Or he bought the shares of a company that was to be acquired by another in an already signed transaction. Now, however, the term has been expanded, and the meaning diluted, to include the Ivan Boeskys and other "risk arbitrageurs" who buy the shares of companies that they believe (hope?) will become the targets of takeovers not yet announced or even in prospect. In the mid-1980s, billions of dollars were committed to various risk arbitrage pools, with effects very different from the traditional operations. First, the "arbs," or arbitrageurs, are no longer simply passive observers of the merger/acquisition process. Collectively, as they swarm around a company that has been identified as a likely target, they may own so much of its stock that the company has effectively been put into play (see *Put into play*). Second, the arbs frequently are buying at prices that already reflect a substantial portion of the expected gain from a takeover. There is therefore a risk, not visible so long as the takeover game continues at full flood, of major losses if and when those putative targets once again sell on their earnings, or whatever other basis the stock market would normally apply to them. At the time the Ivan Boesky scandal first broke, a number of such stocks suffered severe declines, but the lesson was soon forgotten—only to be relearned in October 1987.

Bear raid: A form of stock market manipulation, forbidden since the Securities Exchange Act of 1934, in which an operator or a group, by disseminating misleadingly bad news about a company and selling short its shares to give the same impression, encourages the public to sell out, further depressing the price, at which time the operator can buy back in at a profit.

Black knight: A hostile bidder, one who begins a tender offer for the shares of a target company without its consent, and usually without prior notice. The bidder may not prefer to be seen as hostile, but the dilemma is that, if he proceeds openly, he will give the target valuable additional time in which to prepare its defenses.

Block trading: Trades in blocks or units of at least 10,000 shares. It is a good measure of the dramatically increased trading by institutional investors in the past ten years.

Bridge loan: A very recent development, in which First Boston, Merrill Lynch, and other investment bankers have attempted to overcome the advantages of Drexel Burnham Lambert's hugely successful junk bond operation (see *Junk bond*). Bidders, especially the new breed of bidders with little money of their own, may need access to a billion dollars or more of immediately available credit. Drexel Burnham was able to issue its famous "highly confident" letters, by which it assured the bidder—and the world—that the money could be raised by the sale of junk bonds to its network of clients. Other bankers, unable to match that network, responded by making loans out of their own funds. A bridge loan of over $900 million by First Boston is discussed in chapter 5. In mid-1987, Drexel Burnham, not to be outdone, made its first bridge loan commitment to TWA.

Business judgment rule: Until recently, it was the understanding, if not the theory, that officers and directors were fully protected from claims by shareholders for failure to exercise good judgment, i.e., for any actions that may have turned out badly but were taken in good faith and without any aspect of self-dealing. This understanding was based on the sensible principle that business is a chancy affair, and directors need to take chances without the fear of being second-guessed—at least not in the courthouse. Very few cases can be found in which directors were held personally liable. In a 1985 case, however, *Smith v. Van Gorkom,* the Delaware Supreme Court held liable the directors of a public company for having agreed to sell the company without assuring themselves that the price was adequate. Their liability exceeded $20 million. As discussed in chapter 4, this created quite a stir, and a number of states have taken steps that all but immunize directors from liability.

Capital asset pricing model: Starting from the sensible premise that investors would not knowingly accept greater risks without greater average rewards, modern financial theorists have produced the nonsensical but mathematical model or theory that the prices of common stocks reflect a linear, straight-line relationship between risk and reward. As one popular business school text states, "wise investors don't run risks just for fun."* Risk in this analysis is measured completely by the *beta* of a stock, or the volatility of its recorded stock price fluctuations. Thus if one assumes that Treasury bills yield 7.8 percent and stocks on average earn a total return of about 8.3 percent in excess of the risk-free, or Treasury bill, rate, then the expected rate of return from stocks is "easy" to calculate, depending on whether their *betas* are above or below the 1.0 *beta* of the market average. Implicit in the capital asset pricing model is the conviction, first, that market pricing is highly efficient and, second, that the risk of a stock can be determined without looking at the underlying business, its competitive position, or the like.

Classified, or dual class, common stock: It is possible to create different series or classes of common stock for a variety of purposes. Shares have sometimes been classified with respect to their rights on liquidation or their dividend rights. At the present time, there is a growing practice by which companies, to defend against the threat of a hostile tender offer, have classified their common shares according to voting rights. Under a typical arrangement, one of the two classes would enjoy, either generally or just in the voting for directors, ten times the voting power per share of the other. Even assuming that share-holders willingly accept the inferior class, with the supervoting stock held by management or other insiders, there remains the policy question of whether such arrangements should be permitted (see chapter 6, pages 186–193).

Conglomerates: Corporations with divisions or subsidiaries operating a variety of essentially unrelated businesses. ITT, for example, at one time was engaged in the hotel, rental car, bread baking, insurance, telephone system, and electronics businesses, among others.

Creeping tender offer: When it adopted the Williams Act in 1968, Congress was loathe to restrict much the freedom of bidders. It did not therefore require, as, for example, the British do, that any purchase of shares that would take the bidder above some threshold, e.g., 20 percent of the outstanding shares of the target, must be by a tender offer open to all shareholders. Bidders are free to purchase unlimited quantities of stock in routine, open market transactions, so long as they do not buy in ways that resemble too much the usual tender offer. These ways include for example, pressuring sellers by set-

---

*Richard Brealey and Stewart Myers, *Principles of Corporate Finance* (New York: McGraw-Hill, 2d. ed., 1984), 129.

ting time deadlines for tenders or by offering a premium price. The result is
that some bidders, including those for Evans Products and TWA, acquired
control by a ("creeping") series of open market purchases.

Crown jewel lockup: Probably the best-known example was the agreement by
which Marathon Oil, beset by a hostile bid from Mobil, agreed to sell its
fabulously rich Yates oil field interest to U. S. Steel, the "white knight"
with which Marathon hoped to merge. Mobil could still have bid for Marathon, which would then have had a lot of cash and much less oil. But since
it was oil that Mobil was seeking, there would have been no point to its
bid—which was exactly the point of the lockup.

Efficient market hypothesis: A widely accepted view that the stock market prices
stocks as perfectly as possible, that it is the "smart money" that dictates the
prices of shares. Or, as the textbooks say, you can trust prices. So long as it
remained a creature of academia, efficient market theory worked relatively
little damage. (Those who on graduation went out to manage money still had
to unlearn it, but that didn't take long.) Now that it is widely accepted,
however, it does a lot of mischief. The SEC's chief economist analyzes the
stock price movements over very brief periods, as little as a few days, to
"study" the long-term effects of nonvoting stocks, or whatever else is on the
agenda. Worse yet, investors, convinced that it does not matter which stocks
they own, believe it is rational to buy a market basket of them, an index
fund, without thinking about what's in the basket. The world at large has
begun to accept the scholars' dictum that "seen one stock, seen them all."

Free rider: This is the problem that underlies the Wall Street Rule. According
to the rule, individual shareholders are said to be foolish if they take an active
interest in the affairs or management of a company, because they own only a
trivial portion of the stock. The rest of the shareholders, those owning the
remaining 90 + percent, who have simply sat back, will get a free ride on
their efforts (see *Public good*).

Fundamental-value investor: One who buys shares of a company as if he were
buying the whole company. The primary emphasis is on the likely results in
the business rather than the likely results in the stock market. Five percent,
perhaps even less, of the money under management is managed by fundamental-value principles.

Golden parachute: The very generous severance pay arrangements that are
awarded to senior executives of potential targets. The "cord" may be pulled
by any change in control of the company, even if the executive simply chooses
to leave, without having been pushed out. Some of the payments have exceeded
$10 million. Congress has used the tax law to limit the payments, or at least
to impose a penalty on those that equal three years' compensation. In the

context of large takeovers, the payments are usually insignificant, albeit un-seemly. The argument for them is that they remove the managers' personal interest as a factor, thus reducing some of the litigation and other costs.

Greenmail: In a narrow sense, greenmail refers to the repurchase of a (poten-tially) hostile bidder's shares at a price above either the then current market price, or at least above the previously prevailing price. Greenmailers have thus reaped easy profits of $10 million, $20 million, and more. In rare cases, courts have struck down these arrangements. There is a great deal of ingenuity ap-plied, therefore, to disguising what nonetheless is greenmail. For the bidder if not the target, the result is better if the threatened bid simply puts the target into play, in which case the bidder will get a price as high as or higher than the greenmail price, and with less risk and less public criticism.

Hostile bidder: See *Black knight.*

Index fund: The technique by which institutional investors buy all of the stocks in a given stock index, e.g., the Standard & Poor's 500 Stock Index, and in exactly the dollar proportions that each such stock represents of the index. To the extent that the investor has simply adopted a buy-and-hold strategy, rather than a trading strategy, there are obvious advantages (see *Performance game*). But an index fund goes beyond that, selecting stocks without rhyme or reason. In a larger sense, indexing and performance game strategies are both victims of the same reluctance to exercise independent, long-term judg-ments about earnings and value. The short-term traders mimic what the mar-ket will be doing over the next few months. An index fund, reflecting a similar fear of being left out, mimics the market as a whole. Any such one-decision strategy may work for a time. But it is defenseless against a major overpricing and the consequent correction, such as eventually struck down the growth stock investors of the early 1970s and all the others who at one time or another have bragged that they disregard price and value (see *Keynesian convention*).

Junk bond: There is a much higher tolerance of debt and financial risk in the United States today than for many years past, and junk bonds are one, highly visible aspect of that larger, cultural change. Junk bonds are bonds issued publicly that have far less coverage of interest and other fixed charges than the market would have required just a few years ago. Indeed, in many cases there is no ''coverage,'' meaning that the earnings do not even equal the fixed charges, much less provide the cushion that lenders traditionally demanded. In the near term, the interest payments are made out of the initial proceeds of the loan, thus returning to the lenders some of their own money. Or assets are sold off. Or the lenders agree, by accepting zero-coupon bonds, not to ask for any money for six or eight years. The junk bond is a common stock dressed up as a bond for marketing and accounting purposes. (How else to write a 14 percent coupon drawn on insufficient funds, and still permit the buyer to record the 14 percent as income on *his* books?)

Keynesian convention: A working hypothesis, reflected in efficient market theory and the attitudes and behavior of much of Wall Street, that since we do not know the proper prices for stocks, we might as well assume that the current prices are correct. The convention, as Keynes put it, is that the "existing market valuation, however arrived at, is uniquely *correct* in relation to our existing knowledge of the facts . . . , and that it will change in proportion to changes in the knowledge; though philosophically speaking, it cannot be uniquely correct, since our existing knowledge does not provide a sufficient basis for a calculated mathematical expectation."* There is a lovely connection between the Keynesian convention and efficient market theory. Both ignore the role that opinion, insight, and judgment play in the investment process. It is only new information that will change the price. The difference is that Keynes understood that this was nonsense.

Leveraged buyouts: A buyout or purchase of a business in which the financing is accomplished by an aggressive use of leverage, i.e., from borrowed money. Debt: equity ratios of 6:1 or 8:1 are not uncommon. The buyer typically is a newly formed company, and hence can offer the lenders no security other than that of the acquired business. There are some clear advantages to this kind of transaction, if, for example, it enables the managers of a division of a top-heavy conglomerate to "run their own show." For the process as a whole, however, it's a bit like tuning in to a cowboy movie before the sheriff has buckled on his gun. In recent years there has been an enormous leap in the prices paid for these buyouts, and like junk bonds, the results over the full business cycle have yet to be determined.

Neoclassical economics: There is neoclassical economics, and then again there is neoclassical economics. In one, broadly inclusive sense it is simply the study of what follows from the assumption that economically "rational" individuals maximize their respective profits within the constraints of the markets (or institutions) in which they are functioning. Increasingly, however, the term is used more narrowly to refer to the school of economics that believes markets generally are fully competitive and free of imperfections and externalities, that what is good for the individuals operating in those markets is necessarily good for society as a whole—in short, that the invisible hand theorem is working in almost all cases.

---

*Keynes, *General Theory*, 152.

Pac-Man defense: This is the "I'll gobble you before you gobble me" defense, based on the famous arcade game. The most celebrated instance was the tender offer by Martin Marietta for shares of Bendix, after Bendix had bid for Martin Marietta. Both bids succeeded, if that be success. Each acquired over 50 percent of the shares of the other and therefore of itself. It was impossible to tell who controlled what, and by aggressively borrowing money to buy what in large part were its own shares, each suffered a crippling loss of capital. The tactic has fallen into disfavor.

Performance game: A strategy for investing in which the money manager attempts to perform at least as well as the stock market in virtually each and every calendar quarter that he is to report to the corporate pension manager, or whoever hired him. If the market goes off on a silly tangent, the manager feels obliged to follow. The immediate effect is to generate very heavy trading costs on the one hand and a very short-term investment horizon on the other. The longer-term effects are worse.

Poison pill: An ingenious defensive tactic created by Martin Lipton, who has developed successive versions, in effect trying to stay one step ahead of the bidders. In one common version, the shareholders of a putative target receive presently worthless warrants that entitle them, however, to buy at a deep discount shares of any company that acquires control of the target in an unfriendly bid. The courts have treated the pill much more favorably than had been expected. While there is still doubt as to its validity in many circumstances, it has a substantial deterrent effect, which is after all its primary purpose. Compared to other defensive tactics, this one works no present dilution or loss of value to investors and to that extent is less objectionable. The SEC is hotly opposed to the pill.

Portfolio insurance: There isn't any such thing. Brokers and others who feed on the anxieties of money managers have concocted a scheme, sometimes called portfolio insurance, sometimes other things, in which the broker will begin to sell stock-index futures on behalf of his fund-client, if and when the stock market drops by some previously agreed-upon percentage. The fallacies are too numerous to list, but the most obvious ones are that it is very expensive and there is no reason to believe that it works.

Program trading: By itself and in modest amounts, program trading is hardly objectionable. Typically, it entails selling stock-index futures and buying the underlying stocks anytime there is a spread between the value of the two that exceeds the transaction costs. There is an astonishing volume of program trading, or index arbitrage as it is sometimes called—astonishing because unlike arbitrages in copper or money, nothing turns on whether a stock index is too high by 0.5796 percent or not. Program trading has no redeeming social value.

Pruning deadwood theory: Based on the efficient market hypothesis, the pruning deadwood theory argues that hostile takeovers systematically increase productivity and managerial efficiency. Bidders pay large premiums for target companies, and since in an efficient market everything else is already reflected in the price of the shares, the bidders must be contemplating improved management, better use of resources, or some useful synergies.

Public good: The classic case of a public or collective good is snow removal from the village streets. Each of us gets to use the cleared streets, even if he has not paid his taxes. Second, the use of those streets by any one of us does not detract from or diminish the use by others. Each of us, as economically "rational" actors, will try to use the streets but not to pay taxes. There is, in short, a free rider problem (see *Free rider*).

Put into play: Like the ball on the roulette table, a company can be put into play so that some bidder's number will come up, someone will win the prize, although the winning number will not be known until the last. In the merger and acquisition game, a company can be put into play through a number of different scenarios. There may have been a negotiated merger, which then fell through. Or a hostile bid has been made, or perhaps only threatened. In any case, so much of the stock has come into the hands of arbitrageurs that management is unlikely to find any solution that does not involve a sale of the company or a radical restructuring that is tantamount to a sale.

Shark: See *Black knight.*

Shark repellent: All target company defenses are designed to repel sharks. But the term "shark repellent" refers primarily to those provisions in a company's charter and bylaws designed to make it more difficult for a successful bidder either to achieve the control of the board it ultimately requires or to squeeze out those shareholders who reject the initial bid. There are a number of such provisions, but typical would be the requirement that no more than one-third of the directors be elected in any one year and that directors may not be removed except for cause. Like insect repellents, shark repellents don't work for more than a few hours.

Wall Street Rule: If one shareholder turns activist, investing time and talent in overseeing an otherwise indolent management, the benefits accrue in full measure to all the other shareholders, even if they sit on their hands. Hence the "rule" that investors should not bother to become thoughtful, active shareholders. If they lose confidence in management, the only sensible course is to sell out. What is good advice for any one investor, however, is bad for them collectively, since they cannot all sell out. Even those who do will often have sold at an unnecessarily depressed price. While almost everyone recognizes the dilemma, no one seems much inclined to consider changes. (See *Free rider* and *Public good*).

White knight: A bidder who rides to the rescue of a beleaguered target and, with the advantages of a crown jewel lockup or access to confidential data denied to the original hostile suitor, often wins the bidding. Despite their passionate denials in the heat of the contest, once the deal is done white knights frequently dismantle the target company's operations and management team as cold bloodedly as the black knights whose embrace was so feared.

White squire: One to whom a target issues a substantial block of shares, usually seeking to dilute a hostile bidder's holdings.

Index